RUSSIA THROUGH EUROPEAN EYES

No. 3

General Editor: Dr. A. G. CROSS, University of East Anglia

THE DIARY

OF

GENERAL PATRICK GORDON

PASSAGES

FROM

THE DIARY

OF

GENERAL PATRICK GORDON

OF AUCHLEUCHRIES

IN THE YEARS

1635 — 1699

DA CAPO PRESS · NEW YORK · 1968

A DA CAPO PRESS REPRINT EDITION

First edition	1859
New impression	1968

Library of Congress Catalog Card Number 68-27012

Published by Da Capo Press
A Division of Plenum Publishing Corporation
227 West 17th Street
New York, N.Y. 10011

Published in Great Britain by
Frank Cass & Co. Ltd.
London, England

Printed in Great Britain

TABLE OF CONTENTS.

The Spalding Club.

M.DCCC.LIX.

Patron.
HIS ROYAL HIGHNESS THE PRINCE CONSORT.

President.
THE EARL OF ABERDEEN, K.G., K.T.

Vice-Presidents.
THE DUKE OF RICHMOND, K.G.
THE DUKE OF SUTHERLAND, K.G.
THE EARL OF KINTORE.
THE EARL OF SEAFIELD.
THE LORD SALTOUN.

The Council.

The LORD PROVOST of Aberdeen.

Sir GEORGE SAMUEL ABERCROMBY of Birkenbog, Bart.

JOHN ANGUS, President of the Society of Advocates in Aberdeen.

JOHN HILL BURTON, Advocate, Edinburgh.

CHARLES CHALMERS of Monkshill.

ROBERT CHAMBERS, Edinburgh.

The EARL of CAWDOR.

ARCHIBALD DAVIDSON, Sheriff of Aberdeenshire.

CHARLES ELPHINSTONE DALRYMPLE.

Sir JAMES DALRYMPLE HORNE ELPHINSTONE of Horne and Logie-
    Elphinstone, Bart.

The EARL of ERROLL.

The LORD FORBES.

Colonel JONATHAN FORBES.

JAMES GILES, R.S.A., Aberdeen.

JOHN GORDON of Cairnbulg, Advocate.

GEORGE GRUB, Advocate in Aberdeen.

COSMO INNES, Advocate, Professor of History in the University of Edinburgh.

The Right Reverend JAMES KYLE, D.D., Preshome.

DAVID LAING, Keeper of the Library of the Society of Writers to the Signet, Edinburgh.

WILLIAM LESLIE of Wartle and Drumrossie.

The LORD LINDSAY.

HUGH LUMSDEN of Pitcaple, Advocate.   (Deceased.)

ALEXANDER MORISON of Bognie.

MARK NAPIER, Advocate, Sheriff of Dumfries-shire.

The EARL of NORTHESK.

JOHN RAMSAY of Barra.

ALEXANDER HENRY RHIND of Sibster.

JOSEPH ROBERTSON, Superintendent of the Literary and Antiquarian Department of the General Register House, Edinburgh.

JAMES YORSTON SIMPSON, M.D., Professor of Midwifery in the University of Edinburgh.

The Reverend ALEXANDER TAYLOR, D.D., Leochel-Cushnie.

ALEXANDER THOMSON of Banchory.

GEORGE TULLOCH, LL.D., Aberdeen.

Secretary.

JOHN STUART, General Register House, Edinburgh.

Treasurers.

JOHN BLAIKIE, Advocate in Aberdeen.

JOHN LIGERTWOOD, Advocate in Aberdeen.

_whilst I breath

PGordon

PREFACE.

THE soldier of fortune, whose memoirs are now introduced to the SPALDING CLUB, had been but a short while dead when public attention was turned to the eight or ten thick quartos,[1] in which, for forty years, he had recorded, day by day, the incidents of his eventful life.

So early as 1724, a translation of the Journal from its original English into the language of the thankless country in which the writer was condemned to breathe his last, was

[1] Gordon's manuscripts appear to have been scattered after his death. Some found their way into the archives of the Foreign Office at Moscow; others came somehow into the hands of the widow of a countryman and namesake, who was interpreter in the Admiralty at St. Petersburg. In all, six volumes of the Journal have been recovered:—

Volume I. from 1635 to 1659.
    ,,   II. from 1659 to 1667.
    ,, III. from 1677 to 1678.
    ,, IV. from 1684 to 1690.
    ,,   V. from 1690 to 1695.
    ,, VI. from 1695 to 1699.

No trace has been found of the two, three or four volumes containing the ten years between 1667 and 1677, and the six years between 1678 and 1684.

Besides his voluminous Journal, Gordon seems occasionally to have kept more formal records of the public transactions in which he was engaged. Thus, during his mission to England in 1666, he notes in his journal that he had conferences with Lord Chancellor Clarendon, but refers for an account of what passed to 'my booke of relations,' or, as he elsewhere calls it 'my other booke of my relation.'—(p. 83.) This was doubtless the 'relation of my negotiation,' which he gave in to the Foreign Office on his return to Moscow.—(p. 104.) So, again, in 1686, when chronicling the incidents of his vain attempt to escape from Russia, he refers for a copy of his letters to the Earl of Middleton, to 'my other booke,' or, as he afterwards terms it, 'my other copy book of letters.'—(pp. 162, 163.) 'The copyes of all my remonstrances,' he adds, 'are apart.'—(p. 163.)

begun by Count Ostermann, but abandoned, as it would seem, under the burden of state affairs which gradually pressed upon one who already a Councillor was soon to be Chancellor of Russia. A few years afterwards, Professor Baier drew from the Diary almost everything of value in his relation of the Muscovite campaigns against the Crim Tartars in 1688-89, and of the siege and capture of Asof in 1696. The work was next to fall under the eye of the learned author of the *Origines gentis et nominis Russorum*, Gerard Frederic Muller. This laborious scholar was anxious that the Journal should be translated into German, then much more than now the literary language of St. Petersburg. The task was too much for himself, but it was undertaken by his assistant, John Stritter, upon a plan which cannot be called a happy one. Regarding the work as important chiefly for the military history of Russia, he cut down or expunged almost everything which did not seem to him to bear upon that subject. The Diary, stripped in this way of many of its most interesting and characteristic details, was still farther disfigured by being recast into a narrative in the third person—the ' I marched,' ' I did write,' ' I was at the Czars' hands' of the original being rendered ' He marched,' ' Gordon wrote,' ' He was admitted to the presence of the Emperors. Such as his version or adaptation was, Stritter did not live to complete it, nor did he print any part of what he had finished. Still, in some shape more or less defective, information derived from the Journal continued to find its way to the public, as many as six books built upon its foundations having appeared in Russia between 1766 and 1834. A seventh was projected in England, but was never published, and that it was even contemplated, is now known only by the allusion of Lord Byron in a rhyming letter to his London bookseller, written from Venice in the summer of 1818.[2]

Forty years passed before the first work which professed to give any adequate outline of the contents of General Gordon's Diary, as a whole, began to issue from the press of Moscow.[3] It followed Stritter's ill-planned version, so far as that went. But the editor, Dr. Posselt, carefully collated the original, restored many passages which Stritter had curtailed or omitted, illustrated the text by valuable notes, and supplied the two great chasms in the Journal by information gleaned from other sources. From June, 1692, where his own translation began, he allowed the narrative to run, as in the original, in the first person.

Dr. Posselt's work could scarcely fail to awaken interest in the land of the adventurer whose story it told. It was reviewed, in terms of just praise, in our two chief critical journals,[4] and both urged the publication of at least portions of the Diary in the language in which it was written. The earlier of these reviews was from the lively and accomplished pen of the late Earl of

---

[2] In a bantering excuse for the delay of the fourth canto of Childe Harold, Lord Byron enumerates other works which Mr. Murray is preparing to publish :—
'Then you've General Gordon,
    Who girded his sword on,
        To serve with a Muscovite master,
    And help him to polish
    A nation so owlish
        They thought shaving their beards a
            disaster.'
(Byron's Poetical Works, vol. ii., pp. 394, 395, edit. Lond. 1855.) It was, no doubt, an advertisement of this intended work that led to the belief in Russia that a Life of General Patrick Gordon had been published at London.

[3] Tagebuch des Generals Patrick Gordon, wahrend seiner Kriegsdienste unter den Schweden und Polen vom Jahre 1655 bis 1661, und seines Aufenthaltes in Russland vom Jahre 1661 bis 1669, zum ersten vollstandig veroffentlicht durch Furst M. A. Obolenski und Dr. phil. M. C. Posselt. Erster band: Moskau, 1849. Zweiter band: St. Petersburg, 1851. Dritter band: St. Petersburg, 1853.

The name of Prince Obolenski is dropped from the title pages of the second and third volumes, for which we are indebted to Dr. Posselt alone. That gentleman bore also the chief share in editing the first volume.

[4] In the Quarterly Review for March, 1852, (no. clxxx., vol. xc., pp. 314-332); in the Edinburgh Review for July, 1856, (no. ccxi., vol. civ., pp. 24-51.)

Ellesmere, and it was published in the avowed hope that it might 'induce one of the Scotch clubs, or two or three of them in friendly alliance, to undertake an edition of selections from the original text.' The SPALDING CLUB was specially referred to, and it lost no time in taking measures for accomplishing an object so desirable in itself, and so much in accordance with the purposes of the Association. Its President, the Earl of Aberdeen, then First Lord of the Treasury, made application to the Court of St. Petersburg for a transcript of all the passages of General Gordon's Diary which related to his native country. The request was granted with a prompt and liberal courtesy for which the warmest acknowledgements are due; and the selections which fill most of the following sheets were placed at the disposal of the Club in a careful copy made from the original, in the Imperial Archives of Russia, by the hand of all others best qualified for the task, that of the excellent editor of the German translation. Dr. Posselt accompanied his transcript by a note explaining that while he had been at pains to preserve Gordon's orthography, he had not thought it necessary to retain the many abbreviations which obscure or perplex the original. He adds that it is so faulty in the names of persons and places, especially in Russia, that not a few of them are disguised beyond his power of recognition.

The passages transcribed by Dr. Posselt, and now printed from his copy, are six in number.

The first[5] gives Gordon's account of his birth, parentage, education, and travels, till the summer of 1655, when, at the age of twenty, he took service at Hamburg as a trooper in the army which

[5] Pp. 1-21.

King Charles Gustavus of Sweden was mustering for the invasion of Poland.

The next,[6] a single leaf from the Journal of the winter of 1658, tells how the writer and fourteen of his Cavalier fellow-countrymen, then lying with the Swedish army on the banks of the Vistula, were baffled in an attempt to assassinate the Ambassador from the English Commonwealth to the Court of Moscow, in the mistaken belief that he was the President of the Court which sat in judgment on King Charles the First.

In the third,[7] we have Gordon's relation of the circumstances under which, in 1661, he left the Polish army at Warsaw, engaged to follow the Austrian banner, broke his faith, outwitted the Imperial Ambassador, and posted to Moscow to take a Major's commission under the Czar.

The fourth[8] gives the Diary kept by Gordon, now a Colonel, during his journey on a special mission from Russia to England in 1666 and 1667.

The fifth[9] records a second journey from Moscow to London, after a lapse of twenty years, the reception of the writer, who had now risen to the rank of Lieutenant-General, at the Court of King James the Second, his sojourn in the Scottish capital, and his visit to his kinsfolk and paternal acres in Aberdeenshire.

Last of all, are one or two letters[10] on his family affairs, and a few others on public events, between 1690 and 1696, addressed to the Duke of Gordon and other Scottish peers,[11] by one who, now

[6] P. 28.
[7] Pp. 32-53.
[8] Pp. 55-104.
[9] Pp. 109-163.
[10] Pp. 175-179, 181-183.
[11] Pp. 168, 170, 171, 173, 180, 181, 184, 185.

himself sharing the privileges of nobility,[12] can lament the weariness
of a court life,[13] tell of the large measure of favour and familiarity
which he enjoys with the Czar,[14] and boast that hitherto he has prevailed with the Russian Government to ignore the Revolution, and
know no King of England but the exile of St. Germains.[15]

In printing these selections, an attempt has been made so far to
connect them together, by an outline of Gordon's life in the interval,
with occasional quotations from some of the more memorable pages
of his Journal, such as those in which he notes the beginnings of his
intimacy with Peter the Great,[16] or chronicles the prompt and
vigorous acts by which he quelled the revolt of the Strelitzes.[17]
For the translation of these passages from Dr. Posselt's German
version of the Diary, the editor is indebted to Mr. Andrew Findlater.   Care has been taken to distinguish all the matter thus in-
terpolated by printing it in smaller type.

[12] P. 166. During the first twenty-
eight years of his service in Russia, Gordon
was called, in all official papers, 'Peter
Iwanowsyn.'   In 1689, he received the
style of 'Peter Iwanowitsch,' the liberty of
exchanging 'syn' for 'witsch' being a pre-
rogative of nobility. 'The nobilitie of
Russia,' says Giles Fletcher, 'is of foure
sortes, whereof the chiefe for birth, authoritie,
and revenue, are called *Udelney Knazey*,
that is, the exempt or priuiledged Dukes.
. . . The second degree of nobility is of
the *Boiarens*. These are such as the Emperour honoureth (besides their nobility)
with the title of counsellers. . . . In
the third rank are the *Voyauodey*, or such
nobles as are, or haue bin, generals in the
Emperours warres, which deliuer the honour
of their title to their posterities also. . . .
These three degrees of nobilitie (to wit), the
Udelney Knazey, the *Boiarens*, and the
Voiauodey, haue the addition of *vich* put vnto
their sirname, as *Borris Federowich*, etc.,
which is a note of honour that the rest may
not vsurpe. And in case it be not added in
the naming of them, they may sue the *best-
chest*, or penaltie of dishonour, vpon them
that otherwise shall terme them.'— (The
Russe Commonwealth, ff. 24, 27, 28, 29.
Lond. 1591.)

[13] P. 181.

[14] Pp. 170, 174.

[15] Pp. 169, 170.   According to Gordon's
Jacobite son-in-law, the Czar Peter, alluding
to the good offices of King James I. in
bringing about the treaties of peace at Stol-
bova and Moscow, by which Sweden and
Poland renounced their pretensions to the
Russian throne, was more than once heard
to say 'that he was more obliged to the pre-
decessors of the Chevalier de St. George
than to all the monarchs of the world.'—
(History of Peter the Great, by Alexander
Gordon of Auchintoul, vol. i. p. 54. Aberd.
1755.)

[16] Pp. 168-170, 173, 181, 183, 184.

[17] Pp. 187-193.

Gordon prefaces his Journal with a short explanation of its plan and purpose. But he forgets to tell us when it was that he began thus 'to write the story of his own life.' We may conjecture, however, that it was not until after he had been some time at Moscow—perhaps in 1662 or 1663, when he had completed his twenty-eighth year, had gained the rank of Lieutenant-Colonel, and, after much meditation, had made up his mind to marry. All that is written before this time bears sufficient evidence of being written after the event;[18] and it is here that the author is seen to most advantage. When his Diary really becomes such, when the incidents of each day are recorded as it passes, he too often proves lamentably tedious. It is not merely that his page is filled with trifles—dry, interminable lists of rivers crossed or stages passed, letters received and answered, visits made, or bills paid. But even when historical figures appear upon the scene, it is for the most part only to provoke expectation which is left unsatisfied. We have seldom more than a bare, bald, note of their names. Thus we are told of meetings at London in 1666, with Prince Rupert, with Clarendon, and with Lauderdale; but nearly all that we learn of them is that the first was very sick, that the second was confined by the gout to Berkshire House, and that the third gave Sunday dinners at his house at Highgate, and one evening kept the author waiting half-an-hour, and did not see him after all.[19] So, of a con-

---

[18] Traces of foreign idiom show themselves in the very first lines of the Journal. We have 'as' used in the sense of 'than,' 'by' for 'with,' and the like. Thus, ' I have mentioned no more of publick effaires *as* came to my knowledge'—(p. 3.) ' I cannot tell you a better or truer reason for writing this, *as* that it is to please my owne fancy'—

(p. 3.) ' I was put to lodge and dyet *by* a widdow'—(p. 4.) ' Here wee tooke up our lodging *by* Mr. Menezès'—(p. 7.) ' My mother came foure dayes thereafter, of whom I received the benediction and tooke my leave'—(p. 5.) ' I was very astonished'—(p. 8.)

[19] Pp. 82-90.

versation, at Hamburg, with Queen Christina of Sweden, we are informed that it lasted thirty minutes, but we have not a syllable of what was said.[20] So, again, all the stages of a journey, on horse-back, from London to Edinburgh, in company with Lochiel, are carefully recounted, but we gather nothing more of the renowned Sir Evan Dhu than that his nag broke down at Huntingdon[21]

However this tantalising brevity may be deplored, its excuse is obvious enough; and we should rather marvel at the journalist's persevering assiduity in writing so much than blame him for not writing more. Nor curt or trivial as many pages of his Diary are, must all such portions be pronounced wholly uninteresting. Some little instruction or amusement may be gleaned, at times, even from his accounts of prices, as when at London in 1686, he notes the cost of every article of his apparel, from a peruke at seven pounds to shoes at five shillings a-pair; records that he paid a shilling to the barber ' for trimming him;' that he gave a penny for a newspaper; that the charge for a bottle of wine in a tavern was sixteen pence; that once he had a cup of tea[22] for a penny, although he oftener paid fourpence or sixpence; that a dining-room, a bedroom, and a servant's room could be hired in Pall Mall for eleven shillings a-week; that in Edinburgh, the charge for a servant's meal was

---

[20] P. 100.

[21] Pp. 136, 137.

[22] Pp. 126-135. Tea, not once named by Gordon during his first visit to London in 1666, was used by him daily during his second visit in 1686. Pepys writes in 1660, ' I did send for a cup of tee (a China drink), of which I never had drank before; ' and records as something unusual, in June, 1667, that on going home he found his wife making tea, ' a drink which Mr. Pelling the pothicary tells her is good for her cold and defluxions.' —(Pepys' Diary, vol. i. p. 137; vol. iv.

p 100. edit. Lond. 1851.) Gordon may, possibly, have became acquainted with tea in Russia. His son-in-law tells us, what, indeed, is easily gathered from his Journal, that he had no great liking for stronger potations : ' General Gordon was a sober man, in a country where drinking is much in fashion ; and though he used to be much in the Czar's company, his Majesty, knowing his inclinations, would never allow him to be urged.'—(Gordon's History of Peter the Great, vol. i. p. 138.)

sixpence a-day;[23] and that the northern nobles, from the Duke of Gordon downwards, dined daily in taverns, Crombie's or Blair's, for about half-a-crown, and supped or 'took their collation' at two or three shillings, a-head.[24] Meagre as the glimpses are, which the Journal opens, of high Scotch life[25] on the eve of the Revolution, so very little information of that kind has been preserved, that we should grudge the loss of a single line from the morning on which the Tweed was crossed to the night on which Gordon saw, for the last time, the sun sink behind the headlands of Buchan.[26] The record of the two or three weeks which he passed in Aberdeenshire shows more than usual feeling throughout.[27] There are occasions, also, during his two visits to London, when he warms into something like a communicative mood, as, for example, in his interviews with King James the Second.[28] Between that Prince and himself there was the strong bond of common zeal for a proscribed faith; and it is easy to see what was in the mind of the monarch, during their last meeting at Windsor, when he so earnestly pressed Gordon to make haste back from Russia. The King looked for another Dalyell,[29] and, perhaps, he would not have been disappointed. 'I am sorry,' said Gordon,

[23] P. 142.

[24] Pp. 141-144.

[25] Pp. 140-152.

[26] On one of these bold headlands, almost within sight of Auchleuchries, the ships which bore the first Russian embassy to England were wrecked in 1556.—(Hakluyt, p. 332, edit. 1589; Bishop Lesley's History of Scotland, pp. 257, 258; Illustrations of the Topography and Antiquities of the Shires of Aberdeen and Banff, vol. iv. pp. 106-109; Dr. Hamel's England and Russia, pp. 147-151.)

[27] Pp. 145-152. An attempt has been made in the foot notes to identify the chief persons and places mentioned in this part of the Diary It may be added that 'the Bonny Wife's' where Gordon records (p. 146) that he had a stirrup cup on his way from Schivas to Auchleuchries, was the name given to a house on the Blackhill of Dudwick.—(Inquisit. Spec. vicecom. de Aberdeen, no. 476.)

[28] Pp. 127-131, 135, 136.

[29] This was in the spring of 1686. 'Old Tom of Muscovy,' as King Charles II. used to call General Dalyell, died in August, 1685. It was not until more than a twelvemonth afterwards that Claverhouse was raised to the rank of Major General.

when the news of the battle of the Boyne reached him at Moscow,
'I am sorry from my heart that his Majesty did not, when I was
in Scotland, lay his commands upon me to stay there.   Then might
I at this time have given proofs of my loyalty and what I can do.'[30]
We may well believe that the hand which crushed the Strelitzes
would have been heavy upon the Cameronians; it may be that the
walls of Derry would have fallen before the conqueror of Asof; and
the ready counsel and daring acts which twice saved the throne
of Peter the Great might have upheld the rule even of King James
the Second.

The editor has not had the advantage of access to General
Gordon's family papers, if indeed there now be any in Scotland.
But he has printed in an APPENDIX such notices of the 'goodmen'[31]
of Auchleuchries, and their bleak homestead, as he was able to
collect from the public records, and from private charter chests.

Although no 'laird,' and but what would have been called a
'yeoman' in England, Gordon was well descended on both sides.
Through his mother (from whom, it would seem, he had his nurture

---

[30] P. 170.

[31] 'And this remembers me,' says the
Lord Advocate of King Charles II., 'of a
custom in Scotland, which is but gone lately
in desuetude, and that is, that such as did
hold their lands of the Prince were called
Lairds, but such as held their lands of a
subject, though they were large, and their
superior very noble, were only called Goodmen, from the old French word bonne
homme, which was the title of master of the
family.'—(Science of Heraldry, book i. chap.
ii ; Sir George Mackenzie's Works, vol. ii.

p. 583.)   Mr. Riddell has shown that
'goodman' was used in England, after the
middle of the seventeenth century, as
synonymous with 'yeoman.'—(Peerage and
Consistorial Law of Scotland, vol. ii. pp.
980, 981.)

Auchleuchries, of old a part of the barony
of Belhelvie, and, in the seventeenth century,
a dependency of the barony of Ardendraught,
was held by the Gordons of the Earls of
Erroll, for a yearly rent or feu-duty of eleven
pounds Scots. — (Appendix, no. 57, p. 215.)

in the Roman Catholic faith) he could claim kindred with the noble
house of Deskford and Findlater.[32] His father, ' the younger brother
of a younger house,' was a grandson of the family of Haddo, raised
in Gordon's own day, to the Earldom of Aberdeen.[33] Auchleuchries
was the inheritance of his mother.[34] Its five or six petty farms
appear to have yielded in those days about three hundred and sixty
pounds Scots, or thirty pounds sterling, a-year.[35] But it was so
overwhelmed by mortgages or ' wadsets,' that probably half the
scanty rental went in payment of interest. It is as witness to a
deed by which his father added to the still growing burden of the

[32] Janet Ogilvy, daughter of James Ogilvy of Cullen (the second son, it is believed, of James Ogilvy, the eldest son of Sir James Ogilvy of Deskford and Findlater, who died in 1510), married, firstly, John Gordon of Pitlurg, who was slain at Pinkie in 1547; secondly, James Ogilvy of Blarak, her cousin. By her first marriage she had Sir John Gordon of Pitlurg, father of Robert Gordon of Straloch, the scholar and antiquary. By her second marriage she had James Ogilvy of Blarak and Auchleuchries, who, in 1604, married Marjory Gordon, daughter of George Gordon of Coclarachy. The issue of this marriage was a daughter, Mary Ogilvy, who, in 1633, married John Gordon, third son of Patrick Gordon of Nethermuir, by whom she had six children : (1) George Gordon, younger of Auchleuchries, born in 1634, died before his father in 1665; (2) General Patrick Gordon, born in 1635, became ' goodman' of Auchleuchries on the death of his father about 1675, died in 1699; (3) John Gordon, in Westertoun of Auchleuchries, who, in 1674, married Margaret Forbes, by whom he had issue, and was alive in 1692; (4) James Gordon, in Westertoun of Auchleuchries, who died in 1691, leaving issue; (5) Alexander Gordon, who died before 1682; (6) a daughter, who was alive in 1686.

[33] James Gordon of Methlic and Haddo (great-great-great-grandfather of the first Earl of Aberdeen), who died in 1582, married a daughter of Menzies of Pitfoddels, by whom he had six sons, of whom the fourth, David, was the father of Patrick Gordon of Nethermuir, who had issue, four sons and two daughters : (1) George Gordon of Nethermuir; (2) Mr. Thomas Gordon; (3) John Gordon of Auchleuchries, father of General Patrick Gordon; (4) James Gordon of Westertoun of Auchleuchries; (5) Annas Gordon, wife of James Gordon of Greenmyre; (6) Janet Gordon.

John Gordon of Auchleuchries, his brother Mr. Thomas, and one or two of his tenants, appear among the followers of Sir John Gordon of Haddo in a raid against the Covenanters of Buchan, in April, 1644, when they spoiled the lands and houses of Auchnagat and Kinnaldy, belonging to Alexander Strachan of Glenkindy and his brother, and carried the latter captive to Kelly.—(Spalding's Memorialls of the Trubles, vol. ii. p. 342; Acts of the Parliaments of Scotland (16th March, 1649), MS. General Register House, Edinburgh; Illustrations of the Topography and Antiquities of the Shires of Aberdeen and Banff, vol. iv. pp. 470-472.)

[34] Appendix, nn. 22-35, pp. 204-208.

[35] List of Pollable Persons within the Shire of Aberdeen, 1696, vol. ii. pp. 102, 129 132.

family debts, that Patrick Gordon makes his first appearance.[36] He was then a boy of fifteen, on the eve of setting out to seek his fortune as a foreign mercenary, according to the fashion of a time which taught the country gentleman, however needy, to look on trade with contempt.[37] Twenty years of successful service enabled the thrifty soldier to pay off one heavy encumbrance.[38] He discharged another in no long time afterwards;[39] and when he died, Auchleuchries was freed of all but one inconsiderable bond. But its release was to be short lived. The cloud of ' wadsets' soon began to thicken again, and before Gordon had been thirty years in his

[36] Appendix, no. 41, p. 209.

[37] Gordon's kinsman, Robert Gordon of Straloch, in his Description of Aberdeenshire, written about 1650, says : ' Negotiatio urbanis relinquitur : meliores (magno suo malo) id vitae genus, ut natalibus suis impar, dedignantur ; unde inopia multis ; cui levandae, ad tractanda arma se accingunt, quae, multis locis apud exteros, Belgas praesertim, Germanos et Gallos, semper amicam et illis adamatam gentem, a multis annis, cum laude. exercuerunt ; ingeniis, enim, acribus et fervidis, sive Musis sive Marti se mancipent, non leviter proficiunt.'—(Praefecturarum Aberdonensis et Banfiensis Descriptio, in Collections for a History of the Shires of Aberdeen and Banff, p. 6.)

France and Flanders were the first fields in which the Scottish mercenaries distinguished themselves. The earlier years of the seventeenth century drew them to Germany, then the great theatre of European war. But they had long before carried their arms to the banks of the Nile on one side, and to the shores of the Baltic on the other. So early as 1510, a younger son of Hume of Fast Castle was high in the service of the Mameluke Sultan at Cairo. In 1519, the Scottish Privy Council authorised the King of Denmark to levy soldiers in Scotland for his war against Sweden. The Danish King had Scottish troops again in his pay in 1572.

In 1573, there was a Scottish regiment, commanded by Sir Archibald Ruthven of Forteviot, in the service of the King of Sweden, then at war with the Czar of Muscovy. Before 1591, Russia had Scottish mercenaries in her own ranks.—(Proceedings of the Society of Antiquaries of Scotland, vol. ii. part ii., pp. 160, 161 ; Acta Dominorum Concilii, vol. xxxii. fol. 179, MS. General Register House ; Epistolae Regum Scotorum, vol. i. p. 313 ; Registrum Secreti Concilii, 1571-1572, p. 169, MS. General Register House ; Giles Fletcher's Russe Commonwealth, ff. 39, 40, 55.)

Before the middle of the sixteenth century, Scotland had begun to pour out another class of adventurers—those wandering traders who, in Gordon's day, as we see from the earlier pages of his Diary, swarmed throughout all the Polish provinces. Sir John Skene speaks of ' the Scottesmen of the realme of Polonia' so early as 1569.'—(De Verborum Significatione, voce ' Pede-pulverosus.') Not long afterwards they were of such numbers and importance that a Scottish Consul—Patrick Gordon of Braco—was sent to Dantzic for their protection. He was the only officer of his class of whom Scotland could boast, with the old exception of the Conservator of Scottish Privileges in the Netherlands.

[38] Appendix, no. 48, p. 211.

[39] Appendix, no. 54, p. 214.

grave, his grandson was a landless man, and another race of Gordons dwelt in Auchleuchries.[40]

Patrick Iwanowitsch, as he was called among the Muscovites, was not happy in his children. He was survived by two sons and as many daughters of his first marriage, and by one son of his second marriage.[41] John, the eldest son, entered the Russian army when young, but was dismissed from it for reasons which do not appear. He was next sent to the Scots College at Douay, but showed as little inclination for the school as he had shown for the camp. Settling at Auchleuchries, he married, in 1691, a daughter of one of the few Roman Catholic gentry of the neighbourhood.[42] He visited his father at Moscow in 1693, and died before 1712, leaving five sons and two daughters.[43] The eldest son, who bore his grandfather's name, sold Auchleuchries in 1726.[44] One of his brothers, James, became a member of the Society of Jesus, and he had some reputation as a scholar.[45] Another brother, Alexander, entered the Jesuit College at Bourdeaux as a novice, and is there lost sight of.[46]

[40] Appendix, nn. 61-66, pp, 216, 217. Until a few years ago, Auchleuchries continued to be possessed by Gordons (the descendants, apparently, of the Alexander Gordon of Sandend, to whom it was sold by the grandson of Patrick Iwanowitsch.) It now belongs to one who can appreciate its associations, Mr. Grant Duff of Eden, the accomplished Member of Parliament for the Elgin burghs.

[41] To the last. Gordon kept the day on which he lost his Katharine von Bockhoven as a day of mourning. Thus, in his Diary for 1696, he writes: 'October 10. The anniversary of the death of my first wife— the dear, the beloved.' She died before 1682. Gordon married again before 1686.

A lithograph of the placid features of his second wife, a buxom dame of Dutch extrac-

tion, is given by Dr. Posselt in his first volume, along with a portrait of General Patrick Gordon, which has been reproduced, by Mr. Schenk, for this work.

[42] Appendix, no. 53, p. 213. The poll-tax returns of 1696 shew that the household at Auchleuchries was then six in number— the 'goodman' himself, his wife, their eldest son (for whom the Earl of Aberdeen had stood godfather two years before), one man servant, and two women servants.—(List of Pollable Persons within the Shire of Aberdeen, 1696, vol. ii. p. 129.)

[43] Appendix, nn. 58-60, 63, 64, 66, pp. 215-217.

[44] Appendix, nn. 62, 65, 66, pp. 216, 217.

[45] Dr. Oliver's Biography of Members of the Society of Jesus, p. 23.

[46] The Reverend Mr. Griffin of New

James, the second son of General Patrick Gordon, was at the Jesuit College at Memel in 1686, when his father, ' perceiving that they had there infected him with Calvinism,' removed him to Douay. In 1690 he had a Lieutenant-Colonel's commission under the Czar. He was taken prisoner in a battle with the Swedes in 1700, and at the end of two years made his escape by flight. A petition for the arrears of pay during his captivity is the last mention of him that has been found in Russia.

General Gordon's third son, Theodore, was sent, in 1692, to a Jesuit College in Prussia. Returning to Moscow in 1697, he entered his father's Butirki regiment as an ensign. He had risen to the rank of Colonel in 1709, when all trace of him ceases. Before that year, both he and his brother James had sold or mortgaged the estates of Iwanowska and Krasna, part of the confiscated domains of Prince Golizyn, which the Czar Peter bestowed upon their father.

Of Gordon's two daughters, the elder, born in 1665, was married at the age of seventeen, to Colonel Strasburg, a German, serving in the Russian army. He died in 1692 from wounds caused by an explosion of the fireworks in which Peter the Great took such delight. Eight years after his death, his widow married her kinsman. Alexander Gordon of Auchintoul, and left Russia with him in 1711. She died in Scotland in 1739, having outlived all the children of both her marriages.

Abbey informs me that General Gordon's grandson, James, born in 1702, was sent to Douay College in 1717, entered the Jesuit noviciate at Rome in 1719, and took the simple vows in 1721. He was reputed an excellent scholar, and taught Humanities for four years in the Roman Jesuit province. In 1732 he is found in the Gregorian University at Rome. He afterwards taught for a year in the Scots College at Madrid. In 1735 he was sent from Rome to commence Theology at Douay. Nothing more is known of him.

His brother, Alexander, born in 1708, was sent to Douay in 1721, and after finishing his Rhetoric there, entered the Jesuit noviciate at Bourdeaux in 1726. No farther trace of him has been recovered by Mr. Griffin.

The first nuptials of the second daughter of Patrick Iwanowitsch were graced by the presence of the Czar Peter. Her husband, Major Daniel Crawford, died in 1692. Two years afterwards she married Colonel Snivius, but was again a widow in 1698.

The high place which Gordon won for himself at the Court of Moscow tempted not a few of his kinsfolks into the service of the Czar.[47] The most successful was his son-in-law, Alexander Alexandrowitsch, as he was called in Russia.[48] Leaving the French army, where he had gained a captain's commission, he came to Moscow in 1696, and was at once made major in General Gordon's regiment. He was present at the capture of Asof, and rose in ten or twelve years to the rank of Major-General. In 1711, the death of his father recalled him to Scotland, where he acted as Lieutenant-General of the insurgent army in 1715. He escaped attainder by a mistake in the act, and in 1727 returned to Scotland. He died

[47] There were Gordons in Russia before Patrick Iwanowitsch. Frequent mention of William Gordon, a seaman engaged in the early trade between England and Muscovy, is made in Dr. Hamel's 'England and Russia.' The researches of Dr. Posselt have discovered, among the military archives of St. Petersburg, certain documents regarding a Captain William Gordon in 1631, and a Lieutenant Colonel Alexander Gordon in 1634. The latter, no doubt, is the person of the same name who appears in Sir Thomas Urquhart's 'Jewel,' among 'those Scottish colonels that served under the great Duke of Muscovy, against the Tartar and Polonian.'

I have seen reason to think that more trust may be given to the intimations of the fantastic Knight of Cromarty than may at first sight seem due to them, although I am scarcely prepared to vouch for all that he tells about one of his six Scoto-Muscovite colonels, 'Colonel Thomas Garne, agnamed the Sclavonian and upright Gentile, who, for the height and grossness of his person, being in his stature taller, and greater in his compass of body than any within six kingdoms about him, was elected King of Bucharia.'

[48] George Gordon of Coclarachy, by his first wife, a daughter of Seton of Pitmedden, had two sons, the elder of whom Alexander Gordon of Auchintoul, a senator of the College of Justice for a few months before the Revolution of 1688, married a niece of Lord Gray. The eldest son of this marriage, born in 1669, married, in 1700, Katharine Elizabeth, the eldest daughter of General Patrick Gordon.

at Auchintoul in 1752, in his eighty-second year, having amused his old age by writing a 'History of Peter the Great,' which was published at Aberdeen in 1755.   It is accompanied by a memoir of his own life, the accuracy of which, in so far as regards his career in Russia, is challenged by Dr. Posselt.

Thomas Gordon, a nephew of Patrick Iwanowitsch, distinguished himself in the sea service of Russia, which he entered in 1717.[49] He was made Admiral in 1727, and died in 1741 at Cronstadt, of which he had been governor for nearly twenty years.

JOSEPH ROBERTSON.

EDINBURGH,
12th December, 1859.

---

[49] Dr. Posselt finds him described in official documents in the Russian archives as the son of William Gordon, a merchant. It appears elsewhere that he was born at Aberdeen, and that he married a daughter of Sir Thomas Elphinstone of Calderhall, by whom he had a daughter, married in 1726 to Sir Henry Stirling of Ardoch, baronet.—(Mr. Fraser's Stirlings of Keir and their Family Papers, pp. 120, 121.   Edin. 1858.)

CONTENTS

OF THE

DIARY

OF

GENERAL PATRICK GORDON.

CONTENTS.

CONTENTS.

CONTENTS.

CONTENTS.

CONTENTS.

CORRECTIONS.

DIARY OF
GENERAL PATRICK GORDON.

DIARY OF GENERAL PATRICK GORDON.

I AM not ignorant that it is thought as hard a taske for any man to writt the story of his own lyfe, and narrative of his actions, as for ane artist truly to draw his owne picture ; yet, haveing proposed to my self to writt only by way of a journall, without makeing any reflections by blameing or commending any of the passages of my lyfe (following herein the counsell of Cato, *Nec te laudaveris, nec te culpaveris ipse)*, I think it not uneasy ; especially not intending it for publick view, as also leaving to others, if any shall take paines to read it, the free censure of any thing here done. I have mentioned no more of publick effaires as came to my knowledge, relateing rumours for such and thruths for verity. Some publick effaires (military I meane, for with those of state I have medled very litle, being out of my spheare) I have touched in a continued series, and others interlaced with the story of my owne lyfe (defective, I confess, and that for want of documents and intelligence) being such things the most whereof I have been present at and seen myself. To conclude, I cannot tell you a better or truer reason for writing this, as that it is to please my owne fancy, not being curious of pleasing any bodyes else, seing *omnibus placere* hath been reckoned as yet among the *impossibilia*.

A.D. 1635.

In the year of our redemption one thousand six hundred thirty and fyve, on the last day of March, about three aclock afternoone, being Easter, in Easter Achluichries, within the parish of Crochdan and the shirefdome of Aberdeene, I was borne ; my parents, John Gordon and Mary Ogilvie,[1] heritours and proprietours of the same lands of Achluichries.

A.D. 1640.

I was sent to the schoole at the kirk of Crochdan on Lambe masse day, and put to lodge and dyet by a widdow called Margaret Allan, my schoolmaster being William Logon.

Here I, together with my eldest brother, stayed foure years, haveing proceeded to *Multiplex uno sensu* in the first part of Despauter's Grammer.[2]

A.D. 1644.

My father, dwelling in Achridy, in the parish of Ellon, I was sent to that schoole, my schoolmaster the same, being translated hither, being lodged and dyeted in Alexander Scrogges his house.

I was at this schoole about a year, when, because of the great troubles both before and now, all publick schooles were abandoned. My father tooke a schoolmaster called Georg Murray into his house, who teached us halfe a year very well.

A.D. 1646.

My father, removeing to   , wee were now sent again to the schoole of Ellon, and lodged in John Mill his house, our schoolmaster being Mr. Hary Tom.

Here we learned about a year. My father, in the meane tyme, removed to Achmade, and afterward to his own lands, and dwelled in Westertown.

---

[1] [In a subsequent volume of his Diary, on the 23d August 1698, the Author writes:— " Gott this account of my mother's father. The Laird of Petlurg maryed Janet Ogilby, daughter to the Laird of Cullen, and was soone after killed at the battel of Pinky, leaving him who succeeded unborne, or in the cradle. She was afterwards maryed to one Olgilby of Blarak her cousin, a cadet of the house of Cullen, and of 3000 merks in the Boyne. By him she had a son called James, brother uterine to Sir John Gordon of Petlurge, and unkle to Mr. Robert. This James marryed Marjery Gordon, daughter to Georg Gordon of Coclaraghy. These were my grandfather and grandmother."]

[2] ["Multiplex uno sensu dicatur abundans:
Tignus vel *tignum* sit testis, *pisaque pisum :*
Cum pene innumeris, quae lectio multa docebit."

(Ioannis Despavterii Ninivitae, Grammaticae Institvtionis Lib. vii. docte et concinne in compendium redacti, per Sebastianvm Dvisbvrgensem, lib. iii. ' de heteroclitis,' p. 89, edit. Edinb. 1617.)]

A.D. 1648.

Wee were sent again to the school of Crowdan ; our schoolmaster Mr. Alexander Frazer, who teached us about a yeare.

A.D. 1649.

Mr. Andrew Browne succeeding schoolmaster, I, with my brothers, were continued at schoole, and lodged and dyeted in Alexander Garioch his house, near two yeares.

A.D. 1651.

I was taken from schoole; and, staying at home, did wait upon my father.

Haveing thus, by the most loveing care of my dear parents, atteined to as much learning as the ordinary country schools affoord, and being unwilling, because of my dissenting in religion, to go to the University in Scotland, I resolved, partly to dissolve the bonds of a youthfull affection, wherein I was entangled, by banishing my self from the object ; partly to obtaine my liberty, which I foundly conceited to be restrained, by the carefull inspection of my loveing parents ; but, most of all, my patrimony being but small, as being the younger sone of a younger brother of a younger house ; I resolved, I say, to go to some foreigne countrey, not careing much on what pretence, or to which country I should go, seing I had no knowne ffriend in any foreigne place.

Being thus resolved, there wanted nothing but to have the leave and furtherance of my parents, which I obtained by the intercession of my unkle, and haveing notice of a ship at Aberdeen bound shortly for Dantzick, I made a progress into the country amongst my ffriends and tooke my leave of them.

On the third of June, after a sadd parting with my loveing mother, June 3. brothers, and sister, I took my jorney to Aberdeen in company of my father and unkle, who, after two dayes stay, wherein I was furnished with cloths, money, and necesseries, returned. My mother came foure dayes thereafter, of whom I received the benediction and tooke my leave.

On the twelfth, I went aboord, and stayed at anchor all night in the June 12. roade. The shipp was a large merchant's shipp, with eighteen gunnes, belonging to Dantzick, the skipper called Jacob Bartlman.

On the thirteenth, the merchants and passengers came aboord, and to- June 13.

wards night, notwithstanding it was calme and misty, wee weighed anchor, and, with the tyde, made a slow passage. About sunsett it cleared up, whereof, haveing notice below deck, wee made hast above, and, with many sighes and teares, bidd our native country farewell, which even then seemed to be in a mourning for our departure; but shortly, by a brisk gale of westerly wind, wee were deprived of all sight thereof. Haveing, to ease our minds, laid our selves down to rest, wee were called up by the noise which the mariners made, because of some shippes approaching, who, being come near, were knowne to be Hollanders. They inquired what wee were? from whence come? and whither bound? To all which, receiving satisfaction, they askd if wee had any Parliament men aboard? and if wee had seen an English shipp which had escaped them in the mist? To both which was answered, No; so after salutation with great gunnes, according to the manner at sea, we parted, keeping our course east and by north two dayes with a favorable gale. Then wee were by contrary winds forced very farr to the north, and after two weekes, had a sight of Norway. The wind then beeing a little better, we sailed along that coast, passing by the Nais to Skagen in Jutland, then by the illand Lezow, the Trindell, and the litle illand Arnout, then by a rock called the Kole, where the skippers exact a discretion of every one who hath not passed that way befor. The mariners are ordinarily lett downe thrice into the sea. Wee came in the evening to the roade befor Elsenure, and anchored about halfe a Dutch mile from the strand or shore

The next day wee went ashore, and dined in a Scotsman's house very well for twelve pence a man, and at night returned to the shipp. On the morrow, about noone, the shipp being cleared, wee hoised saile, and made good way, with a fresh gale, by the illands Ween and Roan on our left hand, and the city Copenhagen, the King of Denmark's residence, on our right, holding our course by Valsterboom and the illand Bornholme over to the coast of Pomerell.

July 18.　　On the eighteenth July, new stile, wee had a sight of the coast. In the evening was a great calme, and in the night great raine and thunder, so that wee made no way. The next day wee passed by the Heel, and a litle after, began to throw out our ballast, which was sand and stones. The next day being also calme, and being near the shore, wee were towed near the land by boats, and anchored before the Munde, a strong fort. Some of us went ashore, and walked to Dantzick on foot, being a Dutch mile from the citty, whither wee arrived at noone, and lodged in a Scotsman's house in the Holy Ghost street, our landlord being called John Donaldsone. Here I stayed eight dayes.

On Friday, with a gentleman Thomas Menezes, and three other Dutch men, wee bespoke the ordinary coach for Konigsberg; and Mr. Menezes and I payed each for our share to Brawnsberg a doller and a halfe. On Saturnday at eight acloak wee tooke our jorney, and came the same night to Elving, being nyne miles, and the next day timely to Frawensberg, fyve miles; where meeting with our good friend Mr. Robert Blackhall, who was priest and vicar to one of the chanons there, by his perswasion wee let our coach go, and stayed all night.

This towne lyeth on the lake called the Frish Haffe, being every where open, and all along the foot of an hill, whereon the Dume standeth, wherein ar, as I remember, eight Channons, who have most pleasant houses and orchards towards the fields. The next day, being well entertained by Mr. Blackhall, and hireing an open waggon, with Father Blackhall and Mr. Menezes, I rode to Brawnsberg, being a mile, most of the way being through a wood. *Here Copernicus water worke.*

Brawnsberg lyeth in the bishoprick of Vermia, on the river Passarg, which a mile from thence falleth in the Frish Haffe. Over the river is the new towne, which is divided in two streets, one towards Konigsberg, the other along the river upwards. The townes are joined by a bridge, the old towne walled, the new open every where. Here wee tooke up our lodging by Mr. Menezes his brother, who was a priest called Alexander Michal Menezes, whose charge was a small church in the new towne.

Here being at my studies in the Colledge of the Jesuits, albeit I wanted not for any thing, the Jesuits alwayes bestowing extraordinary paines, and takeing great care in educateing youth, yet could not my humor endure such a still and strict way of liveing.

[A.D. 1653.]

Wherefor takeing my leave, I resolved to returne home againe, and on a Tuesday, about ten acloak, I took my jorney on foot to save expences, for I had no mor money left but seven reichs dollers and a halfe, and one suit of cloaths which I had on. So takeing my cloake and a litle bagge wherein were my linnens and some bookes, with a staffe in hand I pilgrim'd it away all alone. I had not learned any Dutch, by reason of our speaking

Latine in the Colledge, only had enquired and written downe some words necessary for askeing the way, victualls, and such like. My portmantell I caryed for ease on my back, betwixt villages, or when I did see no body ; but comeing to any village or meeting any body, I took it under my arme. Thus accoutred I went privately round the old towne, P. Menezes only convoying me to the high way. I walked the well knowne way through the wood to Frawensberg, pleasing my self either with trifling fancies or such objects as offered in the way.

Being come to Frawensberg, I resolved not to go to Father Blackhall for fear of being chidden for leaving the Colledge, he haveing alwayes diswaded me from takeing any other course as to be a scholler and turne religious. And so excuseing my self to him hereafter by a letter, pretending my being in company who would by no means make any stopp there, I went through the towne without going in any where; and keeping the high roade, about half a mile off, I did meet a coach with some gentlemen in it, who, stopping, look't very ernestly upon me, and asked me in Dutch something, which I not understanding passed by on my way. A mile and a halfe further, at the entring of a wood the way divideing, I was doubtfull which to hold, yet the midle being the liklyest I entred that. After I had gone a pretty way into the wood, and doubting whether I was right or not, I began with serious thoughts to consider my present condition, calling to mind from whence I was come, from my most loveing parents and friends, and where I was now, among strangers, whose language I understood not, travelling my self knew not well whither, haveing but seven doliers by me which could not last long, and when that was gone, I knew not where to gett a farthing more for the great jorney and voyage which I intended. To serve or work I thought it a disparagement, and to begg a greater. With those and such like thoughts I grew so pensive and sadd, that, sitting downe, I began to lament and bewaile my miserable condition. Then, haveing my recourse to God Almighty, I, with many teares, implored his assistance, cravving also the intercession of the Blessed Virgin and all the Saincts in heaven. Then getting up, I went forward, continuing in prayer with great fervency, when on a suddaine, from the right hand, came an old man rideing, whose gray haires might exact and force reverence from the haughtiest heart. He, seing me crying, in crossing my way said to me in Dutch, which I understood so : Cry not my child ; God will comfort you. I was very astonished at his suddaine appearance and words, and also ashamed that any

body should see me in such a plight. However, keeping on my way, I
began to recollect my self, and to think that God had sent this old man of
purpose to divert me from such passionate fitts; the conceitt whereof made
me rouse up my self and walke on more chearfully. And, truly, as well
now as very many times hereafter, as you shall hear, when, in my necessities
or any extremity, I betook myself to God Almighty by prayer, I found His
extraordinary assistance.

At night, I came to a village, and tooke up my lodgeing in the krue or
alehouse. When I came in, I called for halfe a stoup of beer, the table being
covered. The landlord asked me diverse questions, to which I could returne
no answer, because I did not understand him. Only I told him from whence
I came and whither I was bound. He desired me to sitt downe and eat with
him, to which I readily condiscended, and calleing for another halfe [stoup]
of beer, which, and supper being ended, I asked one of the maids where I
should ly, and she laughing, went and fetched me a bundle of fresh straw,
and told me I might ly in an empty waggon in the place where the waggons
and horses were; to the which I went, and makeing my straw bed, I laid my
cloake one halfe under and the other above me, with my coat and portmantle under my head; and so, being exceedingly wearyed, I laid me downe.
But by and by came the maid, and reaching me a pillow, began to laugh
downright, then jumped away in such hast as if she had been afrayed of
some infection. I made but one sleep the whole night, and gott up halfe an
hour before the sunne, and bringing in my pillow to the roome, asked what
I had to pay. The landlady told me a stowp of beer, which I payed, and
then asked what I had to pay for victualls; and she answering nothing, I
thanked and went on my way.

This place being a mile or litle more from Elving, one halfe whereof
was downe a hill, about eight acloak I came in to the towne, where I mad
no stay. Only buying some excellent white bread called semels, and apples,
I walked directly through. When I was without the towne, I made a halt,
to see if I could light on any company going that way; when by and by
came two sturdy fellowes, of whom I enquired if they were going to Dantzick, and they answering yea, we jogged on together. These were alwayes
troubling me with questions, to the which I could answer nothing, only that
I understood not Dutch. Haveing walked a mile, one of these fellowes left
us: the other being a dogged-like bare fellow, who was still eying my cloaths
and cloak, and our way being towards a black like thick wood, I began to

conceit that this fellow had brought me out of the way, and intended to lead me into that wood, and there to murther me for my cloaths, or anything also he thought to find by me. This conceit of myn strongly encreasing, wee came to a little house, where he asked me if I would drink any beer. I told him I had no money; so he calling for beer, I took out my purse, wherein were seven or eight grosses, all in small shillings, which I on purpose shewed him, telling him it was all I had to bring me to Dantzick. I called for small beer for two shillings, which, haveing drunk, my guide and fellow traveller, whom I would have very faine been ridd of if I could, brought me on a way towards the left hand, and by and by to a village.

Wee went into the inne, where my fellow traveller called for beer, and I for small beer; wherat the landlady wondering, was satisfyed at last by the information she received from the fellow that cam with me. At my comeing in, I saw, in the other roome, a fellow standing befor a pack, measuring of lawn; and haveing heard in Brawnsberg that there were diverse Scottishmen who used this kind of trade in Prussia, I began to suspect this was a countreyman. The landlady understanding that I could speak no Dutch, nor Polls either, called out this packman, who haveing asked me something in Dutch, and receiving my usuall answer, that I understood no Dutch, he asked me what contreyman I was. I told him a Scotishman. Then asking me, very confidently, from whence I came, whither I was going, what course of life I intended to take, and why I travelled in company of that fellow (whom he knew, as he said, to be a robber, and wondring that I had travelled so farr with him unrobbed), he told me, if I had a mind for Dantzick, I should go along with him to his house, which was but a mile off, and stay three or foure dayes, and he would take me upon a waggon to Dantzick. I answered to every thing as circumspectly as I could, and thanked him for his kind profer, telling him I must be precisely in Dantzick the next day. He urged my going along with him, and the mor he urged, the mor jealous I was that he had some designe upon me; and so, shifting him fairely off, I made ready to be gone. My countryman diswaded me from going any farther with that fellow, but I told him that I had found nothing in him as yet, and intended at night to hire a waggon for the next day.

So wee went away together, and came to a house called Weyershoffe, and being sett downe in the inne, which is hard by, my fellow traveller told me that he was to stay there; whereat I seemed sorry, but he enquireing, lighted upon other two fellowes, who were bound for Dantzick, to whom he recommended me, and so we parted. These fellowes took a near by-way, ferrying over many ditches, and passeing others upon planks; and came towards night to a village about a quarter of a mile from the river Vistle. Here I lodged all night, supping on such ordinary fare as they use there.

The next morning, I was not able to go any further. My feet, not being used to such hard travell, was full of blisters, and the skinne off in many places; wherefor, going owt to the high way, which lay by the end of the village, I waited upon some occasion of finding a waggon. There droved by, in short tyme, diverse waggons or kolesses, as they call them, none whereof would take me along. At last came a very civill man, haveing another sitting by him, at whom I asked in the best manner I could, if he would take me along to Dantzik, and what he would take for fraught; who, first askeing halfe a dollar, at last told me he would take no less as a reichs-ort; which I promiseing, went to the inne, and paying for my supper, fetcht my portmantle, and gott me upon the kolesse. Here, as every where, I was troubled with questions, which I did not understand. Wee crossed the Wistle in a prumme, and gott to Dantzick by eleven acloak, being three miles from the prumme; where, paying my fraught, I went to seek out my old lodging, which, after much wandring up and downe, I found, where I was kindly welcom'd by my landlady, who was a notable resolute woman.

Here I found my self in great anxiety and perplexity, not knowing what to begin; for all the ships were gone, and so no hopes left of getting home to my owne countrey; no acquaintance of whom I could borrow any money to subsist with untill the next shipping; my cloaths and linnens beginning to looke bare; and, the worst of all, no person to whom I could reveale my necessities, being bashfull and ashamed that any should know that I was re-dacted to such streitgth. But my landlady guessing, by my retirednes and melancholious behaviour, my condition, began to presse me to declare my intentions. I told her my resolution was to returne to my parents as soone as I could; which, my intention, she communicating to diverse of my contrey-men who frequented that house, and withall, that she thought me to be scarce of money; so, the next day at dinner, these merchants began to perswade me to turne merchant, to the which I, fynding my nature averse, answered in fair termes, however, not being willing to disoblidge any. They began to tell me, that it would be nyne or ten moneths ere I should fynd an occasion by sea to Scotland; to travell by land would be very expensive, and to stay there no lesse.   But findeing me averse to engage my self, and resolute to returne home, they left off, and told me I had best travell up to Polland, where I might, one way or another, passe the ensuing winter, and then take what course I thought fittest in the spring; and that there was a countreyman and namesake of mine liveing in a towne called Culm, about twenty miles off, who was a very civill man, and would be very glad of my company; which counsell I embraced, and desired their assistance in findeing au occasion thither.

The next day, I was informed of a flatt-botomed vessell, ordinarily called skute, which was to returne to Swets, a mile from Culm; which way of travelling, albeit longsome and irkesome, yet because cheape, I willingly choosed. So upon a Tuesday, . . . August, haveing contented my landlady for my dyet and lodging, being very favourably used, I walked to the vessell, wherein I was to travell; and about two houres befor sunsett, haveing all ready, wee sett forward.   This, as I said before, was a flatt-bottomed vessell, which is so made because of the many shallow places in the river Vistula.   It was about fyfty or sixty ordinary paces in length, and breadth conforme.   There were fifteen or twenty Polles, or rather Russes, in the boat, who could not speak a word Dutch; only he who had the command of them could speak a litle.   I took up my lodgeing in the most convenient place I could find, being in the open part of the boat, being guarded from the raine by the long hanging cover of the cabine.   Here was no hopes of any exercise but lying and sitting, there being no convenience for walking, only where the steerman's place was, which was very cumbersome.   My best pastime was my booke; only sometimes I went on land and walked a good pace befor, going in now and then to some boures house or another, wher I bought milk.   I had very litle pleasure, for, the most part of the way; the Vistula being hemmed and kept in with great dammes on either side, which hinder the prospect of the countrey, only the toppes of the houses and trees were to be seen.

About foure miles, being so much by water, and three by land, wee passed by a towne, on our right hand, called Dirshaw, lying on a high ground, and fortified with walles.   A mile and a halfe below this towne the Vistula divideth, one arme going for Dantzick, another falleth into the Frish Haffe.   The point at the division, called Dantziker Hooft, hath been diverse

tymes fortifyed and garrisoned, to the great detriment of the adjacent
countrey. About two miles further, we passed by that arme called Nogat,
which falleth also in the Frish Haffe, after it hath passed by Marienburg.
The point here is called Montospilts, and hath been also fortifyed and
garrisoned in the warres. About two miles further, wee passed by the
Meve, on our right hand, lying on a high ground, and fortifyed with
stone walles. About a mile off, on the left hand, Marienwerder, a town
fortifyed with a stone wall, and belonging to the Duke and Elector of
Brandenburg, did show itself. Some foure miles further, wee passed by
another towne, called Nyenborg, situate also on a high ground, and
fortifyed with a stone or brick wall; and, three miles further, by Graudents,
a well fortified towne, with a castle, which being situate on a high
ground, hath a very fair prospect over a most fertile and most inhabited
country. Three miles further wee came to Swetsh, which lyeth in a
low ground, and hath, it seemes, in former times, been well fortifyed
with a brick wall, but had only now a castle, half ruined. It lyeth off
from the river to the right hand, by a little rivolet, called [Schwarzwasser.]
Here I was conducted, by one of these who came along with me, to the
house of John Smith, a merchant, and very civill man, where I lodged all
night, and was very well entertained. The next day I gott a waggon, and
after noon, I crossed the Wistula by a prumme, which is a flatt bottom'd
vessell, wherein waggons, horses, and every thing else are transported over
rivers in this country.

Towards night I came to Culm, being a mile from Swets, and was conducted to my namesake his house. This Culm is very ancient, and hath
been of great account in former tymes, which may appear by its giveing
name to all that district; and the common law, which is observed throughout all Prussia, is ordinarily called Culmish law. It was fortifyed by the
. . . wi . . . with a very strong brick wall of a large circumference. It is but meanly inhabited, and slenderly builded; only about the
market place are some very faire houses, with wealthy indwellers. Albeit,
it hath many gates, yet hath it but three which they make use of; one which
leadeth to the river, the other to Culmsee and Grawdents, the third to
Torun. It is under the jurisdiction of a bishop, who hath his title from it,
and resideth in a towne about fyfteen miles from thence, called Libava. It
hath its owne magistrates, and peculiar lawes of very great and ancient
priviledges. It is very pleasantly situated on a large corner of the high

continent. Below, towards the river, and all along the side of the hill, towards Graudents, ar many fair orchards and gardens, as also by the river a large suburb, called the Fishery. It hath within the towne three monasteryes, a Dominican, Franciscan, and of Votaresses, and a large cathedrall. There ar fair lands belonging to the towne, which is divided among the burgers; who, of beer brewing, and buying of cornes, for the most part have their livelyhood.

Here I passed the tyme during the winter, when falling in acquaintance with one John Dick, who was prentice to a merchant called Robert Sleich, I was perswaded by him to travell further up into Polland; and, because I was much inclined to be a souldier, he told me that Duke Ian Radzewill had a lyfe company, all or most Scottismen, where wee would without doubt be accommodated.

[A.D. 1654.]

So, takeing my leave of friends here, I began againe a jorney on foot, in company of the foresaid John Dick, who had left his service. My stock was much the same as I had when I came from Brawnsberg, haveing gott foure dollers from a friend upon my way; but my habit was farr changed, for, towards the winter, I had translated my cloak into a Polls upper coat, and lyned it with sheepskines. The first night, wee went to a village, and lodged by a Skotsman, who lived there. The next day, we passed by a gentleman's house, called Gzin, and so the direct way to Thorun. When wee were within a mile of the town, two waggons, with wood did overtake us, to whom wee, being wearied, gave each two pence to lett us sitt up to the towne. We entered the towne towards night, and tooke up our lodging in a great house, on the west side of the market place, in the old towne.

Here we stayed foure dayes, and then haveing with two Dutchmen, who were bakers, hired a waggon for Varso, giveing each eight florens, wee sett forward on Saturnday, betimes in the morning. The next day, wee passed by Cuiafsky Brest, so called to distinguish it from another Brest in Littaw, through Cowale and Gambin, two little townes, to Varsaw, which is thirty miles from Thorun.

Wee tooke up our lodgeing in the suburb Lesczinsky, so called from a pallace-like house hard by, built by noblemen of the family of the Lesczinskyes. The seym or parliament was sitting at this tyme in Varsaw, where we hoped to have found Duke Radzivill. After wee had stayed eight dayes, expecting his comeing, wee were informed that he was not to come at all, which put us upon new projects. My comerad had been two or three years in the countrey, could speak Polls and Dutch, had some skill in merchandising, and so, for getting a livelyhood, had many wayes the advantage of me. But my purpose of turning souldier here failing me, I resolved to persue my former resolution of returneing to my parents. Here were many merchants of our countreymen, into whose acquaintance I was ashamed to intrude myself, and they shewed but very litle countenance to me, haveing heard of my intention to turne souldier, and fearing lest I should be burthensome or troublesome to them. I had but eight or nine florens left, wherewith I was not able to subsist long here, or to travell farr either. I began, however, to enquire for the neerest way for Scotland, and was informed that Posna, the cheife citty of Great Polland would be the most convenient place I could go for first; whither an occasion shortly after offered, with a gentleman called . . . who had been at the seim, and had bought some horses, so that, by the recommendation of a friend, he promised to take me along, and keep me free of expences, which was a very good occasion, considering my condition.

So, upon a Tuesday early, we tooke horse, being three persons and six horses. The gentleman, his servant, and I, drove the horses along; but when wee came to any towne he would have me lead one, and the servant the other two spare horses. The first night, we rode five miles, and lodged in a village; the next morning, through the litle towne . . , and dined in Lovits, which is a large not well fortified towne. The arch-bishop's castle-like faire house is fortifyed with a wall and moatt. This night we lodged in a village; the next night in a litle towne, Piatek; and, crosseing the river Warta twice, at the second crossing wee passed by a very fair gentleman's house haveing large orchards and parkes. Foure miles from Posna, we passed through the little towne Szroda, where the seimiks or country committees for choosing of commissioners are kept; and, being Palme Sunday, according to the new stile observed in Polland, about midday wee passed through a pretty wood of firres about half a mile in breadth, the way being streight, about thirty or forty fathome broad, ascending gently, which made a very pleasant prospect. At the coming out of this wood wee had a sight of the fair citty of Posna, which we entered about one acloak afternoone.

Posna or Posen, of all the citties in Polland, is the most pleasant, being very well situated, haveing a wholesome aire, and a moste fertile countrey round about it.   The buildings are all brick, most after the ancient forme, yet very convenient, especially these lately builded.   The market place is spacious, haveing a pleasant fountaine in each corner, the shopps all in rowes, each trade apart, and a stately radthouse.   The streets are large and kept cleaner as any where else in Polland.   It hath on the west side, within the towne, on a hill, a castle built after the ancient manner, and somequhat decayed.   The river Warta watereth the east side thereof, makeing an iland, which is inhabited by Germans, most whereof being tawners, giveth the name of the tawners suburb to it.   There is a fair street which leadeth to the thume eastward, being halfe a mile in length.   The thume is a stately structure. There are diverse monasteries of both sexes, and several orders, and a vast cathedrall, which make a stately schow.   The suburbs are large and decored with churches and monasteries.   The citty is fortified with a brick wall, yet very tenable by reason of its wastnes.   But that which surpasseth all, is the civility of the inhabitants, which is occasioned by its vicinity to Germany, and the frequent resorting of strangers to the two annuall faires, and every day allmost: the Polls also, in emulation of the strangers dwelling amongst them, strive to transcend one another in civility.

The gentleman who brought me along, had his house or lodging in the Jewes street, where I dined with him; and after dinner he took me along to a Skotsman, called James Lindesay, to whom I had a recommendatory letter.   At first, he was imperiousely inquisitive of my parents, education, travells, and intentions.   I answered to all his demands, with an observant ingenuity.   One passage I cannot forgett, which was this.   When, upon his enquiry, I had told him what my parents names were, he said in a disdainfull manner: Gordon and Ogilvie! these are two great clannes, sure you must be a gentleman!   To which, albeit I knew it to be spoken in derision, I answered nothing, but that I hoped I was not the worse for that.   However, afterwards, he was kind enough to me.   There I was persuaded by my countreymen to stay and wait some good occasion or other of prosecuting my jorney.

Dureing my abode in this place, I was kindly entertained by my countreymen, to witt, Robert Ferquhar, James Ferguson, James Lindesay, James White, James Watson, and others.   I was afterwards, by their recommendation, entertained in the suit of a yong nobleman, called Oppalinsky, who was, according to the custome of the Polonian nobility, going to visit foreigne countryes. At my departure, my kind countreymen furnished me with money and other necessaries very liberally, so that I was better stocked now as I had been since I cam from my parents.

[A.D. 1655.]

In this noblemans company, as one of his attendants, I came to Hamborgh, being very civilly used the whole way. It was the midle of Februar when wee arrived here; and the nobleman, after eight dayes stay, takeing post for Antwerp, I tooke my leave of him.

Here, at this tyme, were the Sweds officiers, very busy levying and listing of souldiers. All the innes were full of cavaliers, ranting and carousing. When my lord departed, Wilczitsky, his paedagogue (who spoke good French, Dutch, and Latine) agreed with the landlord of the inne where wee lodged, for my dyet, chamber, and bed, for four markes a weeke; only, when there were no other strangers, I was to be content with such ordinary fare as the house affoorded. Here I stayed eight weeks, when it chanced a cornet and a quarter master to lodge in the same innes, who, haveing inquired at the landlord what I was, and understandeing my condition, began to be very kynd to me, and to sheu me all respect in the tyme of dinner and supper, which was the only tyme I was forced to converse with them; I either passing the other tymes with walking or keeping my chamber. In all their discourses they extolled a souldiers lyfe, telling that riches, honour, and all sorts of worldly blessings lay prostrate at a souldiers feet, wanting only his will to stoop and take them up; then, falling out in commendation of our contreymen, than whom no better sojors were of any nation to be found, and that, albeit, nature had endued them with a genius fitt for any thing, yet did they despise the ease, advantage, or contentment any other trade might bring, and embraced that of a souldier, which, without all dispute, is the most honourable. Albeit I understood most of their discourse, and was well enough pleased therewith, yet was I not able to render any satisfactory answer, negative and affirmative being all I could affoord them; and, being jealous that they had a designe to engage mee, I shunned, as much as I could, any familiarity or conversation with them.

One day at dinner, the quartermaster told me that a countreyman of mine was come, called Gardin, which, according as he pronounced it, seemed to me Gordon. He told me he was a ruitmaster, a very pretty discreet man. In the tyme of my being in this citty, I had not sought to be acquainted with any man for severall reasons, but especially for saveing of expenses; but now I could not be at rest untill I had gott notice where this ruitmaster lodged, and thereupon resolved to give him a visitt, not without thoughts of engadgeing my self. Being come to his lodging, I enquired for him, and, by accident, light upon a servant of his called Andrew, who was a Dutchman, but spoke good English as haveing lived in Scotland some yeares. He brought me immediately above to the ruitemaster, who was in company with two or three other officers. I told him, that, hearing of a person of such quality as he was being come to this citty, I could not be satisfyed with myself untill I had payed my respects to him with a visitt, hopeing that he would pardon my abrupt intrudeing myself into his company at such a time, where, perhaps, he was bussied with weighty effaires. He answered me that I was very welcome, and that he had not such weighty effaires as could hinder him for giveing that entertainment which was due to a friend, especially a countreyman and stranger. And, haveing desired me to sitt downe, he began to enquire of my parents, wherein, having received satisfaction, he asked me if I knew one Major Gardin. I told him I had heard of him, but had not the honour of his acquaintance. He told me that he was his brother, and that I must be their kinsman; then, calling for a glass of wine, began to be very merry, remembring all friends in Scotland; and then, falling to particular healths, in a short tyme we were all pretty well warmed. All along, both he and the other officers were a battering downe my resolution for Scotland, telling me that I would be laught at when I should come home, and that they would tell me I had been over sea to see what a clock it was, and returned as wise as I went out; and what comfort or content could any man of spirit, who had nothing to care for, have to stay at home, when the countrey was enthralled by an imperious insulting enemy, and no way of redresse left? The only way for those who bore honourable minds was to pass the tyme abroad, and better their judgements by purchaseing experience at least. But what needed many perswasions, it being a course to the which I was naturally enclined? So that, without any further circumstances, I give my promise to go along, and that, without makeing any capitulation. So ignorant I was of such matters at that tyme.

The next morning, when I had slept out, and began to reflect upon my last night's engagement, I found myself in such a labirinth of perplexed thoughts, that I knew not how to wind myself out of them. However, of necessity, according to my promise and duty, I must go wait on my ruitmaster; whither being come, he brought me below to the stable and showed me his horses, here being three prime horses for his owne sadle, any of which, he told me, should be at my service and for my use, and that his servant should be as ready to bring my horse as his, and that he would use me as a loveing kinsman, with many fair promises more, which satled my wavering thoughts; so that, now come what will, I resolved to try my fortune this way. The ruitmaster his occasions carrying him from this citty to Stade, I stayed in my old lodgeing, not at my owne but his charges now. He told me, that, in a few dayes he would call for me.

Here I continued a fortnight, when, by intemperancy (to the which my nature was alwayes averse) or by some other accident, I fell into a feaver, which the phisitians commonly call the remitting feaver, which continued me bedfast eight dayes, and then turned to a tertian ague. After I had stayed three weeks longer, which made up in all thirteen weeks, I rode with the ruitmaster to Ratzeburg, the residence of the Dukes of Saxen-Lawenburg, one whereof called Frantz Artman was our collonell, and from thence, the next day, to Lubeck, where the ruitmaster left me, I not being able to travell. After foure or fyve dayes stay, the ruitmaster, being on his march, sent for me. I was in this march in a very pittyfull condition, being hardly able to ride that day which I was free of the ague; and that day I had it, I was forced to ly on an open waggon, above the ruitmaster's baggage, and was very glad of such a convenience.

Wee continued our march through Pomeren to Stetin. I am sorry that I can give no exact account of my jorney and march now through this pleasant and fruitfull countrey, being hindred in my jorney to Hamborg by rideing in a closse waggon and want of the Dutch language, and now by my tedious sickness, which took away all appetite to my curiosity. Wee had very good accomodation on this march; and by that tyme that I was come near Stetin, I was pretty well recovered. I was sent befor to Stetin to buy some necessaries, or swords and boots, for some troupers who wanted.

On the fourteenth of July, I rode out of Stetin, and the next morning came to the army, when they were drawing up in a large meadow. It consisted of thirty brigades of foot and 7000 ruiters, being in all about 17,000 July 14.

men, with a gallant traine of artillery. It was a most delightfull and brave show, the ruiters being very well mounted, and the foot well cloathed and armed, and above all, the officers in extraordinary good equippage.

[Here the Diary digresses 'from the method of a journall, which,' says the writer, 'I only at first intended,' into a formal recapituation of 'the reasons which the King of Sweden alleadged for his invadeing of Polland.' It is needless to print this dry catalogue of hollow excuses. Gordon clearly enough discerns the true motives of the war, in the bold, restless, and ambitious spirit of Charles Gustavus.]

These were the pretences of the King of Sweden for his invadeing of Polland. It would be too tedious to mention the Polnish objections and reasons, and the Swedish replications. But, to tell you briefly, the maine reason was this. The Swedish King, haveing been bred a souldier, and haveing now obtained the crowne, by the resignation of his cousin Queen Christina, would needs begin his reigne with some notable action. He knew that the remembrance of the honour and riches obtained by many cavaliers in the German warrs, under the Swedish conduct, would bring great confluence of souldiers to him, when it should be knowne that he was to arme, which, by reason of the late universell peace in Germany, and the many forces lately disbanded, would be mor easily effectuated. Haveing in his conceit already formed an army, there was no prince or people, except Polland, to which he could have the least pretence, (albeit princes, indeed, never want pretensions to satisfy their ambition, and will have their pretences lookt upon as solid and just reason). Besides, he could never gett such an occasion, perhaps, as now ; Polland haveing been for some years tossed by their prevailing rebellious Cosakes, who had not only gott the Tartars to joyne with them, but had the last year procured the Moscovite to espouse their interest, who, with very great armyes, had made a great impression in Littau, and, at this time, had brought most of it under his subjection. He wanted not, also, good intelligence and encouragement from some of the discontented Polnish nobility ; and [Hieronymus] Radzievsky, the banished under-chancellour of Polland, added fuell to his ambition; so that such a tyme, accompanyed with such advantages, was not to be omitted.

The Swedish ricksrades were very forward, and levyed three regiments on their owne expenses. Cromvell also (who was never backward to make work abroad, that strangers should not have leisure to pry into his designes and actions at home), advanced money, for the which four regiments were levyed in stift Bremen and Verden.

[The Swedish army began its march from Stettin, upon the sixteenth of July. Crossing the July 16. river Netz, it encamped near Posen, which offered no resistance. Here Gordon had an oppor- July 29. tunity of revisiting his countrymen who had befriended him a twelvemonth before, but whose joy on again seeing him did not appear to be immoderate. He notes more than one instance of the extreme severity of the discipline enforced by Field-marshal Wittenberg—'not justice, but tyrrany,' as Gordon calls it. 'A boy of fourteen was hanged for flinging a stone at a Pole August 2. who was searching the camp, under an escort, for horses which had been stolen from him. A August 7. soldier, pursued by the reproaches of a woman, was carrying off a pot of milk from a farm house, when the Field-marshal happened to be passing. The trooper in his terror dropped the can, as well he might, for it was in vain that the good dame whom he had robbed begged his life upon her knees. He was hanged upon the spot.' Gordon was told, on good authority, that between Stettin and Konin, where the King joined the host, and rebuked this excessive rigour, 470 persons were put to death for slight offences, within little more than a month.

On the thirty-first of August, the army resumed its march, the signal being given by great August 31. kettle-drums, each of them as large as nine or ten hogsheads. They were carried on a broad waggon drawn by six horses: the drummer stood behind, and the sound might be heard at a distance of two German miles. Four or five days brought the Swedish force to Sobota, where September 3-5. Gordon, while foraging, encountered some personal adventures. The army rested for a day September 8. beside a Jesuit monastery, from which the inmates had fled into Silesia. The place, having been plundered of everything but its library, the Field-marshal sent his secretary to select some books for his own use. Gordon was called in to assist in the task, and so had an opportunity of providing himself with a few volumes. Three days afterwards, the rear guard, in which he September 11. happened to ride, was, through the imprudence of the officer in command, surprised by the Polish cavalry, which took the whole body prisoners except a corporal and eight troopers, of whom Gordon was one. On galloping up to the main army, they were at once taken to the Field-marshal. That personage had a fit of the gout, and, on hearing that no more than nine had escaped, 'wished only that the devil had taken them too.' In this affair, Gordon received a dangerous wound under the ribs. The surgeon was unable to find the ball until the second day; and such was the pain for a week afterwards, that, every time the sore was dressed, the patient fainted. But by the assiduity of the leech, and care in diet, he soon recovered.

When the Swedes came in sight of Cracow, they found the northern suburb in flames, the September 25. Poles having set it on fire lest it should give shelter to the invaders. On the second day of the September 26. siege, Gordon, who was sent out to reconnoitre, narrowly escaped being taken prisoner. A fort- October 10-11. night afterwards, he was engaged, under his countryman General Douglas,* in the attack and

---

* This successful soldier was the youngest son of Patrick Douglas of Standingstane, the ninth son of William Douglas of Whitting- hame, a judge of the Court of Session from 1575 to 1590. Joining the banners of Gustavus Adolphus, along with his three brothers, Wil-

route of a body of about 10,000 Poles, who occupied certain heights from which they annoyed the Swedish foragers. The pursuit was entrusted to Colonel Konigsmark, who, finding that 400 of the fugitives had taken refuge in a fortress, summoned them to surrender at discretion. They complied, and were hanged to a man. In this engagement, which cost the Swedes 1600 men, Gordon had his horse killed under him, and received a shot in the leg.

October 17.   Cracow having capitulated on what are called 'good terms,' although a contribution of not less than 300,000 rix-dollars was exacted, Gordon succeeded in obtaining his discharge from Rittmeister Gardin, in whose company he had hitherto served. He continued free until the army was about to leave Cracow, and to retire into winter quarters, when he engaged to serve as a volunteer under his countryman, Rittmeister Duncan, in the regiment of the Swedish Count Pontus de la Gardie.

A.D. 1656.

January.   Having one day been sent out to reconnoitre, Gordon found, on his return, that his regiment had left its quarters. As he was riding after it, he was captured by the Poles, and taken to the house of one of their nobles, into whose hands he was persuaded to commit his money and valuables, worth in all 150 ducats. The noble promised, from this store, to supply the young captive's wants, but failed to keep the promise. Gordon, meanwhile, was carried to Sandets, where he was kept in close arrest for seventeen weeks. At length the intercession of a country-man, 'P. Innes, Provincial of the Franciscans,' procured his liberty, but only on the condition that he should take service with the Poles. So much choice being left him, he entered as a dragoon in the company of Constantine Lubomirski, the Starost of Sandets, the most dis-tinguished of three distinguished brothers. So ended Gordon's first brief service with the Swedes.

His first and not more lengthened service with the Poles began with a march, the day after he joined their banner, from Sandets towards Warsaw. That capital, then in possession of the Swedes, had already been beleaguered for three weeks, by the Lithuanian army, which had opened trenches and made approaches towards the walls, before the arrival of the force in which July. Gordon served. The appearance of these troops decided the fate of the city, which was so feebly fortified, that, after a brief siege, and several partial assaults, the Swedish garrison capi-tulated. During these operations, Gordon was placed as guard over a village, a few miles from the city, belonging to the brother of his commanding officer. Here he found an excellent op-portunity of learning the Polish language. The wife of the Podstarost, Arcziferski, in whose house he seems to have had his quarters, treated him with great kindness. She herself was elderly, but she had a daughter who sang Polish love songs to the young Scot, puzzled him with Polish riddles, and was indefatigable in teaching him the right Polish pronunciation. Mean-

liam, Archibald, and Richard, all of whom died in the Swedish service, Robert Douglas had risen to the rank of major-general in 1645, when he captured the baggage of the Empe-ror Ferdinand II. after the battle of Jankowitz. Three years afterwards he was lieutenant-general. He obtained a birth-brief, under the great seal of Scotland, on the 1st of November, 1648. He appears as general in 1655, and as lieutenant field-marshal in 1656.

while, he neglected no opportunity of gaining experience in his profession, never failing to repair to the camp on the eve of any feat of arms, in order that he might take part in it. Some
of his own more private proceedings show considerable likeness to what was known in his own
country as the levying of *black-mail*. Some peasants had taken refuge with their goods and
chattels on an island in the Vistula, and, in return for a weekly pension of sixteen guldens and
four florins, Gordon undertook to guarantee their safety so long as the siege lasted. He confesses another practice still more closely resembling the artifices of the Highland freebooter.
Comrades in the camp, with whom he was in concert, would drive off the cattle of the nobles in
the neighbourhood of Gordon's station. His aid in recovering the missing herds would then be
sought by the owners, and his successful exertions duly rewarded by them. Thus passed his
days, neither unpleasantly nor unprofitably, during the siege of Warsaw. By the time that the
city surrendered to the Poles, it was obvious that the Podstaroste's daughter had lost her heart
to the Scottish trooper. Nor did the mother conceal her willingness to accept him as a son-in-
law. But Gordon had no mind for the match.

In less than a month after the Swedes had been driven from Warsaw, it was once more in
their hands, as the fruit of the sanguinary defeat which they inflicted upon the Poles in the great
battle of three days, fought within sight of the Polish capital. Soon after this conflict, Gordon
was taken prisoner by some Brandenburgh troopers. They carried him before his countryman
and former commander General Douglas, a soldier who had so highly distinguished himself on
every occasion, that the King of Sweden had created him Lieutenant Field-marshal. Gordon's July 18-20.
explanation that he had been forced into the Polish ranks, was readily received, on one hand;
and he, on the other, as willingly agreed to serve again with the Swedes in a picked corps of
Scots which Douglas was about to organise as a training school for officers.

Gordon's second service with the Swedes extended to three years. His first act was to go to
Warsaw to seek recruits among his countrymen for the Douglas company, 'Here,' say the
German editors, 'some three pages of the original Diary are taken up with interviews which
he had with the daughter of his former host, the Podstarost, and her parents, in which'—so they
are pleased to say—'the reader can feel no interest.' Gordon returned from Warsaw with
twenty-four men. The Swedish standard, indeed, was in such favour with the adventurers from
Scotland, that, as we are told, a month or two previously, 'Lord Cranstoun arrived at Pillau with
2,500 Scotch for the Swedish service.' *

The rittmeister of the company in which Gordon served was John Meldrum, and its success

---

* Under the date of March, 1656, a Scottish annalist records that 'at this tyme lykewyse the King of France and the King of Swadin sent over thair commissioneris to Scotland for [levying] of sodgeris. The King of Swadin, by the Lord Cranstoun his commissioner, re-savit multitudes; the uther, for France, was not so weill ansuerit.' (Nicoll's Diary of Transactions in Scotland, p. 175.)

'Whatever be the originals of the warre,' writes Principal Baillie, in September, 1656,

'yet, to me its evident, that the ruine of the King of Sueden is the hazard of all the Pro-testants round about . . . We will stand on our watch-tower, and look on with ane earnest desyre of any thing may come out of all these dangerous commotions, which may look to-wards the performance of the Lord's great promises, Antichrist's ruine, the bringing in of the Jews, the breaking or Christianing the Turks and other Pagans.'—(Letters and Jour-nals, vol. iii., p. 321.)

in driving cattle was such, that Gordon's share of the booty in a short time amounted to a hundred rix-dollars. When orders were given for a march towards Dantzic, he had to provide himself with two horses, which he obtained, by the help of his servant, without money. He confesses that this was wrong, but adds that it could not be helped. The state of the Swedish army was such, that he who could not make up his mind to live by plunder, must be content to be eaten up with vermin, or to die of hunger and cold. He told the rittmeister how his horses had been come by, and that officer made no scruple in allowing him to ride off before the rest of the troop, so that the stolen steeds might not be reclaimed by their owners upon parade. The company was recruited in its march by forty-three Scots who had come to join the Swedes. It lost several by the plague, which was then desolating the district. Gordon believed that he felt its symptoms after burying one of his comrades, and, as a measure of prevention, drank his own urine.

There was now to be a change in the fortunes of the war. Hitherto the Czar Alexis had been labouring for the overthrow of Poland, but, with the prospect of its falling into the hands of the Swedes, his policy altered. Concluding a twelvemonths' truce with the Polish King, he determined to make a diversion in that monarch's behalf, and, marching through Livonia, presented himself before the gates of Riga at the head of 100,000 men. On tidings of this event reaching the camp, the Scottish adventurers were ordered to the relief of the beleaguered town. Gordon's chronicle of the siege is interesting chiefly for the glimpses which it discloses of the state of the Muscovite army. All the superior officers seem to have been foreigners—the commander-in-chief being a Scot from Aberdeenshire, Sir Alexander Leslie.* After the failure of one or two attempts upon the place, Leslie was ordered by the Czar to summon a council of war, and to make a written report of its deliberations. The issue was unfavourable; and although the Czar and his ministers believed that the town might be taken, were it not that the foreign officers were unwilling to subject the King of Sweden to such a loss, they determined to raise the siege.

The footsteps of the Scottish regiment were now turned toward Dantzic, which was held by the Poles. The besiegers seem to have been left to support themselves as they best might. Some Scottish gentlemen, who had newly joined the standard, had not yet learned to live by plunder, and, receiving no part of their promised pay, were reduced to great straits. In order to free himself of their importunities, the Field-marshal ordered them on an expedition, under Major Sinclair, to collect nails for a bridge about to be built. The device succeeded—before the novices came back they had acquired the art of pillage. One day a troop, of which Gordon was one, found itself surrounded by superior numbers of the enemy, but cut its way through so gallantly, as to be praised by the King. In this affair Gordon was wounded in the forehead.

---

* 'At one time,' says a memoir of the family, in Macfarlane's Genealogical Collections (MS. Adv. Lib. Edinb.) 'three Lesleys were generals of armies in three kingdoms, as Walter Count Lesley, in Germany; Alexander Lesley, Earl of Leven, in Scotland; and Sir Alexander Lesley of Auchintoul, in Muscovy.' The Russian commander sprang from the stock of Crichie, —the same branch of Balquhain which, planting an offshoot in Ireland, produced, in a subsequent generation, the author of the 'Short Method with the Deists.' Alexander Leslie appears to have entered the Muscovite service shortly before the Wars of the Covenant broke out in his native country. A commendatory letter from King Charles I, dated in March, 1636, introduced him to the notice of the Czar Michael Fedorowitsch. He died at an advanced age, Governor of Smolensko, in the year 1663.

A.D. 1657.

He was less fortunate on the next occasion. Some Polish peasants, in the garb of soldiers, surprised him in a solitary ride, and carried him into Dantzic. They searched him by the way, but were so little expert, that he was able to conceal from them a purse with fourteen dollars They next proposed that he should take off his new English boots, in order to exchange them for a pair of theirs; but, perceiving with whom he had to deal, the Scot refused in a high tone, and threatened that he would report them to the commandant of the city. That person, on learning that the captive was of the Douglas company, exclaimed, 'Ha! have we got one of these birds?' Gordon was sent to prison under the charge of a corporal, with whom he dealt earnestly for the recovery of his Latin Thomas a Kempis. The corporal was deaf to his prisoner's entreaties, and Gordon is at pains to chronicle the revenge which he afterwards wreaked upon his obdurate jailor.

He was urged to take service with the Poles, but, like most of his Swedish fellow captives, refused, and in no long time was set free by exchange. Lieutenant-Colonel Drummond, Major Fullerton, Lieutenant Scott, and others of his countrymen, obtained their liberty about the same time. Among those who tempted him to follow the Polish banner, was a countryman and namesake, if not also a kinsman, Patrick Gordon of the Steel Hand.* The owner of this re-doubtable name, who was then a captain in the Polish cavalry, at once asked if he was not a son of Gordon of Achleuchries. Gordon no sooner returned to the Swedish camp than he pro-ceeded to extort from the peasants who had entrapped him, compensation for the horse and equipments which he had lost. An attack of fever now stretched him on bed, in a village which was one day surprised by the Poles, when seventy Swedes were killed, and forty made prisoners. The woman of the house n which Gordon lay passed him off as her sick husband; and his countryman and attendant, Alexander Keith, hid himself in a barn. They were the only two of their party who escaped. The Diary here records an example of the impetuous temper of the successor of Gustavus Adolphus and Christina. A complaint having been pre-

* Patrick Gordon, 'with the Steel Hand,' was, along with Lord Lewis Gordon, young Leith of Harthill, and other northern royalists, excommunicated by the commission of the General Assembly of the Kirk of Scotland, in June, 1647, for rising in arms with the Marquess of Huntly. In December, 1650, the brethren of the presbytery of Strathbogie, in their visitation of the kirk of Rothiemay, made inquiry of the laird if the minister, Mr. James Gordon, (author of the 'History of Scots Affairs, from 1637 to 1641,') 'conversit frequently with malignants,' and, 'particu-larlie, if he conversit with Patrick Gordon, *alias* Steilhand.' The laird's answer was, that, 'in tyme of the troubles, the said Patrick came sumtyme to the minister his hous, but knew not if the minister spoke with him; but, since the forty-seven year of God [when Steel Hand was excommunicated] he neuer knew him to haue come to his hous.' Not many months afterwards. Steel Hand appears to have made his peace with the Kirk. In October, 1651, he presented himself before the provin-cial synod of Aberdeen, beseeching release from his excommunication, and appealing to the testimony of the brethren of the presby-tery of the Garioch for proof of his penitence. The synod appointed three of its members to goe apart and conferr with him anent his sense off his former guiltiness and gross de-bordinges.' The report of the reverend dele-gates was 'that they found in him some signes of repentance;' and the synod accordingly re-mitted him to the presbytery of Aberdeen 'to be relaxed.' His next appearance is, as re-corded in the text, in 1656, when he was a captain of Polish Cavalry. He will be found to present himself more than once in the sub-sequent pages.

ferred to the King against Rittmeister Meldrum, that officer was maintaining his innocence, when Charles Gustavus, bursting into a fit of passion, gave him two cuts on the head, and several strokes across the shoulders, and ordered him into arrest.   In one of their foraging expeditions, Gordon and his comrades came upon a party of Finlanders (serving in the Swedish army), who were maltreating a young Polish beauty.   The interference of the Scots in her behalf resulted in a conflict, in which the Finlanders were beaten, when Gordon rode off with the lady, and placed her in the hands of a kinsman named Koitzi.   Gordon's gallantry was such, that he not only refused the ten ducats which were pressed upon him in name of ransom for the fair captive, but next day sent her a number of articles of female apparel, from the ample store of his booty. Having rejoined his company, he had the good fortune, along with his countryman James Elphinstone, to make prize of a number of horses, of which he gave two to his rittmeister, and bestowed others upon his friends.   Soon afterwards, leaving his baggage behind him, he had to take up his station where there was nothing to pillage, so that, he says, he had ' often to dine with Duke Humphrey'—whom the German editors suppose to be a veritable personage of a hospitable turn of mind.

Field-marshal Douglas was now recalled into Sweden, to meet a threatened attack from the Danes. His Scotch company was left behind him, much to its miscontent. It was slowly retreating, followed by the Imperial troops, when a fierce skirmish took place, in which Rittmeister Meldrum fell mortally wounded, after fighting like a lion, and Gordon was taken prisoner, after his horse had been shot under him, and he himself had been severely wounded in two places. He complains that a Scotch Captain Leslie in the Emperor's service, the heir presumptive of Walter Count Leslie,* showed no interest in his captive countrymen, who were

* 'Walter Lesley, second son of the third marriage of [John Lesley of Balquhaine, with Jean Erskine, daughter of Alexander, Master of Erskine,] would have succeeded to the fortune, next to William his brother. But acquiring a great estate in Germany, he was created a Count of the Empire, and was designed Count Lesley, and staid there all his days. He quit his right to the estate of Balwhaine to his younger brother Alexander Lesley of Tullos, and also he often sent home money both to him and his son, whereby he recovered the fortune to its antient splendour. This Walter served long in the wars, under the Emperor Ferdinand II., against the Swedes, with great honour, being first *supremus vigiliarum praefectus*. But that which raised him so high was the killing of Wallenstein, Duke of Freedland (who was the Emperor's general of his forces, and designed to betray the army to the enemies, as was discovered by his letters to the Swedes, which this gentleman gave up to the Emperor), with John Gordon, a Scotsman, in *anno* 1634, whereby he came to greater honour abroad than any Scotchman in his time. For he was made captain of the Emperor's guard, colonel of a regiment, marshal-general of the Emperor's camp, privy counsellor, governor of Sclavonia and Pitrinia, and a Count of the Empire. Yea, and the patent was to him and to his two brothers, William and Alexander also, and their posterity, that, in case he should die without children (as he did) they might succeed to him in his estate and honours. He was made ambassador both to the Pope and the Grand Seignior, which employment he discharged with great abilities and honour, and so much to the satisfaction of the Grand Vizier, that he acknowledged, in his letters to the Emperor of Germany, that the whole court at Constantinople was better pleased with that goodly person he had sent, than if he had sent a million of presents: and the Grand Seignior himself, beholding his entry into the seraglio through a window, was heard to say, that, in all his life, he never saw such a show. (See Mr. Ricaut, his Preface to the Book of the Turkish Fashions.) He was governor of Verasdan and of the confines of Sclavonia and Petrinia, lord of Pettow and Neostadt, privy counsellor to the Emperor, and marishall of his army. He married Anna

left to support themselves by charity. They were kindly treated by the Imperial officers generally, who laboured by every means to persuade them to join the Imperial standard. Appealing to their royalist feelings, the Austrians urged that true cavaliers ought rather to serve the Emperor, who had befriended their King, than the Swedish monarch who was the confederate of the arch-traitor Cromwell. Gordon answered that it was for sovereigns themselves to requite the benefits which they received one from another; that the King of England would doubtless discharge any obligations of this kind, when he got his own again; but that, meanwhile, his subjects were under no obligation to neglect their own fortunes in foreign countries, out of regard to such considerations of state policy.

Escaping after a confinement of six weeks, in company with a John Smith, Gordon, with no little difficulty, found his way back to the Swedish camp He now demanded his discharge from the Douglas company, urging that, during the whole period of his service, he had never received a farthing, either for pay or for equipment; and that, as he had delivered himself from captivity at the risk of his life, he had a right to look upon himself as a free man. After some little delay he obtained a discharge from the generalissimo, couched in laudatory terms, and recommending him for the place of an ensign in the King's body guard—an appointment which Gordon seems to have been in no great haste to obtain.

Engaging, in the meantime, along with Lieutenant Hugh Montgomery and sixteen others of their countrymen, in a marauding expedition very much on their own account, Gordon had his feet frozen. The doctor pronounced the case hopeless, but an old woman effected a cure. The Scotch adventurers had the good fortune, more than once, to make prisoners of foraging parties of the Imperial troops, by whose ransom they enriched themselves. On one occasion Gordon's party, although numbering no more than eighteen, captured a village in which were twenty three men-at-arms, and thirty five dragoons, and carried them, along with forty horses, in triumph to the Swedish head quarters, where the Field-marshal was boundless in his commendations of their skill and courage. Such a name had the Scots now achieved as successful foragers, that, whenever prisoners were brought in, or any exploit was performed, the credit of it was given to them.

Francisca, the Princess of Dietriechsteine (daughter to Maximilian *aulae Cesareae prefectus*), but had no issue by her. He died (short while after his return from that famous embassy to Constantinople) 4th March *anno* 1667, *aetatis* 61, whither he was sent by Leopold, the present Emperor, which embassy was written by Taferner the Jesuit, one of his retinue." (Genealogy of the Leslies, in Macfarlane's Genealogical Collections, MS. Adv. Lib., Edinb.) The work alluded to in the last sentence was published at Vienna in 1668, under the title of ' Caesarea Legatio, quam mandante augustissimo Rom. Imperatore Leopoldo I. ad Portam Ottomannicam suscepit, perfecitque excellentissimvs dominvs Dominvs Walterus S.R.I. Comes de Leslie, Dominus Pettovij, et Neostadij ad Meltoviam, Sac. Caes. Majestatis a consilijs intimis, et aulae bellicis, campi mareschallus, et confiniorum Sclavoniac et Petriniae generalis, Aurei Velleris eques, succincta narratione exposita, atque illvstrissimo domino, Domino Jacobo S.R.I. Comiti de Leslie, domino Pettovij et Neostadij ad Meltoviam, Sac. Caes. Majestatis camerario, et pedestris regimini scolonello, excellentissimi oratoris nepoti, in perennem laudatissimi patrui memoriam dicata a R[everendo] P[atre] P[aulo] T[rafferner] S[ocietatis] J[esu], itineris comite, et excellentissimi oratoris capellano.' The volume has an engraved full-length portrait of Walter Count Lesly.

A.D. 1658.

[The next passage of the Diary, bearing date in January or February 1658, must be given in Gordon's own words.]

Whilst wee lay in this Werder, an English ambassador, called Bradshaw, having been on his jorney to Moskovia, and not admitted,* returned this way, and was lodged in Lamehands taverne. Wee getting notice thereof, and thinking him to be that Bradshaw who sat president in the highest court of injustice upon our soveraigne King Charles the First, of blessed memory, wee resolved, come what will, to make an end of him; and being about fifteen, with servants, six whereof might be accounted trusty, wight men, the others also indifferent, wee concluded, that doing the feat in the evening, wee could easily make our escape by the benefitt of the strait ground and darknes of the night; and so, being resolved, wee tooke our way thither. Being come near, and asking a boore, come from thence, some questions, he told us that just now some officers were come from Elbing to the ambassadour, and about forty dragounes, who were to guard and convey him to Marienburgh; which made us despair of doing any good, and so wee returned. Wee had resolved to make our addresses to him, as sent with a commission from Field-marshall von der Linde to him; and, being admitted, seven or eight of us to have gone in and stabbed him, the rest guarding our horses and the doore, and so being come to horse, made our escape to Dantzick.

[Not without regret for the free and profitable career which he quitted, Gordon now entered the Swedish regiment of Colonel Anderson as ensign. While on duty at Stum, he one day, in company with his friend Captain Forbes, rode after some Poles who were carrying off horses belonging to the garrison. Falling into an ambuscade, they were set upon by about a hundred of the enemy, when Forbes was wounded and taken prisoner. Gordon, floundering through a bog, dashed through three Poles who had marked him for their prey, and, spurring past twenty others, escaped with the loss of his sabre, his cap, and a handful of hair which was torn with it from his head. His clothes were riddled with shot, and had three arrows sticking in them, one of which wounded him in the side. On regaining the Swedish lines, his colonel, who, with

* [The German editors observe, that, from the death of King Charles I. until the restoration of King Charles II., no English ambassador was received in Russia. The English merchants, in consequence, lost their privileges. There are in the Russian archives, it is added, numerous notices of the friendly feeling which the Czar displayed in different ways towards King Charles II. during his exile from England.]

some other officers, had quietly beheld the whole affair, rode up to him with a cocked pistol, and threatened to shoot him for venturing so far without orders. Gordon made no other answer than that he would not desert his captain; but he was so affected by this incident and by the loss of his friend, that, in despair, he rode back to seek death in another skirmish with the Poles. He escaped once more, and Captain Forbes, after a captivity of six weeks, recovered his liberty.

In a sally by a handful of the garrison against a numerous body of the enemy, Gordon again November 22. fell into the hands of the Poles. He was allowed to walk about on parole, and made the acquaintance of divers of his countrymen serving in the Imperial ranks, among whom was Captain Leslie, son of Tullos, and nephew of Count Leslie.* Proposals to liberate Gordon by exchange were made by the Swedes, but refused by the Poles, who wished to see him again in their service. Nor was he at heart much averse to joining their banner, although he thought it right to affect some outward show of reluctance. The renowned John Sobieski tempted him with the offer of a dragoon company in a body of troops stationed on the Sobieski estates, but this appointment would have withdrawn him from the path of promotion, and was therefore declined. The future deliverer of Vienna—whom he characterises as a 'hard bargainer but courteous'— could offer him no other service, but undertook to speak for him to Field-marshal Lubomirski. The latter, soon afterwards, offered Gordon the rank of ensign in his body guard of foot; but the aspiring Scot had already held the same rank in a Swedish regiment of dragoons, and declared that there was no potentate upon earth whom he would serve any longer as ensign.

A.D. 1659.

At length, after a captivity of eleven weeks, he accepted the appointment of quarter master. 1659. He takes great pains to vindicate this change of standard—his chief reason resolving itself into this, that his main object was to make his fortune, and that the Swedes had too many enemies to have much chance of success. His own experience had already satisfied him, that, 'in the Swedish army, the soldier is in danger of being starved to death by hunger.'

* 'James Lesley, the second son [of Alexander Lesley of Tullos, the third and youngest son of John Lesley, the tenth Laird of Balquhain by his third marriage with Jean Erskine, daughter of Alexander, Master of Erskine,] when young, went to Germany to his uncle, Walter, Count Lesley, and was educate with him as his heir. He sent him to his travels through France, Italy, Spain, Poland, and Germany; and, at his return, he married in *anno* 1666, Maria Theresa, the Princess of Leichtenstein, daughter to Prince Charles of Leichtenstein, Duke of Trappau, and spent at his marriage 50,000 rex-dollars, for there were present at the marriage, for respect to the uncle, the Count, the Emperor, Empress, and most of the nobility at the court. For his uncle and his own deservings, he was in great reputation in the Emperor's court, and was created counsellor and gentleman of the Emperor his bed-chamber in *anno* 1660, and received the golden key that same year, and, in 1666, was made colonel of a regiment of foot, and after his uncle's death was one of the marishalls of the Empire. He at last had some competition with Count Staremberg, whereupon he retired from the court to his city of Pettaw, where he was seized with an apoplexy and the gout, which kept him, till his death in *anno* 1692, without issue of his body. But his brother Patrick, his son James Ernest Lesley, succeeded to him, to whom he left the lordship of Pernegg which he had bought, which was to fall to Franciscus Jacobus, son to Alexander his own brother, if he had no heirs; and he gave the lands of Balwhaine etc., to George the second son of his brother Patrick.' —(Genealogy of the Leslies, in Macfarlane's Genealogical Collections, MS., Adv. Lib. Edin.)

One of Gordon's first duties, in his second campaign with the Poles, was with a party of seven dragoons to protect the Staroste of Libush, not from the enemy, but from the Polish troops as they marched past. This task detained him for six weeks. He is warm in his praises of the kind and friendly Podstaroste, and records that such were the gains of this service, that they supplied him with a new uniform, two horses, a carriage, and a couple of servants, besides a parting gift of one hundred gulders and an old but serviceable Turkish steed. Among the gentry whose hospitality he shared was a German of the name of Milgost, who had an only daughter, whose hand he signified his willingness to bestow upon the young quarter master, if only he would renounce the profession of arms. He had another affair of the same sort at the next place to which he was sent. A wealthy widow, in whose house they were quartered, wished to marry his major, and the major, in turn, wished his quarter master to marry the widow's daughter. To all these proposals the Scot returned soft but evasive answers.

About this time Gordon encountered two countrymen—James Burnett of Leys, whom he found in the train of an envoy from the waywode of Kiew in the Ukraine; and Dr. William Davidson, then physician to Field-marshal Lubomirski, and subsequently first physician to John Casimir, King of Poland.*

The Polish army, under Lubomirski, now sat down before Grandenz. Gordon had often been in the place while he was in the Swedish ranks, and the Field-marshal now consulted with him as to the best point of attack. His counsel was followed, and with a successful issue. The town was taken by storm, but, although the mutinous garrison capitulated, the commandant retreated to a tower of the citadel, and declared that he would rather die than give himself up to ' the knaves the Polls.' Gordon was sent to parley with him, and succeeded in persuading him to surrender to the Imperial auxiliaries of the Polish army. Meanwhile the soldiers pillaged his boxes, nor did Gordon disdain the spoil of twelve or fifteen volumes, from his not inconsiderable store of books. The captured garrison immediately took service with the Poles.

Gordon records about this time the arrival of a letter from his father at Auchleuchries ; the death of Lieutenant Adam Gordon, and of Ensign John Kennedy ; and the vain endeavours of Major Patrick Gordon of the Steel Hand to get the property of the lieutenant, who was his kinsman, out of the hands of the colonel of the regiment. Quarter master Patrick Gordon was pressed into this last business, with the promise of ' a share and half ' of all that might be recovered ; but although he almost came to blows with the colonel, and made a perilous journey to the coast, all was to no purpose. William Gordon, a trader in Konigsberg, who acted as banker for the deceased, refused to give up his moneys to Steel Hand, alleging that there were nearer relatives in Scotland—an argument to which the quarter master could only oppose a threat of future vengeance. This journey gave Gordon an opportunity of sending a letter to October 15. his father, by the hands of Adam Gordon of Ardlogy, whom he met at Konigsberg about to

---

* Of this once eminent physician who, after practising in Paris, where he is said to have held the office of intendant of the Jardin des Plantes, finally settled in Poland, notices will be found in the Biographie Universelle, t. x., p. 617; the Book of Bon-Accord, pp. 316, 317; Fasti Aberdonenses, pp. 400, 403, 404; Father Blakhal's Breiffe Narration, pp. 192, 198; James Gordon's Description of Both Touns of Aberdeen, p. 8.

take ship for Scotland. On his way back to the camp, he waited on the commandant of Pillau, by whom, much against his will, he was constrained to stay to a marriage feast. He was much rallied for his temperance at dinner, nor was it without difficulty that he was persuaded to join in the gaieties which followed. The charms of his host's daughter having prevailed against his dislike of dancing, the officers assailed him with fresh provocations to drink, but he turned a deaf ear to them all.

When he returned to the army, the general sent for him to say that a regiment of dragoons was about to be raised, and that he should have a company in it. His first care was for the health of his men, and for this purpose he repaired to Posen to take counsel with a Jew doctor in great repute for his successful treatment of the plague. Of this practitioner he bought ten dollars' worth of pills. Several pages of the Diary are filled with details of marches and counter-marches, of which the only object seems to have been the subsistence of the soldiers. It was 'the custom of the country' that recruiting parties and troops on march should be supported by the districts through which they passed; but this privilege had been so much abused by self-constituted bands, that Gordon was received very much as if he had been invading a hostile country. His entrance into towns and villages was opposed by the inhabitants in arms; and his men had often to march with matches lighted. He spared a visit to one town, of his own accord, he tells us, because it belonged to a prince who befriended foreigners, and because its 'provost' or chief-magistrate was a Scot. But he repented this precipitate piece of courtesy, for which his countryman showed no gratitude.

A.D. 1660.

He was at the Castle of Lubowna, near Guesen, in the summer of 1660, when the Podstaroste 1660. informed him that the King of England had been recalled to his throne. Gordon was so overjoyed with the tidings that he departed for once from his accustomed abstemiousness. He had to pay the forfeit of his loyal festivities next morning.

Field-marshal Lubomirski, compelled by the jealousy of the nobles to abandon his design of raising a dragoon regiment, proposed that Gordon's company should be merged in his own body-guard, and that that the whole should, in the meantime, be under Gordon's command. In this capacity of Captain-lieutenant, he served in that campaign of the Poles and Crim-Tartars, against the Cossacks of the Ukraine and the Muscovites, which terminated in the disastrous route of the latter at Czudno or Slobodischtsche, in June, 1660. In this battle, June. in which the Russians lost 115 standards, 67 guns, and 36,000 men killed or taken prisoners, Gordon greatly distinguished himself, and received several wounds. His friend Lieutenant-colonel Menzies,* who fought in the Muscovite ranks, was taken prisoner by

* Thomas Menzies of Balgownie, the son of a Roman Catholic family driven from Scotland by the Covenant, has been mentioned in a previous page, as Patrick Gordon's fellow traveller from Dantzic to Braunsberg in the summer of 1651. In the same year ' he wes married at Riga in Leifland with Ladie Marie Farserson, borne of noble and honourable parentage in the dukedome of Curland.' It was given in evidence by Lord Henry Gordon, at Aberdeen in 1672, ' that the said deceast Lievtennant-Collonell Thomas Menzeis, being, in anno 1660,

Lord Henry Gordon,† then a colonel in the Polish army, but died of his wounds a few days afterwards.

A.D. 1661.

1661.   Peace being concluded, the Polish army took up its winter quarters in the Ukraine. Here Gordon, hearing of the happy restoration of King Charles II., resolved to return home, in the hope of obtaining service in his own country. He had already apprised his father of his intentions, and now petitioned the Field-marshal for his discharge. He was easily persuaded,

February. however, to retain his command until the spring, when he conducted his company to Warsaw, where Lubomirski was in attendance on the Diet. Meanwhile the army in the Ukraine mutinied, and choosing leaders for itself, began to march towards Warsaw in order to obtain redress of its grievances. At this point the Diary is again resumed in Gordon's own words.]

The prisoners of the Moscovites taken at Czudnow, Mogilow, and Bassa or Gubarj, were convoyed, with the collours taken, in a kind of procession to the pallace where the parliament sate. The woywods, or generall and principall persons, were brought in to the upper house to the pre-

in that charge, vnder the command of his Imperiall Majestie of Russia, in fighting against the Polonianes beseid Szudna, was deadlie woundit, and takin prisoner be the said Lord Hendrie Gordone, collonell vnder the command of his Maje~tie of Polland, and dyed of his woundes in Vkrain, and wes buried in the fields at Szudna.'—(Miscellany of the Spalding Club, vol. v., pp. 352, 353.) Cf Spalding's Memorialls of the Trubles in Scotland, vol ii., pp. 236, 372, 433, 441.

† Lord Henry Gordon was the youngest son of George, second Marquess of Huntly. ' Born in France, he was,' says the historian of the family, ' by Dr. Davidson carried to Poland, with his youngest sister twins : he served there several years in very honourable employment, and came home [before 1666] and died at Strathbogie.' The querulous Robert Mylne writes that Lord Henry, 'quho was a little hair-brained, but wery couragious, in his latter dayes married one Mrs. Rolland, ane innkeeper in Aberdeen.'—(Genealogie of the Familie of Gordon, collected by R. M., *anno Domini* 1707, MS. in the Library at Skene.) The same work gives this account of Lord Henry's twin sister: "Kathrine, daughter to George, second Marquis of Huntley, went abroad to France, and thereafter she and the daughter of the Cardinall of Arquien went to Polland with the Queen thereof, Mary Lodovica de Gonzaga, daughter of the Duke of Nevers, of the house of Mantua, in order to marry Uladislaus, King of Polland ; and the two were both her maids

of honour ; and this Queen procured Kathrine Gordon to be married to [John Andrew] Count Morstein, great thesaurer of Polland, betwixt quhom was procreat the Count of Chateau Villain, quho was killed at the seidge of Namuir, quho had married a daughter of the Duke of Chevreuse, by whom two daughters. This Count Morstin had also a daughter married to Count Bielinski, great chamberlaine of the crown of Polland. This Kathrine, Countess of Morstin, was ane active woman, and had as much credite among the nobility of Polland, as over her husband's mind anent the election of the Prince of Conti to be King of Polland. This Count Morstin is descended from the cheife of ane old family in Polland, and was great thesaurer thereof, but, haveing more regard to his own private intrest than the publict benefit, sent all the riches of the thesaurary into France, quhairunto he retired himself, *anno* 1683, to prevent the Diets calling him to ane account. He purchased in France the whole county of Chateau Villan, worth 100,000 livers a year." Lady Catharine Gordon had a birth-brief under the great seal of Scotland, on the 21st of August, 1687.

Lord Henry Gordon, in 1658, obtained for himself and his heirs, the right of Polish nobility. In 1667, King Charles II. gave instructions that he should have a life annuity of five thousand merks Scots from the estate of Huntly, which was at that time estimated to be worth about thirty thousand pounds Scots a-year.

sence of the King, the collours being carryed befor, and throwne downe on
the floore at the Kings feet.   They were ordered to do their reverence to
the King as they used to do to the Tzaar, which they refused, especially the
Kniaz Gregory Affonasseovits Koslofsky, who also openly upbraided them
with breach of the capitulation.   But he was silenced, and reconducted to
the quarters allotted them.   These collours were afterwards, on Corpus
Christi day, caryed in procession to the new towne, to the church dedicated
to the Blessed Virgin, with great solemnity.

The Swedish ambassadour, Graffe Steno Bielke, received satisfaction;
for albeit the peace had been allowed by a convocation of the estates the
yeare befor, yet it was now fully ratifyed and confirmed.

The newes from the Ukraina, of the confederacy of the armyes, was the
greatest perplexity; and Lubomirskij, being disgusted, though best able,
yet contributed least to the composeing of this mischieffe, and most because
his method and counsells were not allowed nor followed.   And surely nothing proceeded from him which did please the court, he being suspected to
act against its interest; and, even now, they suspected him to be the *bote-
feau* of the armyes confederacy, whereof at this tyme, he was, without
doubt, guiltles.   But, if hereafter, when he was forced into a foreigne
countrey, he fomented the dissension or division betwixt the King and
army, as it is said, I cannot tell: only I say this, which I had great reason
and occasion to know, haveing been, in a manner, his domestick, and constantly present at table, and many private discourses, and likewise being
very intimate with his secretaryes and chieffe servants for the space of two
yeares and a halfe, that I never heard, nor could perceive any thing from
him, but setled and constant resolutions to adhere to the setled constitutions
of the realme, a hatred against innovations, a great zeale for the preserva-
tion of the libertyes and priviledges of the people.   And truly he was by nature a great lover of vertue and vertuous persons, and as great a hater of
vice; a good sojour; a great politician as to the understanding of state
effaires, but no good practicioner, as the event showed; very prudent and
just in all his private actions.   This, in short, I do in verity affirme of this
noble prince.

The Prince Bogoslaw Radziewill went away from the parliament disgusted; his former behaviour, in the late warrs, being objected to him in
parliament by some of the senatours; he being forbidd also to let his chap-
laine preach in his lodging, because it belonged to the church, he haveing

hired it ; the lodging or house belonging to that family not being built since its ruine by the Sweds.

The parliament not comeing to any resolution concerning the contenting the army and prosecuting the warr against the Moskovite, save only the sending some deputies to the army, to perswade them to returne to their obedience and duty, with promise of contentment at the commission, which was shortly to be held at Reusse Lemberg ; wherewith the army, not being satisfyed, marched out of their quarters to a generall rendevous by . . . where they choose to themselves a generall director ; and all or most of the superiour officers being absent, they choose out of their owne number persons to command them ; whereby the fairest opportunity that the Polls ever had, since the beginning of the warr, of reducing the Ukraina, was lost.

The parliament breaking up befor things were thoroughly regulated, and most of the nobility quitting Varso, the King, being much perplexed with the newes comeing from the confederate army, that they were not satisfyed with the results of the parliament, sent for most of the nobility to consult upon the meanes to satisfy the army, and bring them to their duty ; but whatever measures were taken here (the fates of Polland not permitting it), the army remained still dissatisffyed, which afterwards turned to an intestine warr, like to have utterly ruined that nation.

Shortly after my comeing to Varso, I received a letter from my father, giveing me notice of the receit of myne of the third of May the year befor, wherein I had written, that hearing of his Sacred Majesties happy restauration, I intended to come home, in hopes to be accomodated under his Majestie. But, my father informing me that the armyes were disbanded, and that only a few troops were continued in pay, and that the charge of these were given to the nobility, and to such persons who had extraordinarily deserved and suffered for his Majestie, and that without a good stock it was very hard liveing in Scotland ; this deterring me from thinking of going home, I resolved not to quite the service wherein I was, and so not to mention or seeke my passe.* Yet, haveing sollicited my pass with so great

* [Gordon could not have foreseen that his religion would have proved an obstacle to his employment in Scotland. By proclamation, dated on the sixteenth of December, 1673, King Charles II. inhibited and discharged ' any person or persons who are of the Popish profession after the first of March nixt to accept of or exerce any public imployment or office either civill or military within this king-dome.' A few days afterwards, the Privy Council removed Colonel Whytford from his company in the Earl of Linlithgow's regiment, and ordered 'the mustermaster generall to give in lists of the haill officers of the militia troupes and regiments, that it may be knowne who of them are Popish that order may be taken with them conform to the late proclamation.']

pressing earnestnes, and haveing rejected or refused the conditions offered me in Crosna, by Collonel Laniziinsky, to take a compagny, and which, he told me, he did by the generall's command ; being afrayed that it might be objected to me hereafter, I thought fitt to looke about me for other service, though not to engage but upon good conditions. And, first, I had great temptations from the Moskowitish ambassadours ; for haveing, by ordor, conducted some of their chieffe officers to them, about their ransome, as also, they haveing ransomed two officers from me, they very earnestly desired their colonells to engage me in the Tzaars service, to the which I seemed to give halfe a willing eare. So they promised that I should not be longer detained as three yeares, one yeare whereoff to serve for major, and two for lievtennent-colonell. Yet did I not accept of these offers, but only kept them in hand, to have another string for my bow ; nor, perhaps, had ever embraced them, if another accident had not fallen out.

About the same tyme, the Roman Emperours ambassadour, the Baron d'Isola, gott orders from the Emperour to engage officers to levy a regiment of horse ; to which purpose he engaged Lievtennant-collonell Gordon, commonly called Steelhand, who, useing all the pressing reasons he could to perswade me to engage with him, telling me of the honourable service, the good pay, with the advantage and easines of the levyes at this tyme, wherewith being overcome, after mature consideration, I resolved to engage ; and so wee entered into capitulation, fowre of us, to levy a regiment of 800 horse. The persons were Steelhand, colonell ; Lievtennant-collonell John Watson, Maior Davidson, and myself. I engaged to levy two compleet compagnyes, being to receive for each horseman forty reichs dollars, the nominating of the officers being the colonells ; and I made an apart capitulation with the colonell, being to take on officers for the two compagnyes, except the ruitmaster, I myself to be eldest ruitmaster, and to have thirty-fyve reichs dollers for each horseman that I should bring to muster place or rendevows above my two companyes. One of the reasons which induced me to engage here, was the great advantage I expected by the levying ; for I had notice that the Elector of Brandeburg had disbanded foure regiments of horse in Prussia, so that many would be glad to enter into service againe, and I doubted not to bring my companyes and more to the locality which wee were to have in Silesia, and the rendevous, at the rate of fyfteen or twenty reichs dollers a horseman, besides the advantage

I should have had by my officers, who must have furnished so many horsemen according to their charge. I gave surety or caution for my levy-money, James Birney, Georg Gordon, and James Wenton, all merchants and indwellers in Zamoisiz.

Being fully resolved now to engage in the service of the Roman Emperour, upon the above said conditions, I thought it tyme to desire my passe ; and haveing watched a fitt opportunity, with great difficulty, I obteined a grant of it, the generall commanding me to cause writt it myself, which I did in plaine termes, without any hyperbolicall or superfluous praise or expressions, and haveing delivered it to his excellency, he was pleased to read it, and seeming not well satisfyed, gave it to the secretary, Bartholomeus Pestritsky, commanding him to writt it over, saying, He deserveth a better recommendation. Two dayes thereafter, my pass being ready, and brought to the generall, I standing by, he was pleased to ask me, if I would not resolve to stay in the service ? I answering that I could not, he gave me my pass, the exact and true copy whereof I have here inserted.

Georgius Sebastianus Lubomirsky, Comes in Wisnicz et Iaroslaw, Sacri Romani Imperii Princeps, Supremus Mareschallus Regni Poloniae et Generalis Exercituum Dux campestris, Generalis Minoris Poloniae, Cracoviensis, Chmielniviensis, Nizinensis, Casimiriensis, Olstinensis, Pereaslaviensisque Gubernator .

Universis et singulis, cujuscunque status, gradus, honoris, dignitatis, officii et praeeminentiae personis, hasce nostras visuris, lecturis, aut legi audituris, humanissimam officiorum nostrorum contestationem . Quicunque egregiis clarent factis, praesertim illi quorum generosa pectora militari sese efferunt laude, omnes tales a ducibus sub quorum gubernatione militarunt, decore gloriaque meritorum suorum debere ornari omnes postulat aequitas . Hinc generosum Patricium Gordon, natione Scotum, nobili in suis partibus genere ortum, per menses octodecem sub nostra legione dragonum legionarii hospitiorum magistri, et per duodecem menses sub praesidiaria corporis nostri cohorte capitanei locum tenentis muneribus functum, dimitti a nobis postulantem, nec non alias in partes quaerendae fortunae causa conferre se volentem, nequaquam testimonio promeritarum laudum privandum esse arbitrati sumus . Itaque coram omnibus et singulis, ad quorum notitiam praesentes venturae sint, testamur, cum omnibus in proeliis, conflictibus, occasionibus quaecunque sub tempus servitiorum illius contra plurimos regni istius hostes, nempe, Suecos, Moschos, Cosacos acciderant, interfuisse depugnasseque strenue, et ita exactum boni simul militis et officialis munus implevisse, ut tam sibi laudem honoremque paraverit, quam nomini gentis Scoticae virtute bellica ubique inclitae optime corresponderit . Huic ergo praenominato Patricio Gordon non tantum liberam ex more et ritu militari cum honore dimissionem, et amplam meritorum attestationem concedimus ; sed etiam pro eodem tanquam Sacrae ac Serenissimae Regiae Majestati domino nostro clementissimo huicque reipublicae ac nobis optime, strenue fideliterque probato militi, omnes et singulos pro ea qualis cuiquam secundum suam congruit dignitatem et statum, observantia requirimus, ut sive in Scotiam patriam suam, sive in exteras nationes conferre se statuerit, [eum] cumprimis decenter, libere honorateque dimissum reputent, gressum, regressum, commorationemque ubivis locorum tutam concedant, omni honore, benevolentia, ac humanitate, complectantur, ac ad quaevis in re militari, promotionis, officiorum, graduumque incrementa habeant commendatum . In cujus rei fidem meliorem praesentes liberae dimissionis commendationisque nostrae literas extradi illi jussimus manus nostrae subscriptione et soliti impressione sigilli munitas . Datae Varsaviae die 2 mensis Julii, anni Domini 1661 .

Georgius Lubomirsky (*l. s.*)   Bartholomeus Pestriecky
                                         suae Excellentiae Secretarius .

Haveing gott my pass, I made preparation for my jorney to Prussia, and wanted nothing but the maine business, the levy money.

The tenth of Julii, by an express from Vienna, the Roman Emperours July 10. ambassadour received an order not to engage any officers, or to capitulat for levying of men, and, if he had engaged any already, to discharge them the handsomest way he could ; whereupon he sent imediately for Steelhand and imparted his orders to him, and I comeing thither at the same tyme, was made acquainted therewith also ; whereat, I being surprised and greatly troubled, said that none was a losser by it but I, haveing disengaged my self of such good service, and thereby even disobliged the best and powerfullest prince in the countrey ; that the great desire I had to have served the Roman Emperour had ruined me, not knowing where to find such service againe; with which the ambassadour was very much moved, Steelhand also regrateing my condition. At last, the ambassadour recollecting himself, profered me, if I would go with him to Vienna, he should procure me the place of a ruitmaster or capitaine of horse, under a standing regiment, or then give me a thowsand reichs dollers to beare my expences and losses; which, seeing I could not otherwise do or better, I accepted. He offering me a writeing, I modestly refused it, telling him that I trusted his word. He desired me also to come and stay in his lodging, where, as upon way to Vienna, I should be defrayed; which I promised to do, how soone I had set my business in order.

Two dayes thereafter, I comeing to wait upon the ambassadour, he told me that he had found a way to make me deserving to the Roman Emperour; which was, that haveing letters and business of great concernment which he must despatch very soone, he would entrust me with these dispatches, as being well acquainted with the countrey, and haveing such an ample passe, whereby I should be knowne at court, and have a pretension upon the account of service; whereof I was glad, and promised to performe it with all care, fidelity, and diligence.

In the meane tyme, many of my acquaintances and ffriends hearing of my determination to engage in the Roman Emperours service without levying, and of the conditions proffered me, began seriously to diswade me from it, telling me that a peace being lyke to be concluded, betwixt the Roman Emperour and the Turkes, soldiers of fortune, unless of great merit and long standing in that service, would be hardly admitted, and little regarded; that, if at last I should obtaine a company in a standing regiment, the officers in such regiments, at least the captaines, being, for the most part, men of great birth and rents, or well stocked and acquainted with the wayes of that countrey, where quarters, accidences, and shifts are the greatest part of their subsistance, I should not be able to beare out an equall part with them without running my self in debt, or makeing unusuall and not allowable shifts; that I might dance attendance long enough at court, befor I could be accommodated, and albeit in the tyme of my waiting for a charge, I might get some allowance for a subsistance, which would even be very difficult to obtaine, yet would it come farr short of what I should be obliged to spend there; that, by putting my self in a garbe fitt for appearing at court, and conversing with persons of quality, I should soone spend the small stock I had; as for the 1000 reichs dollers promised me, I might possibly wait for that some tyme too, and spend the most part of it befor I should get from thence; and so, at last, being dismounted and ill provided of money, and without ffriends or acquaintance in any other place, in a tyme of peace, a lyvelyhood or honourable charge would be very difficult to gett.

These and many other things considering, I began to waver in my resolution, and, at last, found my self very apprehensive of the foresaid reasons, and convinced so that I resolved not to go to Vienna; to the which the great sollicitations and promises of the Russe ambassadour, Zamiaty Fiodorovitz Leontiuf, and Colonell Crawfuird, with others, contributed very much. The only difficulty was, how to come handsomely of from the ambassadour d'Isola; for, albeit, I should have been very welcome againe to the crowne and Feltmarshall; yet was I ashamed, and feared to have it objected to me hereafter; and also, albeit, I should have been accommodated in the crowne or Littawish army, with a charge to my contentment, yet durst I not, for fear of offending such a prince, who had been so gracious to me, and who was of so great power, and whom I had already but too much offended by solliciting for my pass, and quitting the service. So, haveing made sure with the Russe ambassadour, and let of the most of my servants, I went to the Roman Emperours ambassadour, and desired to know how long it would be befor his dispatches would be ready. He told me that it would be eight dayes. Then I told him, that I had all my best things lying in Thorun, thirty miles from hence, and that he would permitt me to go and fetch them, promiseing to returne precisely against that tyme; which he granting, and desireing me not to delay, nor disapoint him, I tooke my leave.

I had nothing now to do but to prepare for my jorney; so, haveing gott Colonell Crawfuird and Captain Menezes* ready, I tooke leave of my ffriends, and, to make clear with the Roman Emperours ambassadour, I left

* [Paul Menzies, the younger brother of the gallant boy who bore the royal standard in Montrose's last battle, was a son of Sir Gilbert Menzies of Pitfoddels, by his marriage in 1623 with Lady Ann Gordon, daughter of John, twelfth Earl of Sutherland. He entered the Roman Catholic College of Douay when at the age of ten, in the summer of 1647. In 1661, he appears as a captain in the Polish ranks. Joining the Muscovite banner in the same year, along with Patrick Gordon, he rose to the rank of major in 1663. He was in Scotland in the beginning of 1672; and, in the next year, was sent as envoy from the Czar Alexis to the Republic of Venice, the Pope, the Emperor, and the Elector of Brandenburg. When at the court of Rome, he prevailed with Pope Clement X. to sanction a service in commemoration of St. Margaret, Queen of Scotland.—(Pinkert. Vitt. Antiq Sanctt. Scotiae, pp 304, 369) He died, a lieutenant general in the Russian service, on the 9th of November, 1694.]

two letters by a trusty ffriend, one dated three dayes befor the tyme I had promised to returne, giveing him notice, that, upon my comeing to Thorun, I was fallen into a heavy sicknesse, being a hott feaver, so that I could not be able to come at the appointed tyme, promising how soone I were recovered to make all possible hast ; the letter not writt by myself, but subscrived ; the other letter, dated a fortnight thereafter, from the same place, informing his excellency that the violence of sickness was relented, but that I was taken with a sort of a quotiduan feaver, and want of appetite, which had weakened me, so that I was out of hopes of being able to travel in hast, makeing a great regrait, that, by this misfortune, I had lost the honour which I thought to have had to serve his Imperiall Majesty, and such expressions more.

July 25.
stylo novo.

July 26

Haveing taken my leave of ffriends, I crossed the river Vistula, and lodged in the Prague all night ; and the next morning after breakfast, and a merry cup with the ffriends who had convoyed us, wee began our jorney. Colonell Crawfuird, being a prisoner to the Colonell Lord Henry Gordon, was not only maintained by him at a plentifull table in Varso, but dismissed ransome free, and gave him a pass for a capitaine of horse. Captain Pawl Menezes had a pass for a capitaine of foot. The colonell had a servant, and I fowre, so that wee were in company but eight persons, I acting the chieffest by the way.

July 27.

The first night wee lodged in a village fyve miles from Varso ; and the next day afternoone came to Vengrova, which is twelve miles from Varso, where wee lodged and stayed the next day, exspecting Andrew Burnet and William Guild, who had promised to go with me.

July 29.

Wee went from hence, and, crossing the river Bug at a ruined towne called Ostrow, wee came to Tikoczino, where is a strong castle by the river Narew. Here is also a Jewish sinagogue, and very many Jewes. From thence, wee went down by the river syde, and crossing the said river at Wizna, wee lodged there. Wee crossed thereafter the river Leck, where the Polls and Tartars beat the Sweds and Brandeburgers, and tooke Duke Bogoslaw Radziwill prisoner ; and comeing to Raggrod, wee dined there ; then passing by Augustowa, Bokalarzova, and Philippova, where the same Polls and Tartars were, eight dayes thereafter, beat by the Sweds and Brandeburgers, and Duk Radzivill recovered. This was done, *anno Domini* 1656, in September.

Being come to Znin, wee lodged there all night, and were merry with

Captaine Portes and Ensigne Martin.   Wee crossed the river Niemen at
Vilsk, where wee lodged all night; and the next day to Kiadany.   This
towne belongeth to the family of the Radzivills, where is the publick exercize of the Protestant religion, and, because of that, many Scotsmen here
liveing, by one whereof wee lodged, and being welcomed by some of our
countreymen with a hearty cup of strong meade, it did so enflame my blood,
that the same night a hott feaver seized me.   The next day I caused blood
to be let.   Towards night I gott ease, and slept indifferent well.

The next day, being Sunday, I went to church, where the feaver againe
seized me, so that I was not able to heare out the devotion, and with much
ado gott to my lodging.   The feaver continued very violent, with a delirium.
On Tuesday, by the help of a glister, I gott ease.   On Wednesday I kept
bed till noone, and then rose.   On Thursday wee dined by Maior Karstares,
were very kindly entertained, and not pressed with drinking.   On Fridday,
haveing bought a kaless to sitt in, wee tooke jorney, and lodged in a village,
a mile and a halfe from Kiadany.   In the morning Maior Karstares sent a
note with a long gunne to me, desireing to have my tent, which I sent to
him.   We dined in a towne called Novymiasto, and the next day to Len-
kova, where was a market day.   Wee dined, and, setting forward, came to
Gemelly, the best towne of Samogitia, where wee lodged; and came the
next day to Bowsky, a towne belonging to the Duke of Churland, where
finding Dutch people and good beer, wee made merry, and took a guide to
show us over the river [Aa] without the towne.   At the confluence of the
two rivers Mussa and [Niemen], is a castle well situate and fortifyed for a
siege.   Wee lodged in a krue, where wee had of the same Bawskyes beer,
and made merry among ourselves.

The next day wee rose early, dined by the way, and crossing the river
Dwina came to Riga, and tooke up lodging in the suburb without the Sand
Port; where hearing that the Generall Duglas was gone but two or three
[houres] befor towards Derpt, and that he was to lodge two miles from Riga,
being very desirous to have seen him, and to ask his advice concerning my
going to Russeland, (for I was upon the repenting the whole way from Var-
schow, as Captaine Menezes also), so that, if he had but diswaded me (which
he was sure to do) I was resolved not to go further, unles it had been to put
Colonell Crawfuird in a sure place, and then returne.   But, to my great

misfortune, I could not gett for any money horses to hire, and my owne being weary, all the horses being taken up for those who convoyed the Generall, and who did not returne till evening ; so that being disappointed of such an occasion of comeing of handsomely, I was very sorry, and so went into the towne to looke out for acquaintance. Comeing to the market place, I did meet with my old comerades and ffriends Alexander Landells and Walter Airth, with whom I went to a taverne and tooke a glass of wine, to whom I revealed my intentions. These being out of service themselves, haveing been lately disbanded by the Sweds, were in a poor condition and willing to engage any where, and told me that no service was to be had among the Sweds, and besides, that it was so poore, they haveing but pittyfull allowances, that it was not worth the seeking ; that they heard that the Moskovites pay, though not great, was duly payed, and that officers were soone advanced to high charges ; that many of our countreymen of great quality were there, and some gone thither lately ; that they themselves, with many others of our countreymen and strangers, were resolving to go thither, not knowing how (in such a conjuncture of tyme when a generall peace was concluded by most, and shortly exspected by others), to do better ; so that the considerations of a certaine (at least) lyvelyhood, preferment, good company, and my former promises and engagements confirmed me in my resolution to go to Mosko. So, haveing promised to writt to them from the first garrison of the Moskovites, wee parted.

Haveing conferred with Colonell Crawfuird about the engageing of some good officers in the Tzaars service, I went the next day into the towne againe ; and meeting with the same ffriends againe, at a hearty morning draught, I engaged them further, promiseing each of them a degree of preferment, and that they should bespeake so many as they could of the charges of captaines, leivtennants, and ensignies.

Haveing hired a fuirman with two horses to Kokenhausen, more upon the accompt of showing us the way as of any need wee had of him, haveing horses of our owne enough to serve our turne, wee went from Riga about noone, rideing along by the river Dwina, and lodged in a village about foure miles from Riga ; which Riga is distant from Revel fyfty miles, from Derpt thirty, from Vilna forty, from Konigsberg in Prussia sixty miles ; a strong and well fortifyed towne.

Wee rose early, and, towards evening, came to Kokenhausen, a towne and castle situate by the river Dwina, on a high rocky ground. Herein was a garrison of the Moskovites. I seeing the streets so dirty, and every where such nastines, the people so morose, and the houses so decayed and wast, I presaged, *ex ungue leonem*, a great change; for, considering that I was come from a countrey pleasant, citties well inhabited, neat and cleanly, and a people generally well bred, courteous, and civill, I was much troubled. The governour here was called Basilius Volshinsky. Here was also a Dutch colonell called John Meves.

The next day, wee dined at a christening feast, with the governour, by a captaine called John von Arnheim; and, haveing gott some post horses, after noone wee went from thence and lodged in the fields. Wee tooke jorney early, and rode through a pleasent but depopulated countrey, and lodged in the fields. Here did overtake us Captaine Smith and Lieveten-nant John Muris, with their wiwes, who were come from Riga, and going for Mosko to serve. They had gott posthorses, but scarse to serve their turne, and were in a very poor condition. Wee were glad of their company, and so jogged on together. Wee came to a ruined place called Marienburg. Here is a castle within a lake, wherein a Russe garrison. Wee went to wiew the place, but non was permitted to enter the castle but the Colonell. The governour sent us some small provisions and a sort of small drink called quass. Being come to Niewenhausen, wee found the Sweds takeing pos-session of the barneyards and corne, which was standing in the fields; for by the treaty of peace or truce, this and the former two places which they had taken in Liefland, were to be restored to the Sweds. In Kokenhausen, I had seen some great cannon, which they retired from Riga, and which, by the treaty, the Sweds were to furnish horses to bring to Plesko.

Haveing lodged by a barneyard at Niewenhausen, the next morning, about three verst from thence, wee passed the borders and came to Petshure, a ruined towne, where a monastery environed with a stone wall. This place is called Petshure, of the subterranean caves. Wee lodged in a village not farr from the lake Peipus, where I sold my passeganger for nine rubles copper money, imageining each ruble to be two reichs dollers. He cost me thirty reichs dollers in Varso, and that from a good ffriend, but was growne lame by the way, and I could not get any body to cure him.

About midday wee had a sight of Plesko or Opsko, which had a glorious show, being environed with a stone wall, with many towers. Here are many churches and monasteries, some whereof have three, some fyve steeples or towers, whereon are round globes of six, eight, or ten fathomes circumference, which being covered with white iron or plate, and thereon great crosses covered with the same, make a great and pleasant show. One of these globes, being the biggest, is overgilt.

This citty was a free principality in former tymes, and had suffered many changes, untill subdued by Tzaar Ivan Vasiliovits, *anno Domini* 1509, who sent most of the principall inhabitans to Mosko, and returned colonies of Moskovites in their places. It hath since rebelled diverse tymes, and as often reduced. It hath held out diverse sieges of the Sweds and Polls. It had freedome of coyning of money. The Sweds and Lubeckers have their houses of traffick without the towne, on the other side of the river Velika Reka, or the great river, which some versts below the towne falleth into the lake Peipus, and so to Narva, below which it emptyeth itself into the sea. This citty is distant from **Riga** and **Velikij Lukij** sixty Polonian miles; and from Novogrod thirty six.

Here I perceived the low rate of the copper money; and finding everything so deare, and the extraordinary morosnes of the people, I was almost at my wits end with vexation. Here one William Hay, who was lately come from Scotland, came to us and made one of our company to Mosco.

Haveing lodged in the towne, which stunk with nastines, and was no wise answerable to the glorious show it hath afarr of, and our expectation, wee breakfasted with Madam Hayes, who furnished us also with plenty of provisions upon the way. Wee tooke jorney through a pleasant wooddy countrey, the particular description whereof I thought not worthy of my paines, nor had the patience, being out of conceit with the people, to take notices of the places of their habitations. Being come to a large village called Solnitsa, sending our horses by land, wee went in boats down the river Solona into the lake Ilmen, and so to Novogrod.

The lake Ilmen is twelve miles or sixty verst broad, and eighteen Polonian miles or nynety verst long, receiveth about seventy small rivers, and letteth out one called Volcha, which, running by Novogrod, falleth in the lake Ladoga, a hundred and eighty verst, or thirty-six Polonian miles below the citty. The principall rivers which fall into this lake are Solona, Lowat, Mpsiaga, *etc.* The towne of Novogrod, called the Great, haveing been one of the three greatest market cittyes of Europe, giveth name to a large dukedome, and the greatest of all Russia, where Rurick, from whom all the Russian princes and dukes draw their originall, did reigne. It is distant from Mosco a hundred and fyve miles, or fyve hundred and twenty fyve versts, from Plesko thirty-six, and from Velikij Lukij, and Narwe forty miles.

Anno Domini 1570, Tzaar Johannes Basilides began a warr with the Novogrodians, which lasted seven yeares, when, haveing beat their forces at the river Solona, he forced them to submitt, and placed a governour over them. But thinking that he had not such ane absolute power over them as he would, by the meanes of Theophilus the archbishop, he gott entrance into the towne ; where, what cruelty he used to the citizens and to the archbishop himself, I referr to those who have written at large thereof; as also concerning their idoll Perun, from whence the Perunsky monastery hath its denomination.*

Being provided with a large boat, wee went up the river Msta to Brunits, twenty fyve verst, where, by an order from the governour of Novogrod, the boyar Kniaz Ivan Borisovits Repenin wee had ten post horses given us, which were changed at diverse stages, and so my horses were spared. Wee crossed the river Volga at Twere, which giveth name to a great tract of land with the title of duke, and had in former tymes dukes of its owne, till of late, when it, as well as others, were swallowed up by the great Duke of Mosco. It is distant from Mosco thirty-six miles.

Wee came to Mosko, and hired a lodging in the Slabod, or village where the strangers live. *September 2. stylo veteri.*

Wee were admitted to kiss his Tzaarsky Majesties hand at Columinsko, a countrey house of the Tzaars, seven werst from Mosko, below by the river of the same name. The Tzaar was pleased to thank me for haveing been kind to his subjects who were prisoners in Polland ; and it was told me that I should have his Majesties grace or favour, whereon I might rely. *September 5.*

In the morning, the boyar Elia Danielovitz Miloslavsky, who being the Tzaars father in law, had the command of the stranger office, ordered me to come in the afternoon to a field without the citty called the Gartoly, and to bring the other officers who came in with me along. Being *eptember 6.*

---

* [The German editors here think it necessary to warn the reader that Gordon's historical notices are not always to be implicitly relied upon.]

46 DIARY OF PATRICK GORDON. [1661

come into the field, wee found the Boyar there before us, who ordered us to take up pike and musquets (being there ready) and show how wee could handle our armes; wherewith being surprized, I told him, that if I had knowne of this, I should have brought forth one of my boyes, who perhaps could handle armes better as I myself; adding, that it was the least part of an officer to know how to handle armes, conduct being the most materiall. Whereat, he, takeing me up short, told me, that the best colonell comeing into this countrey must do so; to which I replyed, Seing it is the fashion, I am content. And so haveing handled the pike and musket, with all their postures, to his great satisfaction, I returned.

September 9. On Moonday, it was ordered that I should be enrolled for maior, Pawl Menezes for captaine, William Hay for lievtennant, and John Hamilton for ensignie, to foot, under the regiment of Colonell Daniell Crawfuird, and a gratuity for our comeing in or welcome to the countrey, being to me twenty fyve rubles in money, and as much in sables, foure ells of cloth, and eight ells of damask; the rest accordingly, and our monthly pay equall with others of these charges. But the chancellour,* being a most corrupt fellow, delayed us from day to day in expectation of a bribe, which is not only usuall here, but, as they think, due; whereof I haveing no information, after expostulateing with him twice or thrice, and receiving no satisfactory answers, I went to the Boyar and complained; who, with a light check, ordered him againe, which incensing the Diack more, he delayed us still. But when, after a second complaint and order wee received no satisfaction, I went a third tyme to the Boyar, and very confidently told him, I knew not whither he or the Diack had the greatest power, seing he did not obey his so many orders. Whereat, the Boyar, being vexed, caused stop his coach (he being on his way out of the towne to his countrey house) and caused call the Diack; whom, being come, he tooke by the beard and shak'd him three or foure tymes, telling him, if I complained againe, he would cause knute him The Boyar being gone, the Diack came to me, and began to scold; and I, without any respect (whereof they gett but ever too much here), payed him home in his owne coyne, telling him that I cared not whither they gave me any thing or no, if they would but permitt me to go out of the countrey againe. With which resolution I went to the Slobod, and now began in

* [That is, as Gordon immediately afterwards calls him, the *dyak*, or scribe.]

good earnest to consider how I might ridd myself of this countrey, so farr short of my exspectation, and disagreeing with my humour. For, haveing served in such a countrey, and amongst such people, where strangers had great respect and were in a great reputation, and even more trust as the natives themselves; and where a free passage, for all deserving persons, lay open to all honour, military and civill; and where, in short tyme, by good husbandry and industry, an estate might be gained; and, in marrying, no scruple or difference was made betwixt the natives and strangers, whereby many have attained to great fortunes, governements, and other honourable and profitable commands; as indigenation, also, being usually conferred on well qualifyed and deserving persons; where a dejected countenance or submissive behaviour is noted for cowardice and faintheartednes, and a confident, majestick, yet unaffected, comportment for virtuous generosity; the peoples high mindednes being accompanied and qualifyed with courteousnes and affability, wherein, meeting with the lyke humours, they contend for transandency. Whereas, on the contrary, I perceived strangers to be looked upon as a company of hirelings, and, at the best (as they say of women) but *necessaria mala*; no honours or degrees of preferment to be exspected here but military, and that with a limited command, in the attaining whereof a good mediator or mediatrix, and a piece of money or other bribe, is more availeable as the merit or sufficiency of the person; a faint heart under faire plumes, and a cuckoe in gay cloths, being as ordinary here as a counterfeited or painted visage; no marrying with natives, strangers being looked upon by the best sort as scarcely Christians, and by the plebeyans as meer pagans; no indigenation without ejeration of the former religion and embraceing theirs; the people being morose and niggard, and yet overweening and valuing themselves above all other nations; and the worst of all, the pay small, and in a base copper coyne, which passed at foure to one of silver, so that I foresaw an impossibility of subsistance, let be of enriching my self, as I was made beleeve I should, befor I came from Polland. These, and many other reasons were but too sufficient to setle my self for disengageing my self of this place. The only difficulty was, how to attaine to it, which troubled me very much; every one, of whom I asked advice, alleadging it impossible. However I resolved to try and not to take any of their money, albeit I had gotten at Plesko and Novogrod some for expenses on the way.

Hearing that the Boyar was to stay a weeke out of the citty, I resolved

not to go to the prikase untill he should returne, and then give up a petition
or request for my dismission; bringing in for my reasons, that the ambass-
adeur Zamiaty Fiodorovits Leontiuf, with whom I capitulated in Polland,
had promised me to be paid in silver or other equivalent coine, which I
found farr otherwise now, and that I found the constitution of my body not
agreeable with this climate.   But the Diack, getting notice of my intentions,
and fearing the wrath of the Boyar at his returne, colluded with my
Colonell to entice me into the towne; so that I being come one morning to pay my respects to my Colonell, he desired me to accompany him to
the towne, which after some tergiversation I did; and being come and
takeing a walke on the piazza, a writer, with a couple of catchpoles
with him, came to me and desired me to come into the prikase, which
I refused.   He told me, that he had order to force me, if I would not
come fairely.   Being come into the chieffe writer, Tichon Fiodorovits
Motiakin received me very courteously, desireing me to sitt downe; and then,
after some very civill discourse, presented me with orders to diverse offices
for money, sables, damask, and cloth for me and those who came with me;
which I absolutely refused, telling him that I would stay untill the Boyar
returned, with whom I hoped to prevaile and procure my dismission out of
the countrey.   This writer, being a courteous person, began to reason with
me very civilly, showing me many reasons to divert me from such resolutions; and haveing sent for my Colonell (who was not farr to seeke) they
both tooke me aside, and among other reasons told me, that it would be my
ruine to desire out of the countrey, because the Russe would presume that
comeing from such a countrey, with which they were in open warr, and
being a Roman Catholick, I was come to spy out their countrey only, and
then returne; and that, if I mentioned any such thing, they would not
only not dismiss me, but send me to Sibiria or some remote place, and that
they would never trust me thereafter.   This, indeed, did startle me, considering the nature of the people; so that, with great reluctancy, I consented
to accept of the orders for our comeing into the countrey.

September 17.   I gott orders to receive from a Russe seven hundred men, who were to
be in our regiment, being runneway sojours out of severall regiments, and
fetched back from diverse places.   Haveing received these, I marched
through the Sloboda of the strangers to Crasna Cella,* where wee gott our

* [The German editors explain *cella* or *selo*   would have been known to Gordon as a *kirk-*
to be a village with a church—what in Scotland,   *town.*]

quarters, and exercized these souldiers twice a day in faire weather. I re- September 20.
ceived money, twenty fyve rubles, for my welcome ; and the next day,
sables, and two dayes thereafter, damask and cloth.

I received a months meanes, in cursed copper money, as did these who September 25.
came along with me.

About thirty officers, most whereof I had bespoke in Riga, came to September 27.
Mosko, most of them being our countreymen, as Walter Airth, William
Guild, Georg Keith, Andrew Burnet, Andrew Calderwood, Robert Stuart,
and others, most whereof were enrolled in our regiment.

I marched, by order, into the utmost great towne, and to the Sloboda October.
Zagrodniky, and tooke up my quarters

At the first, some contentions did fall out betwixt the officers and sojours,
with the rich burgesses, who would not admitt them into their housès.
Amongst the rest, a merchant, by whom my quarters were taken up, whilst
my servants were cleansing the inner room, he breake downe the oven in
the utter roome, which served to warme both, so that I was forced to go to
another quarter. But, to teach him better manners, I sent the profos* to
quarter by him, with twenty prisoners and a corporalship of sojours, who,
by connivence, did grievously plague him a weeke ; and it cost him near a
hundred dollers, befor he could procure an order out of the right office to
have them removed, and was well laught at besides for his uncivility and
obstinacy.

During my abode here, two notable passages happened, which follow :

The first : The souldiers takeing a liberty to keep brandy for their owne
uses, and sometimes to sell, which being prejudiciall to his Majesties revenues (the profitt of all strong liquor brewed or made in his countrey, comeing into his treasure), it is not only strictly forbidden to all to sell any by
smalls, but the breach hereof most severely punished ; spyes and searchers
being every where, who, getting notice of the selling of any such liquor,
delate and immediately give notice to the office   On a Sunday afternoone,
whilst I was in the Sloboda of the Strangers, a writter, with twenty or thirty
Streltsees, comeing to a house where the sojours had brandy, the doore being
shutt, befor they gott entrance, the sojours carryed their brandy back into
the garden, so that, after a narrow search, and nothing found, the sojours

---

* [Profos, that is, provost,—the provost marshal.]

pretending themselves affronted, began to convoy the writer with the Streltsees rudely out of doores ; who, being come out into the streets, called their
comerades to help, and breake into the house againe, and into the garden,
where they found the brandy, which they tooke, and some souldiers with it.
But more souldiers comeing upon the tumult, not only tooke back the
souldiers and brandy, but falling by the eares with the Streltsees, drove
them to the citty gates, where, being recruited with others, who lived there,
they drove the souldiers back againe.   By this tyme the partyes encreased,
the Streltsees being about seven hundred, and the sojours about eighty ; but
the street being narrow, and the sojours more desperate and resolute, drove
the Streltsees into the gates of the White Wall, at which tyme six hundred
Streltsees comeing from the maine guard of the Castle, cut of the passage
of those who were gott within the gates, and tooke twenty seven of them,
who, after examination, the next day, were beat with the knute, and sent to
Sibiria.

The next : A Russe captaine, called Affonasse Constantino[witsch] Spiri-
donuf, haveing commanded these souldiers befor wee received them, and
being now in the regiment, and a crafty fellow, had acquired and assumed
such authority among and over the sojours, that he acted many things in-
consisting with command.   I told and forbidd him many tymes, but all would
not help.   I complained to the Colonel [Crawfuird] who, being a person unwilling to be troubled with any business, slighted it ; wherewith, I being not
well satisfyed, and this captaine haveing one night entrapped some souldiers
playing at cards, he not only tooke all the money which they had at play,
but imprisoned them by the provost marshall untill they gave him a great
deale more, in all about sixty rubles, and then let them go ; and all this
without my knowledge, which ought not to be, I haveing the chieffe command.   I being advertised of this the next day, could not containe myself,
but sent for him in the evening, and, haveing dispatched the guard and my
servants, all except one, out of the way, he being come into the roome, I
began to expostulate with him, telling him, that I could not suffer such
abuses any longer, and that I would break his neck one tyme or another.
Whereat he beginning to storme, I gott him by the head, and flinging him
downe, with a fresh, short, oaken cudgell, I so belaboured his back and sides,
that he was scarce able to rise ; whereupon, telling him that I would break
his neck if he played such tricks hereafter, I packed him out of doores.   He

went the next day and complained to the Colonell, who promised to take inquisition and give satisfaction; but I denying all, according to the fashion of this countrey, where there are not witnesses, which, upon his complaint to the Boyar, and in the office, I did also; so that he, seeing the Boyar to befriend me, as one lately come and unacquainted with the fashions of the countrey, desisted from his suite, and made meanes to be gone from the regiment, which was that I wished and aimed at.

Whilst I was here, I was at two weddings, in the Slobod of the Strangers, the one, Ruitmaster Ryter, marryed to the widdow of Lievetennant Collonell Thomas Menezes, who, being wounded by Czudnow, dyed there; the other, Captaine Lidert Lome, marryed to Bannerman, at both which I was merry, and gott my first acquaintance with the females.

By order, I removed and quartered over the river Yausa, in the December. Tagany and Potters Slobod, within the Earthen Wall. Here I had my quarters in a rich merchants house, who used all meanes to gett me removed, and brought two orders out of the court office to this purpose; but, I being loth to quite such a convenience, did not obey them of the stranger office. I would not remove, and keeped the orders by me.

At this tyme ane accident did fall out, which I cannot omitt to relate. At my removall from the Zagrodniky, a Russe liewtennant, called Peter Nikiforuf, came to me with a serjeant, telling me, that three souldiers the night befor, in a quarrell with the Streltsees, were so beat and maimed, that they were not able to remove with the regiment, and that without ane underwritten petition from me, they could not be permitted to stay in their quarters. So bringing a petition and reading it, that they might stay in their quarters fyve or six dayes untill they might be able to remove, which I, suspecting no deceit, unadvisedly put my hand to it. But when I mustered the regiment in the Tagany Slabod, these mens names being called, their comerades answered, that they were let of to their habitations, after which enquireing, I understood, that this lieutennant being bribed by these sojours, had either not read the petition right, or shufled in another into my hands to subscrive; for the petition I subscrived was to let of three sojours to their houses for six weekes. These three comeing to Vologda, where their habitations were, the governour apprehended them, and sent them to Mosko with the petition; which, thereafter, by the malice of the chauncelor, who was my enemy, had like to have bred me great trouble.

December 16.   The Boyar, Elia Danielovits Miloslawsky mustered our regiment, and gave six hundred of them to a Golova,* newly created, to be Streltsees. The Golova was called Nikifor Kolobuf. The sojours grieved exceedingly hereat, and many of them rann away.

December 19   My landlord continuing his solliciting to be freed of me out of his house, a writer, very well accoutred, and attended by twenty fellowes called Trubnikes, such as are called by us catchpoles, came of the court office, haveing a written order in his hand to remove me out of my quarters to another. I being at dinner, and he, admitted into the roome, began very uncivilly to command me to be gone. I desireing him to shew his order, he told me, he would not entrust me with it, because I had kept or torne the two former ; and I telling him, I would not be gone except he shew me the order, he commanded some of the catchpoles, who were gott into the roome with him, to carry out my trunkes ; and he himself layd hold of one of the regiment collours, which were on the wall, to bring it out, which incensed me so, being heated befor by his uncivill behaviour, that getting up, by the help of two officers (who were at dinner with me) and my servants, I drove him and his rude attendants out of the roome, and downe staires, where they rallying with these below, essayed to ascend the staires againe by force. But wee, being on the toppe of the staires, easily repulsed them, they haveing no weapons but staves and sticks, and wee the staffes of the collours, which at the driveing of them out wee had laid hold on. But some sojours by this noise being come together, and seeing this, needed no watchword or command to fall on ; for, immediatly, with their fists, and such clubs or cudgels as they could gett, they so exercized these rude guests, that they were glad to take them to their heeles, and ran downe the street ; the sojours convoying them to the Yaus bridge, and basting them soundly, takeing from them their caps, and from the writer his with pearles, and a necklace of pearle, in worth sixty rubles according as he complained afterwards. This had bred me great trouble, if there had not been at that tyme a great dissension betwixt Fiodor Michaelowitz Artistow, who had charge of the court office, and our Boyar, whereby, after some formall inquisition, the business was slighted. Yet, by perswasion of some officers, who understood the fashion of the countrey better as I, I removed to another quarter.

* [That is, as Gordon explains in the next page, a colonel.]

The Boyar, Elia Danielovitz Miloslawsky, mustered six hundred souldiers of our regiment, and makeing them to a new regiment of Streltsees,
gave them to a Golova called Nikifor Ivan[ovitz] Kolobuf, whereat the
sojours grieved exceedingly.

At the same tyme, I was ordered to teach the said Golova or colonell
the exercize of foot, he haveing never served to foot befor, neither knew
any thing what belonged to the command of a regiment.

We were called into the office to take the oath of fidelity to the Tzaar,
the Hollands minister being to administrate it, and speaking befor us.
When he said that wee should swear to serve his Majestie faithfully and
truly all the dayes of our lyves, I protested, and would not proceed, relying
on my capitulation; which not being allowed, and I remaining constant, I
was detained in the prykase, untill this medium was found, and I forced to
swear to serve so long as the warr with Polland should continue.

[For more than a twelvemonth after his arrival at Moscow, Gordon seems to have been op-
pressed with melancholy. The depreciation of the copper money, caused by an abuse of the right
of coining possessed by cities and individuals, was so great, that although his pay was increased
by a fourth part of its nominal amount, he had difficulty in living upon it. He saw no way of
quitting the country. He had a severe illness, issuing in an intermittent fever, which troubled
him for a considerable time. Altogether, the adverse and unlooked for change in his fortunes
went so much to his heart, that he believed he would have sunk under it, but for constant occupation in drilling his men, and the relief which he occasionally found in the company of the
Scottish officers, with many of whose ways, however, he had little or no sympathy.

He records in his Diary more instances than one of the ignorance and suspicious temper of
the Muscovites. One of their prisoners of war, a Lithuanian officer, named Ganseroski, was
advised by his Italian doctor to sprinkle cream of tartar upon his food. They spoke in Latin;
and the Russian captain of the guard, hearing the words *cremor tartari*, reported that the patient
and his physician held discourse on the affairs of Crim Tartary. It was with some difficulty that
the leech escaped torture. Bribery and corruption prevailed everywhere. Hearing that the
Boyar, Feodor Michaelowitsch Milotawski, was about to depart on an embassy to Persia, Gordon
and his friend Captain Paul Menzies made interest to be included in the number of his attendants. The Boyar's consent was purchased by a gift of a hundred ducats to himself, and of a
saddle and bridle worth twenty ducats to his steward. But Gordon's services were too valuable
to be parted with, and obstacles interposed by higher authority disappointed his hopes of a
journey to the East.

[A.D. 1662.]

In 1662 he reached the rank of Lieutenant Colonel. Sick of the frivolous or dissipated 1662.
society of his military companions, he now resolved to cultivate the acquaintance of the virtuous

of the other sex. But this also had its perils. He found himself so beset with the toils of intriguing damsels and their friends, that he ran the risk of being beguiled into marriage on the one hand, or forced into a quarrel on the other. In this strait, he began to doubt whether his safest course might not be to marry deliberately. His Diary duly records the grave discussion which he held with himself on this question. The first place is given to the objections. Marriage being one of the most important steps in a man's life, he ought to have hopes that it would both increase his happiness and better his position. But Gordon saw little room for cherishing such expectations. Marriage with a Muscovite was forbidden, unless he should embrace her religion. Of the foreigners again of his own faith, especially such as were soldiers, the most were poor, many were of indifferent character, and their children but ill educated For a married man to keep house on the scanty pay of a Russian officer, seemed a hard task. Nor was it to be overlooked that when a man took a wife he lost his freedom, so that it was all but impossible for him to remove to another country. On the other side, he was bound to consider the daily danger to which he was exposed from the snares of the women around him. He might, over his wine, let fall a word which he would rue all his life. Then, again, marriage, if a man were happy in his choice, had its advantages and charms. It promised help in household affairs, comfort in sickness, consolation in crosses, new friends, increased respect, and escape from many temptations. As to expense, he saw that others, with no better income than his own, were able, although married, to keep as good a table, and to wear as good clothes, as himself. Hence, he concluded that God bestowed a special blessing on the married state, since a bachelor's housekeeping cost more than the maintenance of a wife. Marriage, he could not deny, was a sort of servitude ; but then surely it was servitude of the sweetest kind. And, even in the event of his having to shift to another country, the aid and advice which a married man could command, would counterbalance some of his other drawbacks. Finally, he persuaded himself that marriage would serve to restore and preserve his health ; and so, after frequent prayer to God for guidance, while lying in bed one Sunday evening, he formally summed up the the arguments on both sides, and resolved to marry.

He had next to determine with whom he should wed. He had little dread of refusal from the daughter or sister of a soldier, and so he passed in review all his female friends. His choice fell on the daughter of Colonel Philip Albrecht von Bockhoven. She was scarcely thirteen, but was well grown, handsome, amiable in disposition, and had been well educated by an excellent mother. Her father, then a prisoner with the Poles, was of good birth, the eldest colonel in his regiment, and high in favour with the Czar. Above all the family, like his own, was Roman Catholic.

[A.D. 1663.]

1663.
January 12.
He lost no time in preferring his suit. The lady was living with her mother, in the house of an uncle, another Colonel von Bockhoven Gordon, at his second visit, found her alone. She wished to send for her mother who had gone out, but he begged her not to take that trouble as his business was with herself. She had given him a small glass of brandy, according to the custom of the country, and he proposed to drink to the health of her lover. She denied that she had one, and when Gordon pressed the point, repeated the denial. He then asked if she would

accept of him as a suitor. The answer was a blush, which satisfied Gordon that he had nothing
to fear on her part. Her mother and uncle were unwilling to give their consent in her father's
absence, but at last they agreed that Gordon should be received in the house as a suitor, and
that the young lady should not go anywhere in public without him. A few days afterwards, he **January 18**
records that they assisted at the marriage of Lieutenant Colonel Winram with Juliana Keith,
and found themselves very happy, although they were the objects of envy and hatred.

Gordon now devoted himself to the task of procuring the liberation of Colonel von Bockhoven, as a necessary condition of his own marriage. But his exertions, although earnest and
long continued, were unsuccessful; and, at length, the mother and other kinsfolks of his be-
trothed so far relented, that the marriage was celebrated in the beginning of the year 1665.

In the meantime circumstances had arisen which ultimately issued in Gordon's being sent on
a mission to England. They are thus chronicled in his Diary:—]

[A.D. 1662.]

1662.
January 13.

At this tyme a great ambassy was prepareing from the Tzaar to congratulate our Kings happy restauration; Knias Peter Simonovitz Prosorof-
sky being ordained ambassadour, and his colleague Ivan Affonaseovits Zelabofsky.*

. . . . . .

[A.D. 1663.]

1663.
September 6.

Wee had notice of the English ambassadour, the Earle of Carlile,† his
arrivall at Archangell, with his lady, and a great traine.

. . . .

I received a letter from the English ambassador, and another from **October 15.**
Mr. Bryan,‡ showing that some things were wanting for the ambassadors
suit, desireing me to provide them so quietly that no body should know·
The things were, two silver trumpets with banners, wherein my Lords armes

---

* [The German editors add that the embassy
was accompanied by the Dyak Iwan Davidow,
who, on leaving England, was despatched,
along with Zelabofsky or Shelabowsky, to
Italy Prince Prosorowsky returned to Moscow in March, 1664, with a letter from King
Charles II to the Czar, which was translated
into the Russian by Colonel Forret, an Englishman serving under the Muscovite banners.
Glimpses of the embassy during its abode in
London, may be seen in Pepy's Diary, vol. ii.,
pp. 70, 74, 87, 93, 169, edit., Lond. 1851. The
ambassador occupied York House, where, says
the Secretary of the Admiralty, 'I saw his
people go up and down louseing themselves.']

† [Charles Howard, first Earl of Carlisle. An
account of his embassies to the north was published in his own lifetime: 'A Relation of
Three Embassies from his Majesty Charles II.
to the Great Duke of Moscovie, the King of
Sweden, and the King of Denmark, performed
by the Earl of Carlisle in the years 1663 and
1664, written by an Attendant of the Embassies.
London, 1669.' 8vo.]

‡ [Thomas Bryan was an English merchant
settled at Moscow. Letters from the King of
Great Britain to the Czar were often entrusted
to his care; and some of them, which are still
preserved in the Muscovite archives, bear to
have been translated by him into the Russian.]

(which were sent me), twelve halberts or partisans, with fringes of his livery, etc. I returned answer two dayes thereafter, that all should be ready to content, and in due tyme.

. . . .

[A.D. 1664.]

1664.
January 1.
Wee had notice that the English ambassador was keeping his Christmas at Vologda.

. . . .

February 6.
The English ambassadour haveing stayed two dayes at Rostokin, and, on the fifth of February, by a mistake of the posts, who ran all out the Twersky way, from whence the ambassadours from all places usually come, and where all the foot and cavalierie, so well strangers as Russes, were ranged on both sydes of the way; the ambassadour being dissapointed of makeing his entry, and was necessitated to lodge, with very bad convenience, in the small village Prutky, which disgusted him very much, sending a letter to his Majestie, representing the circumstances thereof, and takeing it as an affront, whereof he desired reparation befor he should make his entry. Yet, upon promise of satisfaction, he prepared for his entry. His suit was not so numerous as gallant, the liveries rich, and gentlemen all well clothed. He was received with great splendor after the usuall way, as to ceremonies; the Emperour himself, with the Empress, with all the chieffe nobility, being spectatours on one of the gates of the citty. It was late befor he gott to his lodging, which was on the great street in a large stone house.

February 11.
The English ambassadour had his first audience, being convoyed up in the usuall manner, all the presents going or being drawne and carryed befor him; the infantery being ranged on both sydes of the way, and the Crimlina,* or Castle, full.

13.
The English ambassadour had his second audience and first conference.

17.
The English ambassadour at his second conference.

29.
The Earle of Carlile had his third conference, and all with litle satisfaction.

. . . .

June 28.
I had notice, by my servant and letters, that, on the seventeenth, the English ambassadour had refused the Emperours present of sables, saying

* [The Kremlin.]

it was not fitt that he should make any advantage for himself, seing in his
masters business, for which he came, he had received no satisfaction; and
that, two dayes thereafter, the present which, at his first audience, he had
presented from himself was returned; and that, on the twenty-fourth, he
went from Mosko towards Sweden.

.   .   .   .

[A.D. 1665.]

1665.
June 10.

Doktor Thomas Wilson came to Mosko, and lodged by Doktor Collins.*
But because the pestilence was in England, and he should have holden the
quarantine, befor he came to the citty, he, with one Kenedy, who came
with him, were sent back to stay at Klin, ninety verst from hence, and
Doktor Collins to Veschreseziansky,† where they were to remaine six weeks,
where all who conversed with them had liberty to go and come from Mosco,
but themselves not.

Vasily Yek. Deskow‡ returned, without satisfaction, as to his complaint
against the Earle of Carlile, haveing had but a cold reception; yet, by the
bounty of the King, at his dismission, recompenced.

[During this year, 1665, Gordon had tidings of the death of his elder brother, Alexander, in
Scotland. He now earnestly petitioned for leave to revisit his native country, but was refused.
But in the following summer, the Czar resolved to despatch him on a mission to England, under
circumstances which he himself shall describe.]

[A.D. 1666.]

1666.
June 22.

I was sent for to the possolsky office, but comeing late, was ordered to
come the next day.

I went to the possolsky or ambassy office, where the Dumny Diak June 23
asked me, If I had a mind to go for England? I told him, Yes. He told
me, that his Majesty was to send a letter to the King, and that I should
take that along with me. I replyed, that I had indeed, last yeare, desired
to be let of to England, but that now I had no necessity or businesse there;
and that, if I should go about my owne business thither, I could not well
take such a letter with me, because it should be a shame for me to carry a

---

* [Samuel Collins, M.D., physician to the
Czar Alexis Michaelowitsch. He returned to
England, and published at London in 1671 a
work on the 'Present State of Russia.']

† [Woskresenskoje, forty versts from Moscow.]
‡ [Wassily Jakowlewitsch Daschow.]

letter, not haveing any character ; and that I should be look't upon as one in publick employment, whereby I should be put to great charges and expences ; and that, lastly, I should be tyed to expect an answer. To which he said nothing, but that I should stay untill he returned from his Majesty. After an houre, he came and told me that his Majesty had ordered and commanded me to go for England, and that I should make myself ready in three or four dayes to be gone. I repeating the former reasons, and adding, that I was wronged in not getting my full oklad or monthly pay according to others, and that I had all this tyme but twenty five rubles a month whereas I should have forty, and that I wanted, as the rest also, two whole months ; he told me that his Majesty would allow and cause give me money to beare my charges, and that, for my other grievances, I should bring petitions, and compeer to morrow.

Befor I go further, I shall showe the reasons of sending this message, and of the sending a stranger, and why me and not another.

The English, in their adventures at sea, haveing found out the sea port at the mouth of the river Dwina, had, for their losses and paines, great priviledges conferred on them by the Tzaar,* especially to trade without paying of toll or custome ; whereby encouraged they appointed an agent, which continued many yeares with considerable advantage. But the Hollanders and Hamburgers, haveing found the way hither also, began to trade without any corporation, yet encreased so, that the Hollanders especially, in tyme gott great advantages of the English, and outwitted, to give it no worse terme, the English, and even trapan'd them into many things, and then delated them. For they had gott some of the English to bring up their goods under the notion of their owne, so to avoid the paying of custome, whereby the Tzaar was cheated of his revenues ; so that it was in agitation, by the instigation of the Hollanders and Russia merchants, whom they had drawne to their party, to disannull these priviledges. But there not being sufficient proofes, and the English, forwarned, keeping themselves closser, and by their splendid way of liveing haveing gained the good will of the nobility, and those of the poorest merchants and tradesmen by trusting, the business was delayed, untill the unhappy tragedy of the murder of King Charles the First, whereat occasion was taken, upon a more generous

* [Iwan Wassiljewitsch.]

account, to banish the English, and take away ther privileges. Yet, afterwards, they were permitted to trade, paying custome as others; in which state they continued untill the happy restauration of King Charles the Second, at which tyme the English conceived hopes of being restored to their privileges; for, in the year 1662, the Tzaar, not to be behind with other Christian princes, sent a splendid ambassy (and a person of great birth and quality as had been sent any where befor), to congratulate Great Brittaines King, his happy restauration; which was accepted the better, because, of all Christian princes, the Tzaar alone had never acknowledged, nor kept any correspondence with the usurper Cromwell; as also the King, dureing his exile, had received other good offices from the Tzaar.

These ambassadours, in their conferences and discourses, giveing great hopes of the restauration of the priviledges, the King sent a very eminent person, his extraordinary ambassadour, to Mosko, (it was Sir Charles, Earl of Carlisle, Viscount Hovard of Morpeth, Baron Dacre of Gillesland, etc.), in full hopes to obtaine the priviledges. But his excellency takeing himself to be afronted at his first reception at the sea port, (at Archangel), and then much more at his comeing into Mosko, which, albeit done by a mistake and not of purpose, he urged the reparation thereof with too much heat; whereupon followed some irritations on both sides, so that the ambassadour urging reparation at diverse conferences, and at a private audience, and not getting any to his satisfaction, as also being denyed the priviledges, the chieffe business for which he came, refused the presents, which were sent to him by the Tzaar; which offended his Tzaarsky Majestie so highly, that he dispatched a stolnick, Vasily Yakufleufsin Diaskow,* in the quality of envoy to the King, to complaine of the ambassadour, who comeing into England had but a cold reception, and getting but three dayes defrayment, was permitted to live upon his owne. Yet, the Earle of Carlisle returning into England, upon the relation of his negotiation, was justifyed, and his comportment approved. Thereafter, giveing the envoy a visitt, whereat he was much surprized, he promised his assistance for his friendlyer usage, and so, out of an excess of generosity, interceded with the King so farr that he gott full restitution of what he had disbursed, and was dismissed honourably.

Nevertheless this envoy, at his returne, did so aggravate his hard usage,

* [Wassily Jakowlewitsch Dashkow.]

that it was doubted here whither any intercourse or correspondence should be hereafter betwixt the princes.   But now the warr, which the King had with France and Holland, being like to continue, by the advice of the Moskovia merchants, the King did writt to the Tzaar by post, showing of the warr he had with France and Holland, and how that he was informed that the Hollanders brought much materialls for their shipping from Russia, which he desired might not be permitted them, and that it might be free for his Majesties subjects to buy such materialls.   His Majestie gave notice, likewise, how that the pestilence did rage in his residentiall citty of London, and diverse others places of the kingdom of England.   This letter was kept very closs a while, untill they resolved upon an answer, which being ready, no Russe was found willing to go with it, fearing such cold entertainment as Diaskow had gott; for notwithstanding it was knowne how that he had been sufficiently rewarded and honourably dismissed, yet he atributed all this to his owne dexterity, and the fear the King had of offending his Tzaarsky Majestie, averring that none thereafter would be defrayed but for three dayes, as the ministers of other princes; that all things wer ten tymes so dear as in Mosko; and many difficulties more; which, with the Russes unwillingnes to allow any minister so much money as to maintaine him at any court, and also loth to offend the Hollanders, who had now engrossed all the trade almost here, by a publick message, it was resolved to send some stranger, and me especially, because I had petitioned to go thither the year befor, and being one of his Majesties subjects, might haply have ffriends at court.

It was in vaine for me to refuse, when concluded above by his Majesty and counsell; so being ordered to come to the pricase the next day, I went and made ready my petitions.

June 24.   I went into the office, but there being no convenience to come to his Majestyes hand, I was ordered to come the next day.   I bought a coverd waggon and necessaries for my jorney.

June 25.   I went into the ambassy office, and haveing resolved to take my brother in law along with me to England, I told the chancellour, and that he might come to his Majesties hand with me.   About midday I was brought above, and admitted to kiss his Majesties hand, who was pleased to speake very graciously to me.   I gave his Majestie two petitions, one for my full meanes, and another for two months meanes which was owing me; and his

Majestie was pleased to give order to my satisfaction. Then he asked me, why I tooke the child with me, and whose son he was. I answered that he was Collonel Philip Albertus von Bockhoven his son, and that it was his mothers will, he should go along to see his ffriends. His Majestie commanded me to have a great care of him, and bring him back with me, which I promised to do. Then his Majestie called the chancellour, and spoke to him; who, turning to me, told me that his Majestie had graced me with a hundred rubles for equipping me, a hundred rubles for my jorney, and a hundred rubles of my pay in advance, and so dismissed me.

I waited in the office, till the chancellour came downe; who, being come, ordered mandates to be sent to the treasury for money, and gave that petition for the two months to me, with an order on it to receive for these two months full pay; and, notwithstanding I insisted to have an order on the other petition for settleing my pay for the future, I could obtaine nothing of the cross-grain'd old crabbed fellow, but that, when I returned, I should gett a full order. So that there being no possibility of makeing any address to his Majesty immediately, and our Boyar being sick, no other would medle in it, I was forced to be content with that they gave me.

I made ready for my jorney, and bought diverse necessaryes, and in June 26. some places tooke my leave.

The money was brought to me, with his Majesties letters and instruc- June 27. tions. After noone I was in towne, ordered some business, and tooke my leave there.

I rode to Kuntzow, and tooke my leave of the Boyar, Elia Danielowitz, June 28. and his lady, who, with others there, were very kind to me. When I came home, it was told me, that a writer had been there from the ambassy office, with orders to be gone the next day without fail; so I went the same evening, and tooke my leave of my neerest ffriends.

The podwodes* being come in the morning, I made all ready, and have- June 29 ing dined, most of the Slobodish cavaliers and many merchants came and convoyed me to a bush or wood, within sight of the high way or road to Twere, where wee stayed neer two howres, takeing *bon valet* with numerous cups. The ffriends returning, some of my countreymen as Maior Langdales and Ruitmaster Kieth, and others, who had gone aside, and now came on

---

* [That is, posthorses.]

purpose to convoy me further and stay with me all night, came to me; for whose sakes I pitched my tent short of what I had intended. Wee had scarce setled when the English merchants came with a great magazine of all sorts of liquors, with whom wee spent the whole night in hearty cups and joviall discourses.

June 30.   By day light, bidding farewell to ffriends, I tooke jorney, laying my self in my waggon to sleep. About eight o'clock, I passed by Czirkisewa, where lay in the fields a hundred officers who had been dismissed, and very earnest, some of them at least, to have gone in my company; but being informed of some designe, I excused it, and now strived to shun them. So posting in hast by them, without being discovered, I rode twenty verst further, and turning aside to the right hand to ane obscure place, I rested and dined. Here I mustered up my letters, and some tokens and other things sent along to ffriends in the places and townes through which I was to travell, as also many things and lettres sent to England. Whilst I stayed here, a post overtooke me with letters from ffriends in Mosco to merchants over sea.

Haveing packt up and put all my things in good order, I set forwards; and within fifteen verst of Klin, turning aside againe, I lodged, haveing in company with me my litle brother in law, Captaine William Rae, Peter Pile, a apothecary, Caspar Staden, and two servants, with six yempshiks,* being in all thirteen persons. This night the yempshikes kep't watch.

July 1.   I arose early, and set forward, and crosseing the rivers Sosha and Yanugo, I rode through the lately burnt up towne of Klin; which standeth on the descent of a hill, and is distant from Mosko ninety verst, being lately a stage where horses useth to be changed, but now exeemed by reason of their being burn'd up. I rode further, and crossed a litle brooke at a field called Yamoga, being five verst, and to Spassuf Sauka twenty verst, where I dined; then forwards to Sawidowa, a village, where wee had a sight of the river Volga, which comeing from the west runneth east, and so to a village called Soshia, where, being rainy weather, I lodged. Here the river Soshia, being fifteen verst.

July 2.   Haveing notice that the disbanded cavaliers were encamped on the other syde of the river, and not likeing their company, I rose very early, and pass-

* [Waggoners, or carters.]

ing the river, I passed by them without noise, befor any was stirring ; and driveing forward, I dined by the village Mokry, being about thirty verst from Soshia, haveing, on the way, passed by Slobodka, and seen diverse villages on the other syde of the river Volga, and Grodsha, where an ancient fort, from which it hath the name. Makeing hast, I came to Twere, twenty verst ; where, getting fresh horses, I crossed the river Volga by boat, and turning to the left hand from the high way, I lodged in a meadow. This Twere was once a dukedome apart, hath a stone wall, and its name from the river Twere or Twertza ; which on the other syde, a litle below the towne, falleth in the river Volga, and hath its rise by Visnesloczka. I writt from hence to my ffriends in Mosko, by the yempshikes.

Haveing been tormented the whole night with midges or mosquites, I July 3. tooke jorney befor day, passing through woods, and came to the village Medno by the river Twertaz, thirty verst ; where, dineing and going forward, wee crossed the river Lagovets by the village Marina, thirteen verst, and came to Torizok, seventeen verst, and lodged in the Yempsky Sloboda.*

Haveing gott fresh horses, I departed early. I came to Michailofsky, a July 4. brooke, and a large field, thirty werst, where I dined. After noone I crossed the river Twertza at Vidropusk, being five verst ; then to Cholocholnia river and village, ten verst, and crossed the river Twertza againe by Nikola Stolb, a monastery, seven verst, and over plaine fields to Visnego Vloizka, ten verst, where I lodged.

Here I gott fresh horses, and by day light I crossed the river Msta, July 5. which keeping his course, for the most part north west, falleth in the lake Ilmin, by Novogrod. I came to Chotilow, thirty fyve verst, where I dined ; and refreshing our selves once more, by the river Bresay, twenty three verst, I came to Yedro, twelve verst, and to Ziemna Gora, seventeen verst, where I lodged.

Haveing gott fresh horses, I tooke jorney by day light, and made a stop July 6. at the small towne Balday, three verst. On our right hand is a monastery, in the midst whereof a lake, wherein are about a hundred and fyfty monkes, all Polls or Littawers. The towne is also inhabited by the same sort of people. The lake is about six verst broad, and of an incredible deepnes,

* [That is, the carters' or waggoners' quarter.]

being, as they say, in some places a hundred fathom. A litle of from that lake, wherein the monastery standeth, is another of the same bignes, betwixt which a channel. Out of this last floweth a brooke or river which emptyeth itself into the Msta, as all the other rivers and brookes here about. From hence wee jorneyed over hills to the river Grimatsa, fyve verst. On each side of this river are many kurgans,* where they say that the battel betwixt the masters and the servants was fought in the end of Tamerlanes warr. A litle further wee passed along in a most pleasant road, haveing the river Polumet on our left hand, and hills covered with woods on our right hand. Haveing rode ten verst, wee crossed the river Grimatza againe, where it falleth in the Polumet, and so in company of the river Polumet to Yasulbitsa, a village, fyve verst. Here I dined. Then setting forward, I crossed the river Polumet and Yarmy, ten verst, which the river Polumet receiving falleth in the river Pola, and this in the lake Ilmen, fyfteen verst above the . . . ; then to the village Rechina, fyve verst, and to the yame or stage Kresty, where getting fresh horses, and makeing no stay, wee rode along the river Cholova. Crossing it diverse tymes, wee came to the river Mosnia, twenty verst, which crossing, wee came to the village Wina, fyve verst, and to Sajantsova, ten verst, where wee lodged all night.

July 7.   Haveing gott fresh horses wee came to the village and monastery Lustow, three verst, and to the village Krasna Stanky, twelve verst, through woods and bad bridged ways to the river Nissa, ten verst, which runneth here south, and then turning, falleth in the lake Ilmen twenty fyve verst above Novogrodt. Wee crossed this river by a float, and then came to Brunits, fyve verst ; where takeing boat, wee went downe the river Msta to Novogrod, thirty verst, where getting a quarter, I lodged all night.

July 8.   About midday, haveing gone over in a large boat, wee sailed up the river Volcha to the lake Ilmen. This lake is in some places forty verst broad, and about fyfty long. It is said that seventy rivers fall therein, the chieffe whereof are Msta, Poniedielna, Lowat, Vergot, Solona, Czarna, Verunda, Mpsiaga, Veresa, Polist. Wee passed by many pleasant villages on the right hand, and came late to the river Mpsiaga, and so to the river Solonia, up which to the village Saltzee, which is seventy verst from Novogrodt, whither wee came in the morning.

                    * [Barrows, or earthen mounds.]

Here wee gott horses and waggons, and came to the river Shitnia, July 9 fifteen verst, where wee rested, and refreshed our selves, bathing in the river. Then rideing through woods, haveing the said river Shitnia on our right, a great way, wee came to a ruined village called Opochy, where wee lodged, fyfteen verst.

Getting up early, wee came to the village Dombroona, twenty verst, July 10. where, after breakfasting, I left my baggage, and with Captain Rae, a servant, and a yempshik, rode befor and came to Dubesna, fyfteen verst. Then rideing ten verst further, wee refreshed our selves and horses. Then crossing the river Kep, and it keeping us company a good way, wee came to the river Pskova, being a stony river; by which, on our right hand, rideing, wee came to Plesko or Pskow, as the Russes call it, thirty verst. I enquired here for Colonell Odovern his quarters, and found him lodged without the towne. So takeing up my quarters by him, it was late ere my baggage came. I received letters from my wyfe and mother in law, dated Mosko, the fourth of July.

I went to the Boyar, Kniaz Ivan Andreevits Chovansky, who was July 11. governour here, and delivered him his Majesties letters, who, welcomeing me, told me that he would take care that all should be ready according to the order. Being invited, I dined by Collonell Gulits. I writt to my wyfe and mother in law.

Haveing been by the Boyar, I went and breakfasted by Collonell Kruger, July 12. and dined by Collonell Schein.

A sotnik,* with six Streltsees and podwods, being come, I went and July 13. tooke leave of the Boyar; and, after breakfast, tooke jorney, going over the river Velika Reka by a floating bridge, and takeing the Swedish house in our way; where, with hearty cups, the ffriends who convoyed me remembred ffriends, and convoyed me out into the fields, tooke their leave. Only Ruitmaster Colin, Mr. Laughton, with some horsemen, went along with me. At night, wee came to the monastery and towne Petshure, where I lodged, being forty verst from Plesko.

I tooke jorney early, and came to the borders, being nine verst; where July 14. the Ruitmaster being to take his leave, I caused make ready for breakfast, and with heartly cups remembring our ffriends, whereby the trompets, which

* [An officer.]

wee had from Plesko, sounding, put the countrey in no small alarum. The Ruitmaster parting, I had in place of Captaine Rae and Peter Pile, who stayed at Plesko, the sotnike with six Streltzees   Wee came to Niew-heusel, a old stone castle, three verst, and so forward to Roughs crue or innes, whither wee came about foure aclock afternoone, being from Niew-heusel fyve miles   There being bad beer in the alehouse, and hearing that the priest had good liquor, I sent and desired a litle of it, who very civilly invited me to his house, whereof I accepted, and went. He received me very kindly, and kept me to supper, where wee had good wholesome coun-trey fare by a cup of good beer.

July 15.   I rose early, and came to Vorstuf, three miles, and to the Black River, two miles, where I dined. Crossing the river by a float, wee came three miles further, and lodged in the fields by good convenience of wood, grasse, and water, and kept good watch all night.

July 16.   By day light I set forward, and, dineing in the woods, lodged a mile short of Wolmar.

July 17.   Wee passed by Wolmar, and dined at Papendorf, two miles from Volmar, and sixteen from Riga ; and going three miles further, wee lodged in the fields

July 18.   Wee crossed the river Brasla by a bridge, and lodged by the hill Koshewnik. From hence I dispatched the sotnik, with Caspar Staden, to Riga, with letters from the governour of Plesko to that governour, ordering them to take up a lodging for me in the suburbes.

July 19   I came to the river Gavia, two miles, which crossing, I dined in the fields. Then I crossed the river Iuga, and rideing a mile further, I lodged in the fields, being a mile from Riga.

July 20.   I arose early, and came to Riga, and lodged by the interpreter. In the afternoone, the searchers came to me, desiring to know if I had any mer-chants goods by me. I told them that I had nothing but about one hundred reichs dollers worth of sable tippes for my owne use ; and because they were so civill as not to search my trunks, wherein I had some muscas and other things, I gave them two reichs dollers, wherewith they seemed satisfyed and departed.

Mr. Benjamin Ayloffe and Finlay Downy gave me visitt ; and Mr. Herman Becker thereafter, with some others, to all whome there were letters and tokens. I received a letter from Mr. Thomas Bryan, dated

Mosco, the fyfth of July, [16]66; another dated the twenty ninth of June, the first per post, and the last per ffriend; a letter also from Doktor Colins, dated the fyfth of July.

My old acquaintance the governour, Lievetennant General Fabian de July 21. Fersen, sent an officer to welcome me, and told me he was very desirous to speake with me, inviteing me to his lodgings. I rendred thankes, and bid tell him, that I would pay my respects to him in the afternoone.

Haveing dined, I sent for Mr. Ayloffe, and desired him to accompany me to the governour; whither being come, he received me with a great deale of kindnes, and after much discourse of old passages, he began to insinuate the great inclination they * had to preserve the peace, and seemed to doubt of the lyke sincerity in us; and among other things told me, how that some dayes ago, a party of ours had come to the borders, and in a manner of bravado had made a great noise with sounding of trumpets and shooting, and thereby had put the countrey in a great feare and alarum. Which I considering, told him that possibly it might be a mistake, and that it might arise from my comeing to the borders, whither some ffriends from Plesko had convoyed me, and at parting had, in mirth, shott some shotts, and sounded trumpets. Wherewith he was satisfyed, and partly ashamed, that, without ground, they should be so soone alarumed. Afterwards wee began to pass the tyme with hearty cups. Parting, he sent me home to my lodgings, in a coach, with servants and lacqueyes convoying me. At my comeing to my lodging, I gave to each of the better sort who had convoyed me, a ducat, and to the other, a reichs doller, a piece; which was by farr too much. I writt to Mr Bryan.

I dined at home with some ffriends, and in the afternoone was merry July 22. with them.

I exchanged a hundred rubles for reichs dollers, giveing fyfty eight copikes July 23. for a reichs doller, most whereof Hollands, which was no good bargaine.

Mr. Ayloffe hired my passage in a vessel to Lubeck for twelve reichs dollers for my self and people, and I to have the cabinet, and promissed to provide all sort of provisions for me. I dismissed the fuirment† which I had from Plesko, and wrott with them to ffriends there, and by the sotnik to the governour, thanking him for his kindnes.

---

* [That is, the Swedes.]   † [Postillions.]

July 24.   I did writt to Mosko, to my wyfe and mother in law, to Mr. Bryan, Doktor Colins, and to Almos Ivanovitz, the Dumny Chancellour.*

July 25.   The ship being gone downe the river, I sent my baggage to the boat which lay at the wharfe waiting for us. Here these of the custome house stopped my baggage, exacting four reichs dollers for land toll, and as much for going out, of the hundred reichs dollers of sable tippes; which Mr. Ayloffe payed for me, and I repayed him at breakfast in the towne.

About ten aclock wee went in the boat downe the river, and at Dune-munde skonce or fort, made a halt, where I spoke with Captain John Gordon. Then going to the shipp, wee made forward, haveing pilots to shew us the way. The ship belonged to Lubeck, the masters name Durick Ebler.

July 26.   Haveing sailed all night, about ten aclock wee passed by Dumes Ness, haveing the illand Oesel on our right hand. This ness is eighteen miles from the mouth of the river Dwina, and very dangerous, by reason of the sands and flatts, so that seldome a yeare but some suffer ship wrack here. Toward evening, with a pretty gale, wee passed by Silversoort, nyne miles, and Vendaw, three miles. Then, quitting the Curish coast, wee steered our course more to the north west towards Gothland, whereof wee gott a sight

July 27.   the next day in the evening. This illand is eighteen miles long, and is said to have at every miles end a church.

July 28.   By contrary winds, wee were forced to lie here two dayes. Then the
July 29.   wind proveing more favorable, wee sailed forward to the illand Oeland,
July 30.   which is distant from Gothland seven miles. The south end of Oeland is distant from Vendow forty leagues, and from Bornholm twenty one. Both
July 31.   these illands, by the treaty of Bromsebro, 1645, belong to the Sweds. Wee sailed by Oeland, which is also eighteen miles long, and towards evening lost sight hereof. Wee had ugly unpleasant weather.

August 1.   Wee sailed by Erdholme, which hath a small harbour for necessity. No body dwelleth here; only fishers come from Bornholme, and stay. Towards

* [Dumny Chancellor, or Dumny Dyack,—that is, Lord Chancellor, or rather Lord Secretary of State, ‘The Emperours of Russia,’ says Giles Fletcher, ‘giue the name of counsellour to diuers of their chiefe nobilitie, rather for honors sake, then for any vse they make of them about their matters of state. These are called Boiarens, without any addition, and may bee called counsellors at large. For they are sel- dome or neuer called to any publique consul- tation. They which are of his speciall and priuie counsell indeed (whom hee vseth daily and ordinarily for all publique matters pertein- ing to the state) haue the addition of Dumnoy, and are named Dumnoy boiaren, or Lords of the Counsell. Foure of these are called Dumnoy deiakey, or Lord Secretaries’—(The Rvsse Com- mon Wealth, ff. 34-36, Lond. 1591.)]

evening, wee sailed by it, and Bornholme, three miles distant from it. These belong to the King of Denmarke.

Wee sailed towards the Pomers coast, and came in the view of the illand August 2. Rugia, which hath three hookes or nesses called Wittemund, Diasmund, and Darnbush, which is divided from the illand. This illand is distant from August 3. Bornholme fourteen, and from Lubeck twenty six leagues ; and, keeping our course south west, wee had in our view Stralsund, and, towards evening the promontory Dass, which is the confines of Pomeren and Mechlenburg. Wee sailed by Rebnits, Rostock, and Wismar, which is fyve miles from August 4. Lubeck ; and, sailing by the points called Great and Little Cluisemunde, towards evening, wee came into the river, where the fortress Travemunde ; and with a great deale of worke, all the night, wee winded the ship up the river, and, about fyve aclock in the morning, came to anker just under the August 5. towne, being by water foure, and by land but two, miles from the mouth of the river. I tooke up my lodging at the signe of the Red Lyon, and sent the amber cabinet, which Mr. Bryan desired me to bring hither, to Just Poorten with the letter concerning it.

Haveing, with others, hired a waggon, about foure aclock, wee went from Lubeck ; and, feeding the horses about midnight at halfe way, wee arrived at Hamborg about midday. I tooke up my lodging in the Stone August 6. street, at the signe of the Towne Revall, where I had choice company of cavaliers, only a litle more ranting as was fitting for my humour. I sent immediately for Mr. Nathaniell Cambridge, to whom I had letters of recommendation ; with whom, being come, I consulted about my jorney further. By sea was exceeding dangerous and uncertaine, and by land tedious and expensive, neither without hazard. He promised to ask the advice of other ffriends, and give me his and their opinions, proffering me withall all the kindness in his power. Mr. ver Poorten came to me after-wards, to whom I had also letters, who also very kindly offered me all assistance.

I went in the morning to Altonaw, and heard devotion. After noone, August 7. one Mr. Kenedy came to me, who, at his going from Mosko, had taken letters from us all to Scotland, but lost them all at Riga, he haveing had a fitt of a frensy there.

My ffriends came to me, being very irresolute of giveing their advice. August 8. However, I resolved to travell by land, as the most pleasant and secure, by reason of the warr.

August 9.   I sent such things as I had not occasion for on my jorney to Mr. Cambridge, to be sent to Riga, resolving to go as light as I could.

August 10   I did writt to my wyfe and mother in law, to Doktor Colins, Mr. Bryan, and to the Dumny Chancellour Almais.

August 11.   My ffriends convoying me, I tooke leave of them, and went by boat to Harborgh, two miles ; where, with others, takeing the post waggon, wee came in the evening to Sarnsdorffe, foure miles, where, refreshing our selves and horses, wee set forward, and came in the morning to Witsendorffe, foure

August 12. miles ; where wee dined, and came in the evening to Zell, foure miles.   This is a pretty towne by the river Alre, where the Duke of Luneburg hath his residence.   He is called Georg William, and is of the Lutheran perswasion, being a branch of the house of Brunswick.   Here is a very magnificent pallace, where the Duke resides.   Wee were strictly examined at the gatc of the towne, and all our names written up.   Haveing supped, and gott fresh horses, wee went forward in the evening ; and, travelling the whole night, wee came befor day to Hannover, and tooke up our lodging in a inne befor the towne.

August 13.   This towne is fyve miles from Zell.   The river Line runneth by it.   It hath faire buildings, and a large pallace, where resideth Johan Friderick, Duke of Hannover and Luneburgh, being of the Roman Catholik religion, and another branch of the house of Brunswick.   Here wee hired a covered large waggon, being in company the Baron von Lottrum, Lievetennant Collonell Schwerin, a burgess of Worsel, with his wyfe, and myself, with our servants ; and, about eight aclock, takeing jorney, crossing the river, wee had, on our left hand, a village called Ronnenberg, and a parke on the right on a hill, and halfe the descent thereof.   Wee came to the borders of Schawenberg, being two miles from Hannover, where wee saw Neystadt, a pretty towne belonging to the Duke of Luneburgh on our right hand ; then through Great Brinnendorffe and Horest, then betwixt Lowen Hoffe on the right, and Reymene Hoffe on the left hand, belonging to a gentleman called Munichhausen, to Stadthagen, two miles.   Here wee dined, and gott fresh horses.   Wee rode forward, haveing on our left hand Oberkerchen, belonging to the Landgraffe of Hessen, to Bickeburg ; where wee lodged, paying dear the next morning for our carowsing in Hames kuite.*   This is the

---

* [*Hames kuite*, that is *kuite* or beer brewed   in the town of Hamm in Westphalia. See below, p. 72.]

residence of Graffe Philip of Schawenborg and Lippe, where he hath a faire
house, fortifyed with a wall and moate, one mile.   August 14.

From hence, not very early, wee went towards Minden, passing the
river Weser under the towne, one mile, where wee made no stay ; but getting
fresh horses, wee rode along by the Weser, and rideing up over a hill, which
the river Wesser in a manner cutteth through, the tract of the hill being
on the other syde, though not altogither so high, under which standeth the
towne Hamell, famous for the piper who led away their children, never heard
of againe ; * wee came through villages, and crossing the river Weyer,
two miles, came to Haervoerd, one mile, where wee dined ; then forward
towards Bilvelt. On the way, hearing of a well, breake up some weeks
ago, which cured many diseases, wee went of the way a foot, where were
encamped some hundred of persons come from diverse places, some out of
curiosity, but most for health   The well was environed with boughs, and
benches within.   When wee entred, two magistrates of the towne, who attended, invited us very civilly to sitt downe, and offered us of the water to
drink. I found no different tast from other water, only a litle tartnes.
They told us that, on Sunday last, a thanksgiving was done for upwards of
seventy persons who had been cured in the six weekes tyme ; and they shew
us about thirty crutches hanging on trees, which lame people, being cured,
had throwne away.   Wee went on foot to the towne, which was halfe ane
English mile of, and haveing refreshed our selves, and gott fresh horses, wee
made forward in the evening.

This towne is well built, hath a stone wall, and thereby a strong castle,
on a hill called Sparrenberg. Here hath the river Lutter its fountaine.
The towne is also famous for the great trade of linnen, made here, and ex-
ported.

In the night tyme wee crossed the river Dalke, two miles, and the river
Eems, or Amasis, a mile, haveing on our left hand the castle Rietberg,
which giveth name to a county. A mile and a halfe further wee crossed
the river Hastenbeck, and a litle further, about six a'clock, wee came to August 15.

---

* ['Depuis l'an 1284,' say the learned authors
of the *Nouveau Traité de Diplomatique*, ' les
habitants d' Hamelin, au duché de Brunswick,
datent de la sortie de leurs enfants : *A filiorum
nostrorum egressu.* Cette époque est fondee sur
une fable qui porte que les enfants, depuis l'
âge de quatre ans jusqú à dix ans, ayant été
tirés de la ville par les enchantements d'un
magicien, n'y reparurent plus.' The popular
version of the story may be seen in Verste-
gan's Restitution of Decayed Intelligence,
chap. iii., pp. 85, 86, edit., Lond. 1634.]

Lippstadt, on the river Lippe. This, with Minden, and all the countrey wee had passed from thence, belongeth to the Elector of Brandeborg.

Here I was in great perplexity which way to take, for, at my going from Hamborg, ffriends had advised me to passe the river Rhyne at Collen, or lower, and so through the land of Luick, into the Spanish dominions, so to avoyd going through Holland, according to my instructions. But hearing here that the pest was in every towne on the Rhyne, and that all passing that way must keep the quarantaine in the land of Liege or Luick, which hinderance was very grievous to me, so that, at last, I resolved to go with the company I was in to Wesel, and then there resolve on my farther jorney.

About ten aclock, wee went from Lippestadt, and passed by Hoffestadt, belonging to the Frey Herr von der Heyden, being three howres, then to Ham, fyve howres, where wee refreshed our selves and horses. In this towne, a beer called kuit is brewed, which is carryed to diverse places, and even as farr as Hamborg. From hence, wee rode to Lunen, a litle towne, six howres, where wee crossed the river Lippe, haveing rested all night. The river Lippe is thus farr navigable.

August 16.   Riseing early, wee came to Olphen, a litle towne belonging to the Bishop of Munster, three howres, near which wee crossed a litle river called Sieve. Wee came to a towne called Halteren, all destroyed by the late warr. Wee advanced further, and came to a milne called Wolfen, where wee dyned, and stayed a long tyme, carowsing in Rhenish wyne and Spa water, this being three howres from Halteren. From hence wee rode to Shramburg, or Shermbeck, three miles, and towards evening to Wesel, three howres. Wee were questioned at the gate, and a souldier sent with us to the maine guard on the market place, where the Lievetennant Collonell and the rest being knowne, I was the less taken notice of; so, haveing told where wee were to lodge, they let us go, and immediately sent a writer to write up our names. I had promised the master of the post waggon drink money to conceale me, telling him only that I was a Scotsman, and was afrayed of being detained, upon the account of the warr with the King; so, when the scrivener came, I went back to the stables untill he was gone, and the postmaster gave me a name and office, what he pleased. Here wee were very well entertained, haveing abundance of good wyne, and lodged, paying for all halfe a reichs doller a piece, and for our servants ten stuivers each.

Haveing breakfasted early, and given the postmaster his morning draught, August 17. and a reichs doller for his kindnes, I caused bring my baggage to the boat, without being questioned. Wee went now by water, haveing the towne Santen on our left hand, to Rees, four howres, where wee stayed about two howres; then went further in the sight of Cleve, the chieffe towne of the Dukedome of Clivia, in the possession of the Elector of Brandeburg, where he also sometymes resideth.   Towards evening we came to Emmerick, three howres, which, with the two former, are in the Dukedome of Cleve, and the Hollanders have their garrisons in them.   Here I lodged all night, and the next morning went to the Jesuits church, and heard devotion. The Paters August 8. were but lately returned, haveing been forced to remove, when the warr began with the Bishop of Munster.

Haveing breakfasted, wee sailed downe to Shenkenshants, two howres, where the Rhine divides, and wee stayed an howre ; in which tyme I went a shore, and tooke a view of the fort, which, both by nature and art, is well fortifyed.   Towards evening wee went downe the [Waal] and came to Nimwegen, and lodged in the Toelass, being foure howres, which, in all the Netherlands and Westphalen, they reckon being halfe a Dutch myle. A lievtennant lodged with me, and, albeit wee had nothing extraordinary, yet wee had a pretty dear reckoning the next day.

About six aclock wee went to the boat, and sailed to Tiel, six howres, August 19. where wee stayed about an howre, and refreshed our selves, where wee gott another cavalier in company, and two yong wenches.   Wee sailed by the fort Saint Andrewes, two howres, and to Bommel, two howres, where wee stayed about halfe an howre, and then passing by the house of Lowenstein and Workum, betwixt which the river Maes falleth into the Waal, in going by, I see Sir Georg Aiscue, one of the English admirals, who had been taken prisoner in the engagement the beginning of June.*   Wee came to Gorkum, on the other side, being two howres from Brommell, where we stayed but halfe an howre ; and, going two howres farther, the cavaliers, who had bargained it seems with the wenches, haveing bribed or perswaded the skipper to stay there all night, wee could not by any meanes gett him to

---

* [Sir George Ayscue, knight, admiral of the white, had his flag on board of the Royal Prince, then reputed the finest ship in the world. He signalised himself in the sea-fight off the coast of Sussex, on the first of June, 1666, when his vessel, being disabled, ran on the Galloper sand bank, and was burned, himself and his crew being made prisoners.]

August 20. go from hence.   So here wee lodged, and the next morning came to Dort, two howres.

This towne hath the priority of all the others in Holland, hath the staple of Rhenish wyne, and is a strong, populous, rich citty, and standeth in ane illand.   Short of it I went a shore, and viewed the ruines of the house De Merve, being on our left hand ; for *anno Domini* 1421, by a suddaine inundation, eighty villages and about a hundred thousand people were drowned, one child in the cradle, being a son and heire of this lordship of Merve, being miraculously preserved ; for a cat, getting up upon the cradle, kept the cradle in ballance till it sailing downe the river arrived safely at Dort, called in Latine Dordracum, and in Hollands Dordrecht.

Here, haveing put our baggage over into another boat, I went into the towne, and up through the principall streets ; and returning to our boate, wee set forward about ten aclock downe the river Wael, towards Zeeland.   Wee had a great boat, and store of company of all sorts, and passed the tyme with discourses, tobacco, and eating of bernacles.   I understanding that in the boat was a captaines wyfe, with two children, who, being of English parents, and marryed to ane Englishman called Aiscue, a captain who, being with others, at the beginning of the warr, recalled out of the States service, was gone over to England, and now she was convoying her self and effects over to England as privately as possible ; by meanes of my brother in law, Charles, who had found her out, I offered my assistance and company on the way, whereof she was glad.   We sailed by Wilhelmstadt on our left hand,

August 21. foure howres, and giveing our selves rest in the night tyme, by day light, wee found our selves within sight of Zerick-Zee, it being ten howres from Wilhelmstadt.   Wee passed by it, being a good way off, on our right hand. About midday wee landed at Tervere, being foure howres from Zerick-Zee.

Here wee landed, and tooke coach to Midleburg, being a Hollands mile or howres going.   From thence, putting our baggage on a waggon, I, with company, went a foot to Flushing, being one howres going.   I shall speak nothing of these townes, being so well knowne, and described so often.

This Flushing was so propt up with souldiers and seamen, that wee could hardly gett a house to lodge in, for here was De Ruiter, with his fleet, embarking.   Haveing, at last, gott a lodging, and only roome without bedding or beds, wee had but sorry accomodation, and no ease ; for some Scotsmen were gott into the next roome, who passed the whole night carowsing, swearing, and blaspheming, so that it was a grieffe and vexation to hear them.

This Flushing, with Middleburg, and Toervere, are all in the illand of Walcheren, the fairest illand of all the Low Cowntreyes.

I got up early, and caused our baggage be brought a shipboard, and _{August 22.} following our selves about seven aclock, wee went from thence, and crossing over to Flanders, wee entred a large channel or river, haveing an illand called Catsand on our left hand, and the continent on the right, on each syde a fort, with other small workes of fortification. We sailed up to Sluis, which is about five leagues from Flussing. Wee came just to the shoare by the towne, and found the gates shutt, it being, according to the new style, the first Wednesday of the month, which, by an ordinans of the States, was ordained to be a holy day. All the passengers of the ship, haveing nothing but satchels, went out, and, crossing the river, went a foot to a small fort halfe a mile distant, and from thence tooke boat to Bruges; but I, being entangled with a trunke and other luggage, and engaged to keep company with the captaines wyfe, who had a large trunk and other things, and a litle child, could not stirr. I desired the skipper to procure our entrance into the towne, but he could not, nor gett any other convenience for bringing us to Bruges but a cart, which he hired for us, for two reichs dollers.

The sea beginning to flow, the master told us that, how soone his ship was a flow, he must be gone; so I was forced to take all out of the ship, and harbor it on the shore. I was in very great perplexity here, not knowing what to do, whether to reveale or conceale my self, in both which I found difficulties, and so began to repent my comeing through Holland, fearing to be discovered. I promised the master of the ship a reichs doller for his paines, if he could procure us entrance into the towne, which made him apply himself very cordially and earnestly to procure us passage; and finding two of the magistrates walkeing befor the gate, he made his address to them, who commanded us to be let into the towne. So getting fellowes to carry in our baggage, wee entred the first and second gate, when the officer of the guard came stareing and swearing, and would force us out againe, saying the magistrates had nothing to do or command at his post. I gave him all the good and rationall words I could, and the captains wyfe beginning to speake, he knew her, and so, entring in discourse with her, he connived at my going forward through the last gate. Being come to an alehouse, where the cart was ready, I gott the same people to put our baggage on the cart, and, for joy, rewarded them liberally. In the meane tyme, the captaines wyfe being come, for she had told a long formall story to the officer at the gate, wee set forward to the other gate, which we found shutt, wherewith I was a litle troubled; but the carter telleing me that, how soone as the preaching was done, it would be opened, to avoid examination and telling a ly, I went into a brandewine house, and called for brandy, which, not being able to drink, I spilled unperceived, leaving the captaines wyfe to keep discourse with the guards, which she could very well do, being a notable, talkative, witty woman.

The gate being opened, wee went forward, the captaines wyfe with her litle child on the cart or carr, and I, with the rest, on foot. About a mile off, wee came to Middleburg, where, at first, wee were detained by a Hollander, and at the other end of the towne by a Spaniard, who would needs searche us for merchandise, and from the last, with a great deale of trouble, wee came free. Being come about three miles, wee entred Bruges, where, at the gate, wee were questioned from whence wee came. Wee, as the fuirman had instructed us, said wee came from Ardenburg, that being clear of the pest, but Sluis infected. Being entred the gate, wee gott a great company of boyes after us, crying Geuse! Geuse! which is a name they give to the Protestants here, all who come from the United Provinces being supposed to be such, albeit there be in Hollands not few less Roman Catholickes as Protestants, especially in Amsterdam.

This citty is the best built of any in Flanders, and the citizens the most gentile of all the Low Countreyes. It is fortifyed with a stone and earthen wall, and large ditches, hath a very wholesome aire, and, by a new digged channell, can receive vessels of foure hundred tunne.

August 23.   Haveing lodged with good convenience, I hired a waggon to Ostend. On the way wee found one of our Kings yachts at anker, who had aboard, albeit he would not be knowne, Mr Kyvet, one of the States Generall, who was fled for keeping correspondence with England, and interested in the business of Ruitmaster Buat. I went into the alehouse, where the captain of the yacht was, and was very pressing to take me aboard; but he refused, under pretence that he durst not, being sent expressly about his Majesties business, and so durst not take in any passengers. So I went forward towards Ostend, and, getting a boat, ferryed over the haven, wherein, at this tyme were about a hundred saile of ships of all syzes, bound for severall places, to the other syde, and immediately agreed with the master of a ship for my passage to England, and brought my baggage aboard. I did not go into the towne because the pest was in it, yet wee bought our provisions from thence.

The Kings yacht being come downe and ankered in the haven, I went *August 24.* aboard of her, and revealed to the captaine what I was, and what my errand or business, desireing that he would take me along. But then he was more averse, saying he would have resolved to have hazarded the takeing of a private person, but could by no meanes, without express order, adventure to take me in. So I was forced to desist.

In the morning, it was expected that our fleet should set saile the next *August 25.* day, but notice haveing come that the Hollands fleet was gone from Flushing, they were at a stand what to do.

After noone wee did see the Hollands fleet at sea of from Blankenburg, *August 26.* which put all the confused counsels of the masters of the shipps to a resolution of not adventuring out till a safer season. Whereupon I resolved to returne to Bruges, and take up a lodging there, being more convenient to stay there, as a shipboard, or at Ostend, where the aire was unwholesome and vivres dearer.

I went to Bruges, and tooke a lodging in the Esel street, at the signe *August 27.* of the King of Great Brittaine.

I went to Ostend, and brought my baggage back to Bruges, paying *August 29.* halfe fraught, and that with much ado. I writt to Hamburg, and ffriends in Mosko.

Hearing that Mrs. Plowden was come to Gent, upon the account of *August 30.* entring herself a nunne in that convent, where her daughter was abbess, I resolved to go thither, and perswaded my landlord, Mr. Frazer, a good merry man, to go along with me. Wee went in a great boat along the river or channell called Albertina. Wee had all sorts of company on this boat, and were merry. A mile short of Gent, wee quitted our boat, and lodged in ane innes; the boates not being permitted to go to Gent, because the pestlence was in Bruges.

Wee hired a waggon early, and came to Gent, and lodged at the signe *August 31.* of the Starr. I went immediately and heard devotion, and went to the English Nunnes monastery, and spoke with Mrs. Plowden, who was exceedingly rejoyed to hear of my mother in law and see us.   Haveing dined, wee hired a waggon, and went towards Bruges, and lodged in a village half way, where wee had good wholesome countrey fare.

September 1.   Haveing breakfasted, wee set forward, and came to Bruges about two aclock afternoone.

Here I stayed some weakes, expecting the going away of the fleet from Ostend for England, with a great deale of impatience, albeit I had many wayes to divert me ; for, in the morning early, I went over the way to the monastery of the Capucine Fryers, and heard the masse ; then, at halfe ten, I went to the monastery of the English Nuns, after the Princes Pallace, and heard masse againe ; and getting acquaintance, wee did meet at the place where the Lady Abbess useth to sitt and give audiens at a trally,* and there, with others, heard what passed.   In the afternoone, I either went with the English residents, and other Scots and English, and passed our tyme at the Trey, with a glass of wyne and joviall discourse ; or then went to the Nunnery, where three young gentlewomen lately come from Lowen, and going for England, lodged, and passed the tyme with them at cards or discourse ; or went sometymes and walked about the walls, to see the monasteryes, waterworkes, and other things worthy of notice.   Wee had sometymes in the Nunnery after vespers, at my desire, excellent vocall musick, whereat many people of all nations and religions were often present.

September 13.   I did writt to Mrs. Plowden, desireing her advice for buying in of necessaries and makeing of cloaths for my wyfe and mother in law, to the which I received a very civill and respectfull answer, dated the sixteenth.   Being wearyed of lying or staying in one place, I found fitt to writt to England, and give notice of my being here, and desire assistance for my passage.   So I did writt a letter to the Earle of Lawderdale, and another to Mr. James Mettellane, his secretary, to that purpose, and complaining of Captain Hill of Detford, who would not take me into the Kings yacht.   In the meane, wee heard the sad newes of the burning of the citty of London,† diverse posts haveing been kept up.

September 14.   I did writt to General Dalyell and to Lieventennant Generall Drummond,‡ as also to my father and unkle.

---

* [*Treillis*—a grating, or lattice.]
† [The Great Fire of London broke out on the second, and raged till the sixth of September, 1666.]

‡ [Thomas Dalyell of Binns, and William Drummond of Cromlix, together entered the Russian service in 1656, and having risen, the one to the rank of General, the other to that

I did writt to Sir John Hebden,* informing him of my business and stay, September 16. to my Lord Lawderdale, and father.   I did writt to Russia to my wyfe and her mother, to Doktor Collins and Mr. Bryan, and to the Dumnij Almais Ivanovitz, giveing notice of my tedious and expensive jorney, and my being forced to stay here for want of passage, not dareing adventure by the ordinary packet boat for fear of being robbed, as a Brandeburgish envoy was lately by the piokarowns, desireing and hopeing that consideration should be taken of my expenses.

I received an answer of my letter from Sir John Hebden, desireing me to land at Deptford, and ask the way to Peckham, where he invited me to stay in his house untill so long as cloaths and other things should be furnished, which offer I resolved to embrace.   I received an answer of my letter to Mr Mettellan, giveing me notice that a Kings yacht, which was to land at Newport, had orders to take me in.

I borrowed ten pounds sterling from Mr. Collison and recommended my trunks and other things to Mr. Skeine, takeing only a bagge with my credentialls and other letters, and went downe by boat to Newport, and tooke September 25. up my lodging in an Irishmans house.

Here I was farr more grieved as at Bruges, not hearing any thing of the September 26. yacht, and wanting company.   The next day, the packet boat arriving, one, a Scotsman, told me that the Kings yacht, which had orders to take me over, was forced to land at Bolloigne, and would hardly come to Newport, which grieved me exceedingly.

of Lieutenant General, together returned to their native country in 1665.   It was not with out great difficulty that King Charles II. prevailed on the Czar to allow them to leave his dominions. The severity of the military discipline to which they had been habituated abroad, seems to have been matter of frequent allusion in Scotland. The Covenanting Kirkton speaks of Dalyell as a man whose 'rude and fierce natural disposition hade been much confirmed by his breeding and service in Muscovia, where he hade the command of a small army, and saw nothing but tyrranie and slavery.'— (Hist. of Church of Scot., p. 225.) Bishop Burnet's character of Drummond is, that he had yet too much of the air of Russia about him, though not with Dalziel's fierceness.' Sir John Lauder chronicles the popular murmurs against the 'Muscovian rigour' of Dalyell's military administration —(Fountainhall's His-

torical Observes, p. 28.) Elsewhere he relates how a Covenanter, brought before a committee of the Privy Council, denounced the members as 'bloody murderers and papists,' and railed at Dalyell as 'a Muscovia beast who used to roast men,'—(Fountainhall's Historical Notices of Scottish Affairs, vol. i, p 332.) The same assiduous annalist, in recording an instance of torture by the thumbscrews, in September, 1684, tells us that 'the authors of this invention of the thummikins were General Dalyell and Drummond, who had seen it in Moscovia.' 'But,' he adds, 'its also used among our coilyiars in Scotland, and is called the pilli wincks.'—(Id., vol. ii , p. 557.)

Dalyell died at Edinburgh in August, 1685. Drummond was created Viscount of Strathallan in 1686, and died two years afterwards.]

* [The Russian resident at London.]

September 28.   A litle yacht arrived with some merchandise from England, whereof getting notice, I gott my landlord to go for the captaine, with whom I agreed, and hired his yacht to Dover for sixty crownes, on these conditions, that as many passengers as should go, should agree with and pay me for their passage, any goods or merchandise should pay him for fraught, that he should not go a capeing* on the way, nor do any violence to any, but go streight to Dover.

I knowing that there were many in Bruges waiting for a convenient passage to England, sent by an express letters to the English resident, Mr. Glanvile, to Mr. Skein, Mr. Collison, and to the yong ladyes in the Nunnery, showing them the convenience, and that any who would go, should come the next day, without faile, for upon the Sunday wee must be gone. This

September 29. brought some people downe, especially some Hamburger merchants, with their wives, who payed me the halfe of all I had agreed for, and I was very glad to gett that. I writt to Mosko to my wyfe and ffriends, and to the Russ chancellour Almais, by the way of Hamborg, addressed to Mr. Cambrige there.

September 30.   Wee went aboard immediately after midday, the mariners being all drunk, and the captaine not sober. So displaying the Kings collours, wee sailed downe the river, but were not farr gone, when a ship sailing along by the shore alarumed us; for she, perceiving the Kings collours flying, and thinking us to be a caper, turned towards us, and cast anchor within the buyes. Befor she cast anchor I did not know what to think of it, and our captaine gave orders to have all in readines, he haveing about thirty men aboard and foure litle pieces of cannon. So they haled out of a chest their rusty muskets, and charged the pieces, but how soone I saw them cast anchor, I knew they, for fear of us, came in for shelter within the buyes, and so I told the captaine that he should offer no violence, putting him in mynd that it was in a neutrall place, and of our agreement. But the

---

* [*Capeing*, that is, privateering. Sir James Turner speaks, in 1656, of escaping 'a great many Spanish capers at sea.'—(Memoirs, p. 119) Pepys, in 1667, relates how 'a little East Indiaman' was 'snapt by a French caper.'—(Diary, vol iv., p. 15.) Gordon tells in the same page how the vessel in which he crossed the channel was mistaken for 'a caper.' 'Some caping,' says Sir John Lauder, 'there was in King James his minority, and Queen Marie's Regencie, when war was betuixt us and France and Spain; but nothing like this which began in 1664, which grew to that incredible height of advantage to the owners outreikers, that never nation heirtofor took richer pryzes, nor mo of them, then the Scots capers, who became famous for their activity and cunning diligence in the trade.'—(Fountainhall's Historical Observes, p. 261)]

mariners and souldiers, being beastly drunk, would scarcely hear him, so that in the going by one shott off a musquet at them, whereat, they falling to the ground, when wee were past, they rose up and called out, Go you Tailes, the French are waiting for you in the sea; which so irritated the seamen that they would be turning upon them to revenge themselves, but I, with the other passengers, gott them diswaded from it.

Towards evening, wee sailed by Dunkirk with a soft gale. After sunsett, the wind beginning to blow harder, I went downe below, and lay downe near to the great mast, where I knew the least motion was.

About midnight, being against Calais, our captaine seased upon three large fisher boats, haveing masts and sailes, and put men of his owne aboard of them, and tooke some of their's to him. But I, being awaked with the noise, sent up a servant to know what the business was, whereof being informed, I went above and prevailed so with the captaine and seamen, that they let the men go over in their own boat, and let them go; only their nets, fish, ankers, and what they had about, they tooke from them.

By day light, wee came to Dover, and landing, went to the Red Lyon, October 1. and breakfasted. Afterward takeing post, I rode to Canterbury, being, . . . miles, where, refreashing ourselves, and getting other horses, wee rode forward to Sittingborne, where changing horses, wee rode through Rochester, . . . miles, Gravesend, seven miles, and lodged in the Salutation, where had good accommodation and good entertainment, but deare.

Wee tooke boat, and rowed up the river Thames to Detford, where I October 2. went ashore and tooke a guide, who conducted me to Peckham, where I was heartily welcomed by Sir John Hebden and family. Here I received a letter from Generall Dalyell, dated London, the thirteenth of July, and with one enclosed from my father, dated Achluichries, the twentieth of June. I received also letters from Mr. Bryan, dated Mosco, the sixteenth of August; from Doctor Collins, dated the twentieth of August.

Haveing advised with Sir John Hebden about the putting myself and suite in a decent posture of appearing befor His Majesty, I sent to Mr. Peter Webster and Mr. Georg Grove, to whom I had bills of exchange from Mr. Parker, for money, who immediately furnished me with as much as I had occasion for. So I stayed some dayes here untill I furnished myself and suite with cloaths and liveryes; and, because the Court was in mourning, I thought fitt to conforme myself to that, putting myself in deep mourning; my brother in law, who was to carry befor me the Emperours letters, in halfe mourning; but my servants in my ordinary livery, which, because conforme to my instructions, I was not to have any publick entry or audience, needed not to be numerous.

October 9.   Haveing furnished myself with all things, I went privately to London, which lay smoaking in its ashes, and tooke up my lodging in the Strand, a litle above Ivy Lane, in ane apothecaryes house.   The same day, I desired Sir John Hebden to go to the Earle of Lawderdale, and acquaint him of my comeing, and know his pleasure, how and when I should have the honour of kissing His Sacred Majesties hand; who went and returned with answer that he had acquainted His Majesty of my business and comeing, and, that this evening I should have access to His Majesty.

About six aclock at night I was sent for, and brought to the Earle of Lawderdales lodgings, being accompanyed by Sir John Hebden, and Mr. James Metellane, his lordships secretary.   The Earle of Lawderdale received me very kindly, and, being informed more particularly of the circumstance of my business, he conducted me to His Majesty, who was newly returned from seeing a French ship which was taken.

I found His Majesty standing under a canopy bareheaded, with many nobles about him.   Being entred the roome, and performed the usuall reverences, I tooke the Emperours letters from my brother in law.   After I had the short complement, His Majesty was pleased to receive the letters with his owne hand, and gave them off immediately to one standing by, and asked me for the good health of His Majesty, which I answered after the ordinary way.   Then His Majesty was pleased to say, that this message was so much the more acceptable that the Tzaar had been pleased to entrust one of his owne subjects with it, and caused tell me, that I might use the freedome of the Court.

Being reconducted to my Lord Lawderdales lodgings, I stayed halfe an howre, expecting that my Lord should come downe; but he not comeing, I went to my lodging, whither Mr. Patrick Wast conducted me, and, with others, stayed about two howres with me.

October 10.   The next day I received the visits of diverse particular persons, not haveing in my instructions to give notice of my comeing, or visits, to the ministers of forreigne Princes, upon the account of not makeing any great noise, the Russes being unwilling to disoblige the Hollanders, whom my business concerned most.

Hearing that Mr. Georg Gordon,* brother to the Laird of Haddo, was October 11. in the citty, I sent to seeke him, and desire him to come to me, which he did in the evening, with Mr. James Metellane and John Kirkwood. Wee mad merry, remembring ffriends, till neer midnight.

Received letters from Generall Dalyel, dated Lieth, the second of October, and from Lieutenant Generall Drummond, Edinburgh, the ninth of October. The Kings lock smith, by order, brought a key which opened the doores to the parke, galleries, and other passages in the Court, to whom I gave twenty shillings, and to his attendent fyve, my name being graved on it.

Being not well accommodated in the Strand, I removed to Hay Market, and lodged in Mr. Robert Ranyes, at the signe of the Two Blew Balls, where I had exceeding good accommodation. I sent my brother in law Charles to the dancing and writeing schoole.

Writt to my father and brother.				October 15

I had conference with my Lord Chancellour† in his house, he being October 16 sick of the gowt; the substance whereof in my other booke of my relation.

Being Sunday, I hired a coach and rode to High Gate, and dined with October 21 the Earl of Lawderdale, and returned in the evening.

Writt to my father, and to Mistress Massy in Bruges, and to Mistress October 22 Plowden in Gent, per post.

I had another conference with my Lord Chancellor and Sir William October 23 Morice, the Secretary of State, at the Lord Chancellors house, which is insert in my booke of relations. Received a letter from Generall Dalyel, dated Lieth, the sixteenth of October.

Writt to Generall Dalyell and Lievetennant Generall Drummond per October 25 post. Received letters from my wyfe and mother in law, dated Mosko,

* [George Gordon, second son of Sir John Gordon of Haddo, knight baronet, was born in October, 1637. He studied in King's College at Aberdeen, from 1655 to 1659, when he took the degree of Master of Arts. He was immediately afterwards appointed a regent or professor, and held this office until March, 1663, when he went abroad to study law. He succeeded to the family estate and title on the death of his brother, Sir John Gordon, in March, 1667. He became an advocate at the Scotch bar in February, 1668, a judge in June, 1680, Pre- sident of the Court of Session in October, 1681, and Lord Chancellor of Scotland in May, 1682. A few months afterwards he was made Earl of Aberdeen. He ceased to be Lord Chancellor in May, 1684, and died at Kellie (now called Haddo House) in April, 1720. A memoir of his life, from the graceful pen of the late Mr. John Dunn, is prefixed to the volume of letters addressed to him, printed for the Spalding Club in 1851.]

† [The Earl of Clarendon.]

July the twentieth and twenty fourth, and August twenty fourth and twenty sixth.

October 29   Writt to my wyfe and mother in law, to Doctor Collins, Mr. Bryan, and to Almais Ivanowitsch per post. Writt to my father per Mr. Skeine.

October 30   Received a letter from my father, dated Achluichries, the twentieth of October, and another from Generall Dalyell, dated the twenty third of October, from Lieth; from my brother John, dated Westertowne, the fifteenth of October; from my unkle, dated Bomatuthil, October the fifteenth.

November 1   Received letters from my ffriends in Mosko per post, in an enclosed from Collonell Bockhoven.

November 4   Writt to my father, unkle, and the Laird of Pitfodells, with that from his son Pawl.

November 5.   Writt to my wyfe and ffriends in Russia, and to Collonell von Bockhoven. My cousin, Collonell Patrick Gordon, commonly called Steelhand, came to London, with another Bohemian collonell with him. Mr. Golt came. I received my trunkes and other baggage which I left at Bruges.

Had Madam Hebden and her daughters at the New Exchange, and bought for them gloves, etc., for two pounds ten shillings.

Received letters from Doctor Collins, dated Mosko, the twenty fifth of September; from Mr. Bryan, dated the twenty seventh; from my wyfe and mother in law, whereby I had notice of the birth of a Prince called John.

I sent a memoriall into the Secretary office concerning my business, and was promised ane answer.

November 12.   Received a letter from my cousin, Mr. Thomas Gordon, dated Edinburgh, the twelfth of November, with one from my father.

November 13.   Writt to the generalls * and other friends in Scotland. I had the third conference with the Lord Chancellor and the Secretary of State, where wee debated the business I came for, as also that of the priviledges very sharply. I did writt to my father, unkle, brother, and ffriends in Scotland, sending four small wipps or rings for tokens.

I sent Charles to sollicite about a letter to the King of Polland for his fathers releasement.†

* [Dalyell and Drummond.]
† [Colonel Philipp Albert von Bockhoven, Gordon's father-in-law. He had been made prisoner by the Poles in the year 1661, at a battle in the neighbourhood of Polotzk, and had not yet recovered his liberty.]

Mr. Skein came from Bruges, and brought my note from Mr. Colleson for the money I had borrowed from him in Bruges.

Received letters from my father, dated at Achluichries, the seventeenth November 20. of October; from Generall Dalyell, dated Lieth, the sixth of November.

Writt to my wyfe and ffriends in Russia. Received a letter from Lieve- November 23. tennant Generall Drummond, dated at Lieth, the fifteenth of November; and from Generall Dalyell, dated Lieth, the fourteenth of November.

Writt to Generall Dalyell, and Lievtennant General Drummond.   November 24.

Writt to Mr. Clough. Received two letters from my father, dated the December 1. twentieth and twenty third of November.

Received letters from my wyfe and mother in law, dated Mosko, the December 6. twenty sixth of September.

Received letters from Mistress Plowden, dated Gent, the twenty fifth of December 7. November; and from Mistress Massy, dated Bruges, the twentieth of November. I borrowed fifteen pounds sterling from Mr. Peter Webster.

Received a letter from the Laird of Pitfoddels, dated Aberdeen, the December 8. twenty sixth of November, with an enclosed to his son Pawl; and one from my father, dated the twenty sixth of November.

I went to Peckam, afterwards to Lower Teutin, and from thence rode to Colebrooke, where wee were merry all night, and haveing augmented our company with Mr. Richard Hebden and bedfellow, wee returned to London, where all supped by me.

I went to the Tower, and see the crowne, scepter, juwels, armes, and December 9. magazine, which cost me in wages one pound thirteen shillings.

I had my last conference with the Lord Chancellour in his house. He December 10. told me the Kings resolution, and the Counsells, concerning my business, and an answer which I was to have, and that His Royall Majesty had commanded to give me two hundred pund sterling upon the account of my expences and a gift.

Writt to my wyfe and ffriends in Russia. Received a letter from Mr. Clough. I was entertained very kindly by Mr. Battersly at a dinner.

The Earle of Rothes, being Lord High Commissioner of Scotland, came from Scotland, whom I visited in his lodgings in Suffolk Street, who received me very kindly.

Received a letter from Lievtennant Generall Drummond, dated Edinburgh, the fourth of December, in answer to myne of the twenty fourth past ; as also from Pitfoddels and my father.

Collonell Patrick Gordon departed with litle satisfaction, haveing gott but fifty pund sterling, and that from the Earle of Middleton, but by His Majesties order. He haveing left his skatole with his passes in pledge, of twenty pounds sterling, by Mr. Golt, he desired me to buy it out, giveing me but fyve pounds sterling, so I payed the other fyfteen.

December 17. Writt to my wyfe and ffriends in Russia.

December 19. Received letters from Mr. Skein and my unkle.

December 20. Writt to Generall Dalyell,* to my father, Pitfoddels, unkle, cousin, and to Mr. Skein.

Received letters from my wyfe, mother in law, in a *coverto* from Mr. Bryan, dated the seventh of November. Dined in London with Sir John Hebden and his sons, and visited, in the afternoone, Mr. Towrs.

December 27. On St. Johns day, dined in Peckam with choyce company, and were merry.

December 28. Dined with the Earle of Middleton.

December 29. Visited the Earle of Carlisle at his lodgings.

December 30. Dined with Sir William Davidson† and Sir William Thomson,‡ where was also Doktor Morison,‖ and were merry.

December 31. At dinner with great company, which cost . . .

1667.

[A.D. 1667.]

January 1. Being invited, I rode to Lower Tewtin, where choice company were conveened, and were merry two dayes together.

January 3. Came to London with all the company who supped at the signe of the Cock, and stayed in my lodging all night at my charge.

January 4. Dined in the Rhenish wyne house, at the charges of Sir John Hebden.

January 5. Dined by Sir Georg Ent, § the phisitian.

January 6. Dined by the Knights Errant.

* [It seems remarkable that Gordon should make no allusion to Dalyell's defeat of the Westland Covenanters at Rullion Green, on the 28th of November, 1666.]

† [Conservator of the Privileges of the Scottish nation in the Netherlands. He died in 1689.]

‡ [Probably one of the members for the city of London.]

‖ [Robert Morison, M.D., born at Aberdeen in 1620, died at London in 1683. He was appointed physician to King Charles II. in 1660, and Professor of Botany at Oxford in 1669. There is a memoir of him in Dr. Irving's Lives of Scottish Writers, vol. ii., pp. 177-188.]

§ [President of the College of Physicians.]

Dined by Mr. Carril his father, who was a member of the Innes of January 7. Court in Holborne.

Received a letter from Mr. Bryan, dated Mosko, the fourth of December, and therein letters from my wyfe and mother in law.

A letter was ordered by His Sacred Majesty to be written to the King of Polland, in favour of my father in law, the substance whereof followeth, after titles and salutations :

Whereas Colonell Philippus Albertus von Bockhoven haveing, for severall yeares, served our father of blessed memory and us, and had still so continued in our service, had not the late rebellion of our subjects happened, whereby wee were forced for some tyme to estrange ourselves from our patrimoniall kingdomes, and so consequently our servants were forced to seeke for their subsistance of forreigne Princes :   Amongst those, our distressed servants, the aforesaid Collonell Philippus Albertus von Bockhoven was entertained in the service of our loveing brother, his Tzarish Majestie of Russia, in whose pay and service he continued till the yeare 1660, when, in October the same yeare, he was made prisoner of warr to the Littawish Generall Johan Sapiha, and now doth continue prisoner with the eldest son of the foresaid Generall, now deceassed :   Wee, calling to mind the many and faithfull services which wee received from our aforesaid servant, Collonell Philippus Albertus von Bockhoven, and the desire which wee have to restore him againe into our service, do, therefor, desire of your Majesty to give unto our said servant his liberty to returne unto us and our service, which wee shall acknowledge as a particular kindnes from your Majestie to us, and shall be ready upon all occasions to returne the lyke, when it shall be required of us, *etc.*

I dined with my Lord Middleton, and was very kindly entertained. January 8. Writt to my father, unkle, brother, and cousin Mr. Thomas.   Lievetennant Generall Drummond came to London.

I received the money ordered me by the King, and payed for the fees January 14. as followeth :

	Pounds.	Shillings.	Pence.
For drawing the bill - - - - - -	1	—	—
Fees of the signet and privy seale - - - -	4	—	—
To Sir Philip Sidneyes clerk for the docquet - -	—	10	—
For my Lord Treasurers warrant - - - -	1	10	—
For entring the privy seale at my Lord Ashly - -		5	—

	Pounds.	Shillings.	Pence.
For entring the privy seale at Sir Robert Longs, and the warrant - - - - - - -	–	7	–
For entring the privy seale at the Pells - - -	–	5	–
For entring the privy warrant at the Pells office -	–	2	–
For entring the order at the Pells - - - -	–	6	–
For entring my Lord Treasurers order to strick tallyes for 200 punds at Sir Robert Longs, at the Pells, and Mr. Shadwall - - - - - -	–	7	6
Sir Robert Longs fees for 200 pund sterling - -	2	10	–
The fees at the Pell office - - - - -	1	7	–
The tellers fees - - - - - - -	6	7	–
For the tally - - - - - - -	–	2	–
To the cashirer at the Custome house for expedition -	1	–	–
	19	14	3
For bringing the money from the Custume house -	–	2	10
	19	17	1
To Mr. Perring, who, by order, went through all these difficulties and intricacies, for his paines - -	5	–	–
To his servant - - - - - - -	–	5	–
In all - -	25	2	1

Haveing caused make cloaths ready for my self and suite after the new fashion,* and haveing notice that the Kings letter was ready, I went and tooke my leave of ffriends, first at Highgate, by my Lord Lawderdale, who was pleased to give me a letter to Doktor Davison in Polland, for address of the Kings letter in favour of my father in law, Collonell Philippus Albertus von Bockhoven.

I entertained Mr. Cooke, and these of the Secretary office, where I had

* ['The King hath yesterday, in Council,' writes Pepys, on the 8th of October, 1666, 'declared his resolution of setting a fashion for clothes, which he will never alter. It will be a vest, I know not well how; but it is to teach the nobility thrift, and will do good.' A few days afterwards, in chronicling a visit to the Duke of York, at Whitehall, he adds, 'I stood and saw him dress himself, and try on his vest, which is in the King's new fashion, and he will be in it for good and all on Monday next, and the whole Court: it is a fashion, the King says, he will never change.'—See Pepys' Diary, vol. iii., pp. 304, 308, 310, 311, 313, 325.]

all the Russia merchants, with ladyes and musick, which cost . . . I gave to Mr. Cooke fyve punds sterling, to Mr. Tomkins ten shillings, to the door keepers ten shillings.

Received a letter from Generall Dalyell, dated Kilmarnok, the twenty-seventh of December. Returned an answer to his Excellency the same evening, which I sent in the black boxe.

I went to London, and tooke my leave of ffriends there. Received letters from Mosko, from Mr. Bryan, dated Mosko, the fourteenth of December, with letters from my wyfe and mother in law, to the which I returned answer by the first post.

I went and tooke my leave of Prince Rupert, who was very sick,* and told me he should writt to the Elector of Brandeburg, and to Duke Bogislaus Radzivil, in favour of Collonell Bockhoven, and send the letters after me to Hamburg, commanding Mr. Hayes, his secretary, to mind him when he should be a litle better.

I was sent for to have my last audience of His Majesty, who received me January 18. very graciously, and delivered the letters to the Tzaar out of his owne hand to me, desireing to be remembred to, and salute, his deare and loveing brother, which promiseing to do, I then thanked His Majestie for his great favours to me. So, being admitted to kiss His Majesties hand, I tooke leave, and was reconducted to my lodging; whither being come, and lookeing to the superscription of the letter, and found *Illustrissimo* written for *Serenissimo*, so I desired Sir John Hebden to represent the business to the Secretary of State, telling that I durst not for my head carry such a letter with me, and that it was well knowne what a great deale of stirr there had been in Mosko with the Earle of Carlisle about that word. The Secretary very readily promised to amend it.

The next day I was conducted to His Royall Highness the Duke of Yorke, who, with much favour, received me and dismissed me. I told His Highness that His Majesty had promised that I should have a catch† to waft me over to Flanders, and His Highness said that he would give orders to Sir William Coventry‡ about it.

I went and tooke my leave of my Lord Chancellour, who was still sick

---

* [He was trepanned about a fortnight afterwards. One of the physicians in attendance on the occasion was a countryman of our journalist, Sir Alexander Fraser of Durris.]

† [Catch, katch, or ketch, a fast-sailing ship.]

‡ [Then secretary to the Duke of York, the Lord High Admiral.]

of the gowt, in his lodgings in Barkshire House. He wondred that I had been detained so long.

A clerke brought the Kings letter to me, amended in the title, with the copy of it, and a pass, to whom I gave twenty shillings.

The King sent Sir Harbert Price to me, to bring me to His Majestie againe, whom wee found just comeing out of his bed chamber. The King was pleased to speake to me so :   Colonell Gordon, I have a servant there in Russia, called Gaspar Calthoffe,* for whom I have written diverse tymes to your Emperour. I wonder that, at our desire, he doth not dismiss him. Pray, speake to the Emperour, that he dismiss him. I answered that, how soone I shall have the honour to see His Imperiall Majestie, I shall not faile to show Your Majesties desire and pleasure. His Majesty replyed: Pray do ; I wish you a good jorney. Being returned to my lodging, I went and tooke my leave of Mr. Secretary Morice, to whose kindness being much obliged, I gave him many thankes for his civilities and assistance, and entreated him to be pleased to accept of a paire of sables, worth ten punds sterling, as a token of my love, and not as any recompence for his paines; which by no meanes he would accept of.

I went and tooke my leave of the Earle of Middleton, to whose kindness I was very much obliged.

THE COPY OF THE KINGS LETTER TO THE EMPEROUR OF RUSSIA.

Charles the Second, by the grace of God, King of England, Scotland, France, and Ireland, Defender of the Faith, *etc. etc.*, to our dearly beloved brother, the Most High, Most Potent, and Most Serene Prince, and Great Lord, Emperour, and Great Duke, Alexy Michaelowich, *etc. etc.*

Most Excellent and Renowned Prince, your Imperiall Majesties letters, bearing date the twenty ninth of June last past, came to our hands by your Imperiall Majesties Colonell Patrick Gordon, being in answer to ours, dated from our Court at Oxford, the twenty ninth day of December last, wherein wee are sorry to find ourself somequhat disappointed in our expectation from your Imperiall Majestie. For when we reflect upon your Imperiall

* [It appears, from the Earl of Carlisle's memoir of his embassy to Russia, that as he was preparing to leave Moscow, one Gaspar Kalthoff, who had been for some years in the Russian service, petitioned for leave to accompany him. It was granted, but the embassy had scarcely quitted the city when Kalthoff was ordered to return.]

Majestie, our most dear and loveing brothers most kind expressions in severall former letters and ambassies to us, wherein your Imperiall Majestie declared that the brotherly love and friendship, which your Imperiall Majestie had for us, was more then ever had been befor between any of our Royall predecessours, and that your Imperiall Majesties esteeme towards us, was farr greater than what your Imperiall Majestie had for any other Christian Prince ; upon the confidence whereof wee gave you, our loveing brother, your Imperiall Majestie, notice of the present warr wee have with the Estates of the Netherlands, and of the severall glorious victories which it hath pleased God to give us over them.   In answer to which, wee cannot see by your Imperiall Majesties said letter, that your Imperiall Majestie discovers any greater inclination or concerne for us then for the said States, our enemies.   Also, in our said letter, wee gave your Imperiall Majestie notice that we, our Royall Majestie, had received advice that the subjects of the said States of the Netherlands, our enemyes, did furnish themselves, out of your Imperiall Majesties dominions, with masts for ships, and tarr for the use of their ships of warr, which are employed against us and our Royall navy ; and, thereupon, wee desired your Imperiall Majestie, out of the brotherly love and affection which your Imperiall Majestie hath for us, our Royall Majestie, not only to forbid the said subjects of the States of the Netherlands to export any such navall provisions out of your Imperiall Majesties dominions for the future, but that, on the contrary, your Imperiall Majestie would give liberty to the officers of our navy or their assignes, to buy up and transport, out of your Imperiall Majesties dominions, such masts and tarr as, yearly, for fyve yeares to come, should be, by the said officers of our navy, found necessary for our immediate service, and the use of our Royall navy.   In answer to which, wee find ourself obliedged to you, our most deare brother, your Imperiall Majestie, for the restriction which your Imperiall Majestie hath caused to be made, both upon your Imperiall Majesties river of Dwina and port of Archangell, that no man, upon paine of death, shall dare to sell any navall provisions to the subjects of the States of the Netherlands, nor they to buy or export any such out of your Imperiall Majesties dominions.   But to make the obligation compleat, wee can expect no lesse then your Imperiall Majestie should effectually comply with our former desires, that navall provisions for our owne proper service, and the use of our Royall navy, should be ffreely bought and transported out of your Imperiall Majesties dominions, by such persons as the officers of our navy shall employ, and in such quantity as they shall desire; for, otherwise, wee shall be no better treated by your Imperiall Majestie then our enemyes are, which wil be no waies suitable to the brotherly professions your Imperiall Majestie hath made unto us. That the trade of our merchants is, by your Imperiall Majesties order, forbidden for this yeare, by reason that your Imperiall Majestie hath been informed, by severall Intelligences and printed Gazettes, that the plague of pestilence doth still rage in our Royall Majesties dominions, wee might have hoped that your Imperiall Majestie would not give creditt to the printed papers and artifices of our enemyes, whose practice it hath been, and is, to give out to the world that which may most advance their designes, without any regard to truth or falshood, when, in this very particular, we can assure your Imperiall Majestie, contrary to their malicious rumors, that the plague is totaly ceassed in our Royall citty of London, and in all our ports, for which infinite mercy wee give heartly thanks unto Almighty God ; and as wee doubt not but the knowledge hereof will be most acceptable to your Imperiall Majestie, our most loveing brother, so wee will be confident that, upon the receipt of these our letters, your Imperiall Majestie will recall all prohibitions in that kind, so that the next ships that shall come from our kingdomes may, with their merchants and merchandize, be admitted to a ffreedom of trade in your Imperiall Majesties dominions and ports as formerly. What concernes the restauration of your Imperiall Majesties priviledges to our subjects, the marchants, seeing wee cannot prevaill with your Imperiall Majestie to grant them at present, though wee cannot be satisfyed with your Imperiall Majesties answers to that particular, yet wee do in some measure support our patience with hope to find the same in short tyme granted to us, not doubting in the least of your Imperiall Majesties brotherly inclinations and real performances. So, wishing your Imperiall Majestie, our most dear and loveing brother, long life, with a most happy and successefull reigne, haveing most graciously dispatched your Imperiall Majesties Colonell Patrick Gordon with these, our Royall Majesties letters, wee committ your Imperiall Majestie to the protection of Almighty God. Given at our Court, in our Royall citty of London, the twenty seventh of December, 1666, in the eighteenth yeare of our raigne.

Haveing notice that the Baron d'Isola was come from the Roman Emperour, in the quality of Extraordinary Envoy, and, his suite not being arrived, he kept himself incognito, I sent to him to know if he would be pleased to accept of a visitt without ceremony; which at first he excused, yet, bethinking himself, he condiscended. So I went thither in the evening, and had a long discourse with him concerning the passages of the moderne transactions. All the tyme he looked very earnestly on me, and at last he told me that he had seen me some where else, but could not call to mind where. So I, thinking it uncivility to keep him in long suspence, told him what I was, and of our Varsavian business.* He rejoyed heartily at my good fortune, he told me, and was sorry that I was going from thence so soone. So, with a great many protestations of kindness on both sides, I tooke my leave, haveing great satisfaction to have seen such a eminent person, to whose kindness and inclinations I had been so much engaged.

Haveing given my *valete* dinner to my friends at the signe of the Cock,† where wee were merry with musick, ladyes, and choice company, I caused pack up all, sending my trunks to Mr. Meverall to be sent by shipping. I tooke only two great valizes with me, and a red bagge, wherein the Kings letter, and best papers and things.

I communicated in St. Jameses, and, after dinner, takeing leave of my January 27. good landlord and landlady, as of Madam Lesly and her daughter, Mrs. Charles, I tooke coach and went for Peckham, from whence I did writt the following letter to Sir William Coventry:

Right Honourable,

I should have wished that by this tyme I had been engaged to returne a thankfull acknowledgment to your honour for giveing order for transporting me out of His Royall Majesties dominions. But, being disappointed of my expectation, I could do no less as notify and represent the case to you. The King, out of the affection His Royall Majestie hath for the Emperour my master, was graciously pleased, when I tooke my leave of His Majestie, to grant me a vessell to transport me to Flanders, and His Royall Highness was pleased to second His Majesties will by speaking to you. I question not but it is well knowne to you, that there never cometh any person, of never so meane a character, upon a publick account, from

---

* [See above, pp. 35-40.]
† ['The Cocke, at the end of Suffolk Street, a reat ordinary, mightily cried up.'—Pepy's Diary (15th March, 1669) vol. v., p. 142. Gordon mentions it in a previous page. See above, p. 86.]

any Prince of State to His Imperiall Majestie my master, but is attended from and to the borders of his dominions, and furnished with all the conveniencies the countrey affoords, expecting the same reciprocally from others. It is no wonder if I be troubled at my delay, serving such a master, whose will is no sooner knowne as executed, and will scarcely beleeve, or think it strange, not to heare the lyke of any other Prince, in such a case as myne. If the season of the yeare could permitt, or I be answerable for my longer stay, I would be loth to be so importune, and, likewise, if it were not to betray my trust, I should be very sparing in the relation to my master of the occasion of my detention. But since now, of necessity, I must take the first conveniency, and if that be the pacquet boat, if I shall chance to be rob'd, His Majesties letters and effaires, which concerne the good of the English nation, miscarry, where the blame will ly I leave it to your selfe to conjecture. Yet, hopeing still that you will send an order, which, with your answer, by this my servant, I shall expect at Greenwich, at the signe of the . . .

This produced an order to the captaines of the Swallow and Hawkes, to either of them, lying in the Downes, to take me in and waft me over to Flanders.

January 28.　　I received a note from Lieutennant Generall Drummond, desireing to know where he could speak with me in the evening. I sent him word that, at the Beare at the Bridgefoot,* I should wait for him at two aclock afternoone. So, haveing dined with Sir John Hebden and others ffriends, I went thither, whither also came the Lieutennant Generall about halfe a howre thereafter. He gave me a full power to recover two thousand rubles from Mr. James Cooke, merchant in Mosko, which he remained indebted to him, as also a letter to Doktor Collins, to deliver me his bond. Haveing supped, and remembred our ffriends in hearty cups, wee parted.

James Burnet of Leyes,† haveing most earnestly entreated me for the lend of five pund sterling, I sent a note to Mr. Peter Webster to deliver him the money.

---

* [A tavern of note. It was at this house, it is said, that, a few weeks afterwards, the Duke of Richmond persuaded the beautiful Frances Stewart to run away with him.]

† [Gordon had encountered this fellow-countryman some years before in Poland, in the retinue of an Ambassador from the Waywode of Kiew. See above, p 30. He appears to have been the youngest son of the first knight baronet of Leys.—See Douglas' Baronage of Scotland, p. 42.]

After breakfast, I went to Greenwich, Sir John [Hebden], with his whole January 29. family, convoying me, whither came also all the Russia merchants and other ffriends, where wee supped, and were exceeding merry.

At one after midnight, the tyde serving, I tooke leave of our kind January 30. friends, and tooke boate. Comeing by day light to Gravesend, where breakfasting, I hired horses, and, towards night, came to Sandwich, where I lodged.

I came to Deale, and immediately caused enquire for the ketches to January 31. whom I had orders, but could not gett notice of them.

Sir John Kempthorne lying in the Downes at anchor with his squadron, February 1. I went aboard of him, and shewed him my order. He told me that these (Friday.) ketches might have been here and gone, for any thing he knew, they not belonging to him, and that, without express orders from the Lord High Admirall, he could not affoord me any vessell. Being returned to my lodging, I immediately did writt by post to Sir William Coventry, informing him that there were no such ketches in the Downes as he had given me order to ; who, the next day, returned me answer that, the wind sorving, the ketches, it seemes, had followed their former orders, and that he could not forsee any occasion whereby I could be served in hast. So I resolved to go to Dover, and take the packet boat.

The great Field Generall and Crowne Marshall of Polland, George Se- February 2. bastian Lubomirsky, dyed in Bresslaw.

I rode to Dover, being rainy, unpleasant weater, and lodged by Mr. February 4. Tours, at the signe of the Prince of Orange.

I passed the tyme in viewing from the high ground the coast of France, February 5. which, albeit a darkish day, wee could plainly discerne.

About midnight, we were told to make ready to go aboard, which, haveing payd dear for naughty entertainment and sweet musick, wee did, about two aclock in the morning. Wee were tossed hither and thither the whole February 6. day betwixt Calais and Graveling, and the next night too, and had enough to do the next day to gett to Newport late, I haveing been extremly seasick all the tyme.

Wee went by boat to Bruges, and tooke up my old lodging; afterwards February 8. went with the English resident, Mr. Glanvile, to the Vrie, and, with other ffriends, were merry till midnight.

Haveing heard masse at the Nunnery after the Princes Pallace, and taken February 9.

leave of the Prioress and sisters, being convoyed by the English resident and other ffriends, I went to the boat, and, with good company, gott in the evening to Ghent; and, haveing left orders for supper in our lodging, I went with Charles to the Nunnes Monastery, and spoke with Mrs. Plowden and her daughter, the Lady Abbess. Haveing stayed an howre, and taken leave, I returned to my lodging, where, with two yong Irish men, who were to go for Antwerp, wee made merry the most part of the night in wine.

February 10.   I went early and heard mass in the Cathedrall church, and then haveing breakfasted in our lodging, being the signe of the Great Starr, wee tooke horse, leaving Mr. Divee, with Charles, to come with our baggage. Wee passed through a most pleasant countrey, and, about two aclock afternoone, came to Antwerp, ferrying over the river Sheld, and lodged at the signe of the Bear, on the market place, where, round the court within, on great . . . were painted the armes of diverse Polls, ambitious, if not vaine glorious gentlemen, for a remembrance of their haveing been there. In the evening, I went and visited my good friend and acquaintance, Sir William Davidson, by whom I found Myn Heer Van der Hurst, one of the States Generall, who had fled with Mr. Kivet about the business of Ruitmaster Buat.*

February 11.   My brother in law came with the baggage, and, for reasons, permitted them to lodge at the White Hart. I did writt to Sir John Hebden, and to his son, the esquire. I hired my fraught in a ship to Hamborg. Dined by Mr. Gibson.

February 19.   I tooke shipping, and, the next day, came to Enckhuisen, where, the
February 20.   wind proveing contrary, I payed my fraught, and, going a shore, caused set
February 23.   me over to Staveren; for, hearing of a ballet to be held by the Queen Christina of Schweden, at Hamborg, the fourteenth of March, I intended to gett thither befor that tyme. So, hireing a waggon, wee passed by Bolquerum on our right hand to Hindlopen, from thence to Workum, to Bol-
February 24   swaert and to Leevarden, whither wee came in the morning, then to Dockum, and to Groeningen, whither wee came in the evening, and were very well accommodated.

February 25.   In the morning, wee passed to Dam and to Delfzyl. It being a great

* [A French gentleman, settled in Holland, who was beheaded at the Hague, in August, 1666, for entering into a clandestine correspondence with the English court. His story is told by Lord Clarendon, in the Continuation of his own Life. Gordon alludes to it in a previous page. See above, p. 76]

storme, wee could not gett over to Embden as I intended, so stayed all
night here.   I againe let my self be perswaded to go to sea againe, the
people there assuring me that, in three or four dayes, I would gett to Hamborg, which I could not do by land, and that, whither there be wind or no,
the vessels could go over the Watten, as they call them, which is a passage
betwixt small islands and the firme land.   Wee went aboard of a small February 26.
vessel, and passed by a small island called Bandt, haveing Borkum and
Juist, two bigger islands, further off.   So, haveing the countrey of East February 27.
Frieslands on our right, we passed by the island Northerny on the left,
and, in the night, by the illand Baltring, then by the illands Langeroeg, February 28.
Spikeroog, to Wangeroog, whither wee came the first of March, haveing, March 1.
with great impatience, endured a slow and tedious voyage, for want of good (Friday)
wind, so that I often perswaded the master of the ship to take out to sea,
which he excused for want of ballast.

The wind blowing exceeding cross, wee were forced to stay here at
anchor till the fifth, when, about midday, wee set saile, bidding adiew to the
wast, sandy, barren illand, where nothing but some poor fisher cottages, and
ane alehouse.

Wee sailed in company of sixty or seventy small wessels, with a pretty
gale, by the gulfe or bay, and the river Iada.   A litle further, the seamen
told us of a drowned illand and castle called Mellum, by the mouth of the
river Weser.   Then, casting about, wee came, with a pretty favourable gale,
to the mouth of the river Elbe, and up the river some miles.   Towards
evening, wee perceived a huge tempest comeing downe the river, encreasing
so darke and black as at midnight, which put us in no small feare, and the
rather seeing some vessells, which kept us company hither, putting out to
sea againe, which our master seeing, would needs follow, but I would not permitt him, telling him that when I desired him in fair weather to put out to
sea, he would not for want of ballast, and now how thought he to be able to
keep sea in a storme without ballast?   He proveing obstinate, I told him he
must choyce either to run a shore or ride it out at anchor, which last, with
great reluctancy, he choiced.   So haveing notice of new cables and anchors in
the hold, with the help of my servants and passengers, wee haled them out,
much against the skippers will, who told me he would complaine upon me
in Hamborg, and fastened all so well as wee could.   And, seeing montaines
of ice comeing downe the river upon us, wee provided our selves of long

poles to keep off the ice. So wee continued working the whole night, and,
notwithstanding all wee could do, at day light wee had a mountaine of ice
gathered befor us, much higher as our boyesprit, which wee could not gett
our selves cleared of till after midday, notwithstanding the storme and wind
was much abated. Towards evening wee gott up as farr as Brunsbottel, and
because of the contrary wind, were forced to anchor there againe, and stay
till the next day about noone. Then, with a great deale of labour, wee gott
up to Gluckstat, where I went immediately ashore and tooke up a lodging,
intending to go by land to Hamborg. In the evening, Mr. Deeve, with our
baggage, came also ashore.

March 6.

March 7.

March 8.

Haveing hired a great waggon with four horses, haveing in company a
sea captaine, and another captaine with his wyfe, and it being very cold, wee
caused a great deale of straw to be put into the waggon, which, on the way,
gave occasion of laughter and loss, for the captaines wyfe, sitting on a
bench with her husband, in the midle of the waggon, and haveing a pott
with coales, in a woodden case, as the fashion is, the straw tooke fyre, so
that wee had enough ado to gett from the waggon. Yet, whilst her husband
and the other captaine were striveing to dampfe or stifle it with their hatts
and clocks, I had leasur to throw out our clockbags, which were behind us
in the waggon ; yet I had some holes burnt in my new Ferendine clock,
and Mr. Deeve had a litle bagge with stockens and other things, to the
value of fifteen or twenty reichs dollers, burnt. But the two captaines clocks
and hatts were utterly spoiled ; and what harme the woman had, was only
fitt for her husband to enquire. Towards night, wee came to Hamborgh,
I going to my old quarters to lodge, where I was very welcome. Here to
my grieffe, I was informed that the ballet was the fourth.

March 9.

Collonell Gordon Steelhand, haveing notice of my being come, came to
me, and afterwards Mrs. Cambridge, who brought me a packet of letters
from Russia, from Mr. Brian, dated in Mosko . . . January, 1667 ;
from my wyfe and mother in law, of the same date, and of the seventeenth
December, 1666. Received letters from Mr. Andrew Hay, with a letter to
the Elector of Brandeburg, and ane other to Duke Boguslaw Radzivill, in
favour of Collonell Bockhoven, both under seale *volant* from Prince Rupert,
of whose recovery I had also the glad newes, dated London, the thirteenth of
February. Received letters also from Sir John Hebden, and his son the
squiie.

I went to Altenaw and heard devotion. Being returned, Collonell March 10.
Malyson sent an officer to welcome me, excuseing that he himself was
bedsick, telling me, that hearing I was come in a private way, he desired
me to make use of his coach and servants, which he would take for a
singular courtesy, and that dureing my stay there. I rendred many thanks,
and promised how soone I could to returne his kind visitt. I dined with
Steelhand, whither in the afternoone came Feltmarshall Wurtz,* who,
hearing of my being come to the citty, came of purpose to gett Steelhand
to go along with him, to give me a visitt. I gave him many thanks,
telling his Excellency that I tooke it for a singular favour, and his good
intention for a visitt. The same evening I went and visitted Collonell
Malyson, who was sick and under phisick. He made us very welcome, and
pressed me to accept of his coach and servants dureing my stay, seeing he
could not himself ; which I promised to do. Here I gott notice of my old
master, the noble Lubomirsky, his death, who dyed the second of February,
in Breslaw.

Feltmarshall Wurts gave me a visitt, and stayed, discoursing together March 12.
of old and moderne stories, two howres. The same day, many other
cavaliers came and gave me visitts. I had notice of the thirteen yeares
truce betwixt the Emperour of Russia and the King of Polland.

Finding my lodging unfitt for me, for many reasons, I removed to the
new towne, and lodged in the signe of the White Horse, where I had
better convenience in every thing.

I did writt to Russia to my wyfe, mother in law, Mr. Bryan, and Almais March 15.
Ivanovits ; as also to England, to Sir John Hebden and his son, to Mr.
Andrew Hay ; to Scotland, to my father, to Generall Dalyell, and Lieve-
tennent Generall Drummond ; to Mr. Glanville in Bruges, and Mrs. Plowden
in Ghent ; to Doktor Dawison in Varsso ; to Mr. Gellentin in Dantzick, to
whom I sent the letter from His Majestie of Great Brittaine to the King of
Polland, in favour of Collonell Bockhoven, as also the letter from Prince
Rupert to Duke Boguslaw Radzivil, recommended to him. Writt also to
Lievetennent Collonell Bruce, who was commendant in Magdeborg, recommending to him the letter from Prince Rupert to the Elector of

* [Paul, baron de Wurtz, a native of the   Gustavus Adolphus of Sweden, King Christian
dutchy of Sleswig. He served successively   IV. of Denmark, and the United Provinces of
under the Emperor Ferdinand II., King   Holland. He died in 1676.]

Brandeburg.   Writt also to Mr. Ayloffe in Riga, and to his care letters to Collonells Forrat and Odovern.

I delivered Steelhands writeings and passes to him, but received no money, he remaining, upon this account, due to me fifteen punds sterling. I gave visitt to Field Marshall Wurtz, and to some others who had visitted me.

Queen Christina being here, and I finding it fitt to pay my duty to Her Majestie, gave notice of my desire to kiss Her Majesties hands, which she very readily granted. So I went thither with Steelhand, and, haveing given notice, I was introduced by an Italian Marquesse to a large roome, where the Queen was standing at the upper end of the roome. How soone she saw me, and, that after my first reverence, I advanced, she made hast to meet me ; and, notwithstanding my dilligence, she did meet me near halfe the roome, and, pulling of her glove, she presented me her hand, which, bowing, I kissed ; then spoke in High Dutch to Her Majestie a very short oration. She haveing thanked me, invited me, as it were, to go up and downe the roome with her, which I did, a litle backward, discoursing with Her Majestie about halfe an howre. Then haveing heard a very short masse in the same roome, I tooke my leave, being convoyed down staires to my coach by a gentleman.

Hearing that Mr. Johan van Sweden, with his family, was come to Lubeck, and going for Russia, I went to Lubeck to consult with him about our passage. I lodged a night by the way, and the next day, about noone, came thither. So wee resolved to take our passage from Lubeck by sea ; and, by his perswasion, I resolved to come and stay in his lodging, and take my dyet and chamber here, being mor quiet, and farr lesse expensive liveing, as at Hamborg. So the next day I went for Hamborg againe.

Writt to my wyfe and mother in law, in a *coverto* to Mr. Bryan, and to Doktor Collins, and to Mr. Joseph Williamson. I received eighty reichs dollers, in specy, from Henry Poorten, upon a bill of exchange from Sir John Hebden. Received letters from Mr. Benjamin Glanville, one dated Bruges, the fourteenth of February, the other dated Ostend, the sixteenth of February, with a full power to persue and recover his debts from Henry Krevett in Russia.

I was by Mr. Zelmer, and see his horses, at the Bremer house.

Two collonells, Shults and Olefelt, would needs be going for Russia

March 20.

March 21.

March 23

March 25.

March 26.

March 27.

with their officers, from which I diswaded them, that the Emperour haveing dissmissed so many officers who had served and were acquainted in the countrey, it was not lykely that he would accept of new, sceing, by the peace with Polland, there was litle to do.   And, with much trouble, I got them perswaded to stay so long untill I should returne them an answer from Mosko, if they could be accepted or not ; to which purpose they gave me a memoriall subscrived with their hands.

I was entertained in the English house.   March 28.

I did writt to Dantzick to Mr. John Gellentin.   March 29.

I did writt to Collonell More in Buxtehude, and the next day received March 30. answer.

I confessed, and received the blessed sacrament in Altenaw.   March 31.

Being resolved to go to Lubeck, I tooke my leave of ffriends, as of April 1. Field Marshall Wurtz, Collonell Malyson, and the English merchants, and (Monday) last of all, of Collonell Gordon Steelhand.

I borrowed one hundred dollers of Mr. Cambridge, giveing a bill upon April 2. Mr. Herman Becker to pay to Mr. Benjamin Ayloffe, with a letter of advise to Herman Becker.   This same evening I tooke my leave of the Queen of Sweden, who was very gracious to me.   Received letters from Sir John Hebden, dated Peckham, the first of March.

I went for Lubeck, lodging by the way, the innes where wee should April 3. have breakfasted being in the night burn'd off, wee breakfasted in a house by the same landlord, to whom we contributed largely upon the account of his losse.   By the way, a merchant in the coach shott the master of the coach through the legg, holding a pistoll negligently in his hand.

Writt to Steelhand.   April 6.

Writt to Hendry Poorten, and the twelfth to him also.   April 8.

Received a letter from Hendry Poorten, dated Hamborg, the tenth of April, and from Steelhand, dated Hamborg, the thirteenth of April.

I did writt to Collonell Malyson, thanking him for his civilityes.   April 18.

I was entertained in the Ratsheer Keller.

At a feast by Jost Poorten.

By Johan van Goren, entertained liberally.

Writt to my wyfe and her mother, in a *coverto* to Mr. Bryan.   I was April 20. in Grinaw, with Mr. Van Sweden.

I entertained the officers who had been in Russia. I bought a black stoned horse, and gave forty reichs dollers for him.

April 24.

Writt to my father, addressed to Mr. Rany in London.

Wee haveing hired a galliot to Riga, for two hundred reichs dollers, and the season serving, wee went downe to Travemunde, where wee spent two dayes with shipping in our horses and baggage. And so takeing leave of Mr. Poorten, Mr. Ivings, and . . . who had convoyed us from Lubeck, and stayed here with us so long; and I particularly of Captain Kauffman, who had been my lieftenant whilst I was under the Sweds in Stum, and furnished

April 28.

me now with a bed; wee set saile on the twenty eighth, and, with a gentle gale, made good way.

May 1.
(Wednesday)

Wee passed by Borneholme with a strong gale, which made all of us seasick, the wind being too violent; and the horses, whereof wee had twenty two aboard, breaking the traveses, and no body able to mend them; by the perswasion of the master of the ship, wee returned to Bornholme, being eight leagues, and anchored safely.

May 2.

Haveing mended the traveses, and the wind calmer, wee set saile very

May 6.

early, and, with good weather, arrived in the river Dwina the sixth; the master of the galliot, called Wulffe, professing to have had a very good passage. I went ashore with Mr. Van Sweden, and went to Herman Beckers countreyhouse, whither, by chance, he came and made us welcome; so that, about midnight, we came to Riga, and stayed all night in his house.

May 7.

The next day I went to my owne lodging in the suburbs.

I received letters from Mosko, from my wyfe and mother, and Mr. Bryan, dated the fourth of March; from Doctor Collins, dated the second of March; another from Mr. Bryan, dated the seventeenth of March; from John Gellentin, dated Dantzeck, the twenty second of April; from Doctor Davidson, dated Varso, the twenty first and twenty eighth April, with encloseds from him to my Lord Lawderdale and Sir William Davidson, being answers to myne from Hamborg, and giveing me a account of the letters and business about Collonell Bockhoven; from Lieuetennant Collonell Bruce, also about the same business, dated Magdeburg, the fifteenth of April.

May 8.

Our horses being brought all out of the ship, and passed toll free under my name, the Governour Generall desired that they might be brought through the Castle, which being done, he fancyed my black horse, and sent to me, desireing me to let him have him, and he would give .me either money or another for him. I answered that the horse indeed was not to be sold, yet, seeing he had a fancy for him, he was at his service, and that I would take it for a great favour, if he would be pleased to accept of him; and sent him along to his Excellency with one of my servants. But he would not accept of him, and gave me many thanks for the offer.

I, being invited by Mr. Clayhills to his brandy house, went with Captaine Gordon, Mr. Ayloffe, and Finlay Downy, and were merry. I bought my bay horse from Mr. Clayhills, and gave for him, with sadle, sherbrake, and hulsters, my sable furr, and twelve reichs dollers. He gave me also Cambdens Brittannia.

I hired horses and waggons to Plesko, haveing Mr. Isaack and Mr. *May 9.* Deeve still in my company.

I did writt to Mr. Gellentin, Doctor Davidson, to Sir William Davidson, *May 10.* to Captain Kauffmans and to Steelhand, giveing off Captain Kauffmans bed to the skipper Wulffe. Writt to Mosko to my wyfe, mother, Mr. Bryan, and Doctor Collins.

Being invited to Mr. Herman Becker, I went, and with Mr. Van *May 11.* Sweden and his family, and diverse, were magnificently entertained. The same day, haveing taken my leave of my ffriends who convoyed me out of towne, I went from Riga, and came to Plesko the seventeenth, where the *May 17.* Woywod, upon pretence that the pest was in England, but, in reality, that I would not let him have my black horse, which he fancyed, detained me till the twenty fourth; when, receiving my podwods, our company being *May 24.* augmented with Mr. Henry Munter, and a poor fellow, our pristaw, I tooke my jorney, and the twenty seventh, came to Novogrod, and the *May 27.* second of June, to Torizok, the third, to Twere, the fourth, to Klin, and *June 2.* the fifth, to Axinina, where I had orders to stay, untill I should give notice to the ambassy office, and get licence to come to Mosko. I dispatched my pristave immediately away with the letters from the governour of Plesko, wherein was my testimony or *skaska* that there was no pestilence more in England nor in any place through which I had passed.

About eight aclock in the morning, my father in law, with Mr. Bryan, *June 6.* came, and brought an order, that I should go to the Sloboda, and stay *(Thursday)* there till further orders. I came to the Sloboda, and was, with a great joy, welcomed by my wyfe and ffriends.

The following dayes, I received the visitts and gratulations of my ffriends.

Being at last permitted to come into the prikase, I presented His Majesties letters to the Boyar, and gave thereby my *statine knigy*, or a relation of my negotiation. The Boyar told me that I must have a litle patience befor I could be admitted to His Majesties hand.

I presented my father in law with the black horse, with sadle, pistols, and compleat furniture.

June 25.

According to my promise in Hamborg, I caused enquire if two colonells could be admitted to come in to serve with their officers, but no possibility, seeing so many brave cavaliers had been dismissed, who had served here so long, and knew the fashion of the countrey. Whereupon I did writt to Hamborg to Collonell Shults, and informed him thereof, and also to Collonell Gordon to the same purpose.

Writt to Captain Gordon and Mr. Clayhills in Riga.

[Here the first and largest gap in the Diary begins. It extends from June, 1667, to January, 1677. The events of Gordon's life during this void of ten years, must be gleaned from other sources.

For reasons which do not very clearly appear, he was now visited by the displeasure of the Muscovite court. He was ordered to confine himself to the Sloboda. The Czar would not see him; and he had to wait till the next reign, before he could get payment of the expense of his mission to England. The German editors suggest that offence may have been taken at the letter of which Gordon was the bearer from King Charles II., desiring the release of Kaspar Calthoffe.

A.D. 1670.

He did not lose his regiment; and, in the year 1670, he was sent with it into the Ukraine to assist in subduing the Cossacks of Little Russia. The skill and courage which he displayed, may have been one cause why the Czar kept him in this province for the long period of seven years. He did not allow the time to run to waste, but devoted his leisure to the study of mechanics, fortification, and strategy.

A.D. 1677.

In the year 1677, he was summoned to Moscow to answer the complaints of some troopers of his regiment. His vindication seems to have been triumphant; and he was sent back to the Ukraine, to take part against the Turks and Tartars, who were besieging Tschigirin, the capital of the Saporogian Cossacks. His successful defence of this town, and expulsion of the Mahometans from the Ukraine, gained him high military reputation.

A.D. 1678.

He now renewed his efforts for leave to quit Russia. But the Czar Feodor was on this point as implacable as his father Alexis; and, although the endeavours of the Scottish soldier were backed by a letter from King Charles II., presented by Sir John Hebden, his ambassador extraordinary, they were in vain. The value of Gordon's services in the field was now fully appreciated; and, in the year 1678, he was again sent, with his dragoons and a regiment of Strelitzes, to the defence of Tschigirin from the renewed attack with which it was threatened by the Turks and Tartars. In this task, his skill as an engineer enabled him to overcome great difficulties, and, for four weeks, to fight every inch of ground against overwhelming numbers.

He was repairing and strengthening the ramparts in expectation of the siege, when the twenty-ninth of May called him to celebrate the day of the birth and restoration of the King of Great Britain, by a dinner to the chief officers of the garrison. The feast was spread in his garden; salvoes were fired; there was music of sundry sorts; and all were very merry. The revel was still high, when a letter arrived from Major-General Kosazow, demanding to know the cause of the shots which had so alarmed the camp. The bearers of the dispatch added that the army had been called to arms, and that the cavalry were in their saddles; and they wondered how the Scottish engineer and his company could be so gay and reckless at a time of such anxiety. Gordon, having quieted their alarm, dismissed them with a conciliatory answer.

It was on the eighth of July that the van of the besieging army came within sight of the town. Gordon gathered from deserters that the Turks numbered about fifty thousand men of all arms, and that the Tartars who followed the Khan of the Crimea were about as many. They had four great cannon, drawn each of them by thirty-two yoke of buffaloes; twenty-seven battery pieces of various sizes; a hundred and thirty field guns; six mortars, throwing shells of a hundred and twenty pounds in weight; and nine smaller pieces, throwing shells of from thirty to forty pounds. There were eight thousand waggons, and five thousand camels, laden with ammunition. There were a hundred thousand waggons with provisions, and eight thousand herdsmen. These last, as well as the waggoners and the miners, were Christians from the European provinces under Ottoman rule. The command of this formidable host was entrusted to the Grand Vizier, Kara Mustapha.

The garrison which had to hold Tschigirin numbered rather less than twelve thousand. Gordon had the command of his own dragoons and of a regiment of Strelitzes. He was, besides, the chief engineer, and both constructed the works before the siege began, and directed the subsequent operations. The Russian army on the Dnieper came but slowly to the relief of the beleaguered city, and did but little when it came. Gordon's Diary chronicles the events of each day, and describes in detail the assaults and sallies, mines and countermines, breaches and retrenchments.

He notes that, on the eleventh of July, there were eighteen men killed, and twenty-five wounded, in the citadel; and that 468 round shot, and 246 shells, were cast into the citadel and town. On the next day, the number of killed was fifteen; of wounded, twenty-four; and 542 balls and 183 shells were fired into the town. On the twenty-eighth, 844 balls and 225 shells were thrown, and thirty-seven men were killed, and thirty-five wounded. On the second of August, 1008 balls and 387 shells were shot into the place, killing thirty-four persons, and wounding forty-two.

Neither among the officers nor among the men of the garrison did Gordon find much alacrity in making sallies upon the besiegers; and it was chiefly by assiduous repair of the works over night, and by making retrenchments behind breaches, that the defence was made good so long.

The governor was killed by the bursting of a bomb, on the eighth of August, when the colonels and other officers came to Gordon and entreated him to take the command. On the eleventh, after a furious cannonade, the enemy assaulted both the town and the citadel on all sides. They had gained partial possession of the former, and the garrison was beginning to run away, when Gordon, hastening from the citadel, with a strong guard, occupied the gate of the bridge which led from the town to the camp of the Muscovite army of relief. He thus stopped the tide of flight, and was even able to turn back some of the troops to dispute the narrow streets with the advancing enemy. But so great was the panic, that, if the Turks had pressed onwards, they must have taken the gate, and so cut off all means of retreat. Fortunately for the besieged, the town had been set on fire, and now the flames hindered the enemy from making their way in any numbers in that direction. The sight of Turkish cavalry on the other side of the river, between the town and the Russian camp, as it warned the garrison of the danger of flight, encouraged them to a more resolute defence.

Again and again, Gordon sent urgent messages to the Boyar in command of the Russian army. If six thousand men were sent him, he would even yet beat back the Turks; and if no help were given him, he could scarcely hope to hold the citadel itself. No answer was returned to these representations. Nothing daunted, he at once resolved on the construction of a retrenchment which should secure the communication between the fortress and the gate of the bridge. He was urging on this work, when one of the colonels told him that the Boyar in command of the camp had sent an adjutant with an order that the fortress should be evacuated. Gordon refused to listen to such a message. He had been told, he said, rather to die than to desert his post, or to allow others to do so, without a written order. He therefore commanded each man to do his duty. But seeing how many of all ranks were making their escape, he despatched a letter to the Boyar in the camp, describing the state of matters in the fortress, and asking instructions as to what should be done. Meanwhile, he ordered supper, and in order that it might be seen how far flight was from his thoughts, he desired that his silver service should be used.

Late at night an answer arrived from the camp, having been brought to the gate by an adjutant, who, refusing to proceed further, handed the despatch to a drummer, by whom it was delivered to Gordon. It was an order to evacuate the place, bringing away the lightest of the cannon, burying the rest, and destroying all the ammunition, especially the powder. He now assembled what officers remained, and apportioned the guns to be taken away. Some maintained that it was impossible either to carry off the cannon or even to bury them, their soldiers being exhausted or having fled. Others ran off without saying a word. Only the foreign officers, with few exceptions, stood to their posts, until they had scarcely soldiers left to carry the colours. Gordon then dismissed them; but he himself remained to collect the men still dispersed through the fortress. He had succeeded in gathering them together, after placing lighted torches in the loopholes, when suddenly loud shouts, mingled with the rattle of musketry, were heard in the town below, striking such terror into the soldiers that they threw down their arms and fled. Gordon was now left almost alone, the few stragglers who remained being either so drunk or so intent on plunder, that they would obey no orders. Whatever was to be done, he had therefore to do with his own hand. Having seen to the closing of the gates and sally ports, he turned his steps towards the powder magazine. Breaking it open, he threw in straw and boards, and then set fire to the nearest house. When he returned to the market place, he found his servants fled and his carriage plundered.

Hitherto he had not apprehended any difficulty in making his way to the camp. Three Muscovite regiments had crossed the river to occupy the bridge and gate until the garrison should effect its escape. But suddenly, and without warning, these regiments withdrew, precipitating the retreat of the garrison into a tumultuous flight. The Turks pursued, and, taking possession of the gate without resistance, signalised their victory by the shouts and salvoes which had so startled the citadel. Gordon, finding retreat by the gate thus cut off, followed some Russian marauders, in climbing over a wall, and making for the river. They threw themselves into the stream; but Gordon, who could not swim, was obliged to seek some other way of escape. He walked along the river side until he came to the bridge, where, although it was night, he could see Turks flitting to and fro, bearing the heads of Russian fugitives, killed as they swam to land. This sight somewhat troubled him; but there was no time for hesitation, and so, devoutly commending himself to Divine protection, he rushed across the bridge, with a sword in one hand and a pistol in the other. He met five or six Turks, each with a bare scimitar in his right hand, and a Christian head in his left. Firing his pistol, he dashed past them, and, gaining the other end of the bridge, turned to the right, and ran along the embankment until his pursuers lost sight of him. Stumbling over the headless trunks of the slaughtered Muscovites, he scrambled through the ditch, and made for the camp. When half way, and almost worn out, he met two ensigns of his own regiment, who conducted him to head quarters, where he heaped bitter reproaches upon the Boyar. He had scarcely found a sleeping-place for the night, when a terrible explosion shook the ground. The magazine at Tschigirin blew up, destroying four thousand Turks. Gordon's services in this affair were rewarded by promotion to the rank of Major-General.

Here the Diary is again interrupted by a chasm of five years. The volume which chronicled the events from 1678 to 1684 has not been recovered.

A.D. 1679—A.D. 1684.

It is known, from the military records of the Empire, that, in 1679, he was appointed to the chief command in Kiew. Soon afterwards he was placed at the head of the selected regiments in the Ukraine. In 1683, he was made Lieutenant-General. In the beginning of the next year, he undertook a journey to Moscow, in the hope of obtaining an order for his removal from the provinces to the capital. The Czar Feodor had died in 1682, leaving two brothers, Ivan and Peter. The former being imbecile, and the latter only in his tenth year, the government devolved upon their sister, Sophia. The Scot was graciously received, both by the Princess Regent, and by her favourite and prime minister, Wassilij Wassiljewitsch Golizyn. The former showed him marked favour, and the latter took his counsel as to a projected alliance with the Roman Emperor against the Turk. But neither would allow him to leave Kiew, much less to make a journey to Scotland. Although thus compelled to abide in a position with which he was very much dissatisfied, he did not fail in the zealous discharge of his duty, occupying himself in fortifying Kiew, which was believed at the time to be threatened by the Turks. During his command here, he became acquainted with a foreigner, fated like himself to exercise great influence on the young Czar and the fortunes of his empire—the Genevese adventurer, Lefort. With this eminent man, then in his twenty-eighth year, and serving as a captain and engineer, Gordon formed a friendship which proved life-long.

Towards the end of this year, he had to grieve the loss of a son, for whose tombstone he wrote this inscription: "Hic depositum est quod mortale fuit Georgii Stephani Gordonis, nati anno Domini 1682, Decembris 24, denati anno Domini 1684, Novembris 1. Requiescat in pace.

> " Non tua sed nostra abbreviarunt crimina vitam,
>   Mors te felicem nos miserosque facit.
> Nos lacrimarum tristes in valle relinquis,
>   Dum patriam repetis aethereumque polum.
> Hic Pater Omnipotens nos plecte, ut parcas in aevum,
>   Defunctis requiem tribue Summe Parens."

The learned pen of the Lieutenant-General was employed, in the same month, to write the epitaph of one of his countrymen: "Hic jacet mortalis pars Domini Andreae Arbuthnoti nobili in Scotia genere orti. Vixit annos LXXVIII. Requiescat in pace.

> " Scotia me genuit, tenuitque Polonia quondam,
>   Russia nunc requiem praebet. Amice vale."

A.D. 1685.

Tidings of the death of King Charles II., and of the accession of King James II. on the sixth of February, 1685, reached Gordon not many weeks after the event. He records that, on the twenty-ninth of May, being the birthday of the most blessed King of England, the English commemorated him in mournful wise. On the thirtieth of September, he received a circumstantial account of the defeat of the Earl of Argyle in Scotland, and of the Duke of Monmouth in England; and of the execution of the former, at Edinburgh, on the thirteenth of June, and of the latter, on Tower-hill, on the fifteenth of July. Along with these tidings he got certain copies of Latin verses, which his loyalty thought worthy of being copied into his Diary. The first may be read backwards:

"Sat se jam erutam tenet mature Majestas."

The second runs thus:

"Rex Argile ambit Scotus, Monmutius Anglus,
Esse: perit, Regem qui petit ense suum.
Eruta mature Majestas Anglo periclo est,
Scote tuo Regi, plaude Britanno tuo."

The third, an epigram on Monmouth, borrowed its point from the early history of Rome:

"Mutius ense petit Regem et Monmutius, errant,
Hic caput invitus, sponte dat ille manum."

The last took the shape of an epitaph upon Argyle:

"Ecce sub argillo jacet hic Argile cruento:
Non oculis Argus, sed fraude Argivus Ulysses."

Influenced, no doubt, by the accession of a Prince of his own faith to the English throne, Gordon now determined to renew his efforts for leave to return to his own country. In a petition which he placed in the hands of Prince Golizyn, he recounted all the services which he had performed in Russia, called to mind the promises of liberty which had been made to him, recapitulated his many grievances, and represented that, unless he were allowed to visit Scotland, he was in danger of losing the inheritance which had fallen to him by the death of his parents. If absolute release from the service should not be granted, he prayed that he might at least have leave of absence for six months. The answer to this petition was a summons to Moscow, where he arrived on the first of January, 1686. Here he met his friend Lefort, and stood god-father to his son Daniel. Permission was at last given him to visit England, on condition of a speedy return, for which his wife and children were to be hostages. The incidents of the journey are thus recorded in his Diary:—]

A.D. 1686.

I sollicited the Boyar* about my going out of the countrey, and was bidd bring a petition.

1686
January 18.

*[Wassilij Wassiljewitsch Golizyn.]

January 19

I gave up my petition to be lett out the countrey for a tyme; and had orders to be lett off, my wyfe and children staying in Mosko in pledge.

January 26.

Was at their Majesties hands, receiving a charke* of brandy out of the yongest† his hand, with a command from him to returne speedily.

January 27.

I was at the Princesse‡ her hand, who required me to returne speedily, and bring at least one of my sonnes with me.

January 28.

I went to Czarny Grash, and tooke my leave of the Boyar, who desired me to returne speedily, and not to drowne him my cautioner, and to writt to him by every post.

January 29.

I did writt to Lieutennant Generall Drummond and Mr. Meverell by post, under Mr. Wulffe his *coverto*, informing them of my being dismissed and going from Mosko the next day; and the Lieutennant Generall, my transaction with Mr Cooke, and, because no exchange could be had, of my haveing given the money to Mr. Wulffe, to be remitted from Archangell, hopeing to gett it done ten *per cento* better as now.

I dined with Mrs. Boetenant and diverse others; and afterwards, in the towne, tooke my leave of the Secretary of Estate,§ and Mr. Vinius, from whom I received a verball commission, by order from the Chieffe Minister of Estate,‖ concerning their Majesties effaires.

In the Slobod, I tooke my leave of the Hollands resident, and others my nearest ffriends.

February 4.

In Nowgrod, the Customers wished to inspect my effects. I did not allow it. They assured to have the orders to sight persons of all quality, charge, and condition. I told them that that was to be understood as to merchants and others, and not to military persons, especially of such quality as myself, and instanced them diverse examples of late. They pretended an order of some few dayes old, and I referred my self to the Governours raport or verdict, who declined to medle into it, yet gave me his dispatch as to what concerned himself. I visited him a night; he was exceedingly kind, and repeated what is said befor.

February 5.

I sent againe to know the Governours pleasure, who told as befor, that I might go for him, haveing full dispatch from him; and upon my desire,

---

*[Apparently a cup or glass. Gordon afterwards notes that, at Memel, he bought "ane amber crosse, a *charke*, and three bracelets."]

†[The Czar Peter, then in his fourteenth year. This was Gordon's first interview with him. When at court, in January, 1684, he saw only the Czar Ivan, Peter being ill of the small pox.]

‡[Sophia.]

§[Iemelian Ignatjewitsch Ukrainzow, who was then Dumny Dyak.]

‖[Wassilij Wassiljewitsch Golizyn.]

granted me two Streltsees for a convoy. But, hearing that the Customer was getting all his catchpoles together, and resolving either not to let me out of my quarters, or to stopp me upon the way, I sent againe to the Governour, desireing to know if this was by his order, or if he would authorise such force. He sent me word that he did not, yet that he could not medle in the Customers businesse, they haveing their commission immediately from Mosko, and that I might do as I thought fitt. So haveing dined, I gave orders to make ready, resolving to force my passage through the towne, maugre of all opposition. The Customer, haveing notice hereof, came to me, and desired that, since I would be gone, and not suffer my baggage to be visited, I would let them be sealed, and put in a church or some secure indifferent place, untill order should come from Mosko ; which, indeed, rather as be detained, I had offered at first. But now being encouraged, or rather connived at, by the Governour, I declined; and haveing sent a petition under my hand to the Governour, complaining upon the Customer and his fellowes for affronting me in putting a watch to my baggage and me, and detaining me from my jorney, to my great losse and prejudice, desired it to be written in here and sent to Mosko. Which being accepted, I marched out, and without offering or haveing any violence offered to me, I passed through the towne, over the bridge on the Volcha, and so on my jorney ; and the horses being a litle weary, they baited in a village twenty five verst, and in the night to Mpsiaga, twenty five verst. I payed in Novogrodt, for ten horses, twenty five altins, and here for the same, one ruble, three altins, two dengies. I did writt from Novogrodt, to Mr. Vinius, Collonel Menezes, and my wyfe.

About three howres befor day, I went from thence, and by faire day- February 6. light came to Solnitza, fyfteen verst, where, by a gentleman come out of Novogrodt in the fourth houre of the night, I was informed that the Customer, with the principall persons belonging to that office, had with great importunity obtained of the Governour an order, with a writer and a number of Streltsees, upon podwods, to follow me, and either search my goods upon the place, and, if any merchandize were found, to fetch it back, or in case I should not permitt, then to fetch me back with all, or at least to stopp me where they should find me. Which hearing, and haveing good horses, I promised the yempshiks drink money, and so drove on like Jehu, and came to Opochy, thirty-five verst, where baiting not above half an houre, I came to Zagoria, forty verst, about the third houre of the night, where changing horses, and giveing five kopikes for each horse, I came to Plesko, befor day, thirty-five verst.

The Governour, Kniaz Michael Gregoriovits Romadonofsky, received me very kindly, and ordered my present dispatch, and that, when I was ready, I should come and take my leave of him. I hired horses from the borders to Riga, giveing for each horse one ruble, eight altins, one dengy, and hired in all six; and so, in the evening, haveing taken my leave of the Governour and the ffriends with him, about ten aclock at night I went from thence; and without my knowledge, I being asleep, the yempshiks, being drunk, went into a house about twenty verst and rested. But I awakeing, awaked them with sound stroakes, and made them drive on; and so, in the

first houre of the day, came to the Petsharsky,* and, a little before mid day, to Newhausell, ten miles, where the Commendant, being a lietennant, and named Erich Goth, after I had given him notice in his house in the castell what I was, gave me a note or pass.

Haveing baited the horses a litle, and returned these from Plesko, wee passed by diverse ale houses, this place or countrey being famous or remarkable by nothing, and for three miles, or fifteen verst, a very hilly or rather hillocky country, and lodged in Roughes alehouse or krow, five miles; the villages, which are rare, haveing their denominations, as also the alehouses, from the gentlemen they belong to.

At cockcrowing, wee set forward, and crossing the Black river, dined by it, five miles; then crossing the river Gavia, lodged in ane alehouse standing alone in a wildernesse, five miles.

And resting here about three houres, wee came by day light to a alehouse, six miles, and here only fooding the horses a litle, and crossing the river Aa, wee dined in the alehouse befor Wolmar, two miles, and lodged in a alehouse, three miles. A little befor midnight, wè marched, and

passeing many krowes to Rubina, three miles, and by day light came to Brosla, one mile, where baiting, with badd way, the snow being most consumed, wee came about three miles further and baited. And a mile further, crossing the river Gavia againe, wee lodged in Hilkins krow, a mile further, and three miles short of Riga. Here hard by, in a hoffe called Sarankova, liveth the Baron von Mengden.

*[Petschur, a monastery. See above, p. 43.]

I gott our landlord to conduct us through bywayes where the snow was February 12. not quite consumed, and going from thence at cockrowing, with great difficulty I came to Riga, about eight aclock, and lodged in the Sandstreet, by a barber called Harder.

I did writt the same evening to my wyfe, Collonells von Mengden and Menezes, Mr. Vinius, and Guasconj, and to the Boyar Kniaz Vasily Vasilivits,* by the apothicary Christian Egler, whom I did meet here returning to Mosko, and who came to visitt me with Marcus Luys, a merchant, to whom I delivered diverse tokens from Mosko.

I did writt to the Governour of Plesko, Kniaz Michael Gregorivits February 13. Romadanofsky, and to Joachim Voght, a merchant, who there were very kind to me, so could not but returne thanks. Friends comeing to visitt me, would needs have me to come in and stay in the towne; so I went and lodged in the Jacobs street, in Widow Bevermans house. After noone, Mr. Richard Daniell sent his sledge for me, desiring me to walke on the river Dwina; so with diverse other English men and women, wee fuired a great way downe the river on the ice, and then was invited into a suburb house, and passed the tyme two or three houres. The Customers sent to know if I had any merchant goods along, and tooke notice of my trunks, saying they must be searched.

I dined by Mr. Daniell, and was very kindly entertained.   February 14.

I dined by Mr. Frazer, and supped with Mr. Watson.   February 15.

Hired fuirmen to Memel, at the rate of nine reichs dollers a waggon February 16. with two horses.

I did writt to Mr. Boetenant, informing him how that because I had a February 17. specification of the things in his trunk with me, they let it passe, paying two and a half per cent. for *portorio*,† and the other two, belonging to Messrs. Hartman, and Van Sowme, were taken into the *portorio* to be kept there untill a specification should be brought, and then to be opened, sighted, and valued, which they did not to Mr. Boetenant his. Payed for *portorio* thirteen and a quarter reichs dollers; payed for dyet halfe a doller a day, and for servants ten stuivers.

After dinner, I went from Riga, being convoyed, with Mr. Daniell and Mr. Frazer, to the other syde of the river Dwina, and lodged all night in

---

* [Golizyn.]   † [Toll or custom; and, also, toll-house, or custom-house.]

Shrudens krue, three miles from Riga, and payed a third of a doller, and four poltoraks to the maides.

February 18.   Wee came to Mittaw, three miles.   Here is the residence of the Duke of Curland, in a castell fortifyed with an earthen wall and a moate, haveing a decayed horne worke upwards on the river.   Writt from hence to Pater Makovius, by Pater Sturms convoyance.   The towne is pretty bigge, with a decayed earthen wall about it.   Here wee payed for our dinner, thirty two pence or poltorakes.   Wee passed over three litle rivers, and lodged in Duplins krue, three miles, and payed for bier seven poltorakes, and four for hay, which we lay on.

February 19.   Wee crossed a litle river, and came by Annes church, and dined in Blydens krue, about three miles, paying for bier eight pence ; and went three miles further, and lodged in Fronbergs krue, where payed in all nine pence.

February 20.   We came and crossed the river Wendon, and dined in a house, being four miles.   Here is a stone house, belonging to the Duke of Curland, environed with a tetragon.   Payed here for beer and egges twelve pence.   Wee went two miles further, and lodged in a krue, where payed for beer seven pence, and for hay, to lay on, three pence.

February 21.   A great snow falling out, wee came to a krue, by a gentlemans house, where I bought a litle sledge, giving a doller for it, two miles.   Payed here for beer eleven pence.   Wee travailed with greater speed, and, crossing a litle river by Christburg, wee came to Barta river, which crossing on a floate, wee lodged in a good house, being fyve miles.   Here wee payed for bed and bier eighteen pence, and to the maid a penny.

February 22.   Wee came to Rutzen krue, three miles.   All the snow being gone, I was forced to leave my sledge, neither could I gett any thing for it ; and all by a piece of the juglery of a merchant which came along with me from Riga, who, as in other things, made his advantage of me.   Here payed for bier and egges eighteen pence.   Wee came nearer the sea coast, and, crossing the river Heyligen Agh by a float, wee lodged hard by in a good house, being but two miles and a litle more from the place where wee had dined.   Here wee payed for fyve persons, and my two boyes, for supper, bier, and bed, two florens, and to the maid four pence.   Here wee were on Polnish ground, this being the Starosty of Polanga.

February 23.   Wee travelled to Polanga, a little towne inhabited most by Jewes, two miles. Here toll is gathered by these Jewes, who pay a yearly summe for it. Here I caused tell and said I was a Polnish colonell, yet was forced, according to the custome, to give a discretion, *videlicet*, a doller and twelve pence to the two tolners, twelve pence to each of their assistants; and it cost, for brandy and white bread, eighteen pence. Wee went on to Memell, three miles, two and a half whereof are on the Elector of Brandeburgs territories. Here, all along, the sea, especially in a storme, throweth out amber, which, on the Polnish coast, every body hath freedome to gather that live there; but, on the Brandeburgish coast, none but these ordained to gather it. At the mouth of the river Heiligen Aagh, the English have obtained a priviledg of trading free for ten yeares, they promiseing to make a safe harbour there, whereof litle hopes as yet; there lying great banks of sand befor that river, and it being an open, sandy coast, can hardly be gotten kept clear. In Memell, being required to tell what I was, I told the guards that I should satisfy them in my quarters; whither being come, I did writt a note and sealed it, addressing it to the Commendant, Liewtennant Collonell Krygher, giveing notice what I was, and desireing not to be knowne. The Commendant sent me immediately notice by an officer that he would give me a visitt, and came accordingly about an houre thereafter, welcoming me with great respect, and invited me to take a part of a sojors dinner the next day. At his going away, there was a pikeman from the maine guard sent to stand sentry at my doore.

The Commendant, haveing sent a officer in the morning to invite me to February 24. dinner at eleven aclock, sent his coach for me, and a captaine liewtennant called Chappell, an Englishman, to conduct, there being also halfe a dozen of well cloathed fellowes, besides my owne, about the coach. I was well entertained, and reconducted in his coach to my lodging, but without other attendants as the captaine liewtennant. I gave to the coachman halfe a doller, and a doller to the watch on the coach, and caused feed those who stood sentry at my doore, and gave them halfe a doller drink money when I went away. I payed off the Rigaes fuirmen, they haveing received in all twenty seven hard dollers for six horses and three waggons, besides beer on the way. I hired a waggon, with fyve horses, for ten dollers; Yury Powlson and the apothecary being to bear a share, I haveing but one servant thereon and my baggage. I hired two rideing horses for my self and a servant, paying three dollers for each, and feeding them and the guide with

a third, on the way to Konigsberg, being wearying of tossing upon a
waggon.   I payed here, for dyet, wine, and feeding the sojors, twelve
florens, includeing Yury Powlson.   I gave to the maid fyfteen pence, and
bought ane amber crosse, a charke, and three bracelets, for four and a half
dollers.

This Memell is a very strong place, especially the castle, which is to be
fortifyed yet better, according to a draught which the Commendant did
show me, most of the materialls being already provided.   The souldiers
have duly allowance of six florens a moneth, for two whereof they are provided of bread; two ar given them to buy beer, kitchin meat, and extra-
ordinaries; and two is preserved by their officers for furnishing them with
shooes, stockings, shirts, and other necessaries.   A captaine hath thirty two
dollers a month; a liewtennant, eighteen; and an ensignie, twelve.

March 5.   Haveing hired a coach, at the rate of a reichs doller a day, I rode in it
to Scotland Syde, and, in the Jesuits Church, heard devotion.   In the afternoone, the Rector of the Jesuits Colledge gave me a visitt, to whom I declared my resolution of takeing my son along with me; for, perceiveing
that they had here infected him with Calvinisme, I was afrayed he should be
altogether subverted.   I repayed the visitt to Mr. Browne and Mr. Forbes,
and consulted with the Doctor concerning the boy Daniell.

March 6.   Being invited, I dined by Mr. James Browne, where, with many of our
countreymen, I was very kindly entertained.   I did writt to my wyfe, son
in law, and Collonell Leviston, in Kyow; to the Boyar, Kniaz Vasily
Vasilivits;* Mr. Vinius; to Lievetennant Collonell Kruger, in Memell; and
Mr. Georg Gray, in Konigsberg; the former in a *coverto* to Mr. Georg Fraser,
in Riga.   I hired a shease, with three horses, to Stetin, for eighty florens.

March 7.   Haveing been at devotion by the Jesuits in Scotland Syde, and taken
leave of them, I dined by Mr. Forbes, and was very well entertained.

March 8.   I made preparations to be gone, haveing gott medicines for Daniell, the
ffriends sending me wyne and provisions on the way in abundance.   I went
and tooke my leave of Mr. Browne, Mr. Forbes, and others.   I changed
here forty ducats for currant money.   Money disbursed in Dantzick: For
two paire of shooes, 5 florens; for a clock to my son, 9 dollers 2 florens;
for dyet and wine, 10 dollers 2 florens 10 pence; drink money to the

* [Golizyn.]

maides, 1 doller 1 floren 14 pence ; coach hire, 4 dollers ; drink money to the coachman, 2 florens ; to the inspector, 3 dollers 16 pence ; linnen washing, 1 floren 13 pence ; to Mr. Brownes maid, 12 pence ; to the doctor, 1 doller ; medicines, 4 dollers ; apothecary, 1 floren 4 pence ; postage of letters, 14 pence.

My father* came to Dantzick. Wee began our journy. We ware con- March 9. woyed by the cheif Scotsmen in Dantzick to Harmans, and was interteaned their by them, being the pleasant place, from Dantzick a half myle, and lodged in Sagorski, two myll and a half from Putsky ; and haveing past through Oliwa, wee left the Carthusiane monastery the left hand. Payed for fyve and a half stoup of bear, sixteen and a half grosse; for beddeng, six grosse ; for brandie, wyn, and wages, three gross and a half.

Through a litle towne called Neu Stat, a myll. This is a little open March 10. towne, with many churches and holy places ; and, two mylles further, baited in a crue ; then two mylles further to the towne of Lawenburg, which is the judiciall city of this country. It hath a brick wall, furnished with many quadrat and round toures, and a river running on the wast syde of it, which could be brought round the towne, bot the hill on the east near it, hinders it from being any considerable fortrese. It, with the whole destrict, belongeth in former tymes to the croune of Polland ; bot, by the treatie of Oliva,† it came to the Elector of Brandiburg, whose territors begin two myll and a half eastward of this towne. Wee rod two mylles further, and lodged in a crue belonging to the Generall . . . . .

All this and yesterdayes journy being through a low walley, barran March 11 sande, and stony ground, with hills on both sydes, cloathed with firre, oaken, and other trees, yet, on the left hand, better furnished. Wee crossed only two or three hills which interrupted the walley passage. Given out at midday, nine grosse for three stoup of bear, and three grosse by the way for bear. Lodged by the river Lupon, in the new red crue, belonging to Cornall Grunku, being four mylls from Stolpa. Payed here, for bear, eages, and bedding, twenty two gross and a half.

By day light, tooke journy to the river Russa, where a gentlemans March 12. house, willage, and myll, one myll and a half ; and dyned in Stolpa, by a

* [This, and a few other pages of the Diary, were obviously written by Gordon's son, at his father's dictation.]   † [23 April, 1660]

river of the same name, a small towne, which is accounted from Dantzick eighteen mylles, and from Statin twenty four. Payed here, for bear and boyling of fish, seventeen grosse; and then, for fish, three grosse. Then, through a bair countrey, to a litle towne called Slage, four mylles. This is the Dukedome of Butow. Here, round this towne, runneth a part of the river called Wippet, and many pleasant woods and grotes. This towne has more larg priwiledges then any towne has. Payed here, in our lodging, two gilders and six grosse; and to the maides, three grosse. This towne hath a ruinus brick wall; the touers or flanks thereof are altogither decayed.

March 13. Wee trawiled through a more fertill and better inhabited countrey, and divers villages, wherein churches, to a little towne called Zanow, two mylles, haveing crossed a marishe passe, which is called Wendan, with a draw bridge on the streame called Grabow. Wee were informed that, towards the sea syde, from whence the two or three last mentioned townes are bot about two mylles distante, the countrey is more fertill; and that, all along from Putsky, there lives boures called *heekell* boures, who are rich, and lives so as in the Werder, with their feilds inclosed. At this a toll is collected by the Electors officers. It is an open place. From thence wee rod over the hill called Goldenborg, from whence a very fair and large prospect over all the countrey round about, and then came downe to the low grounde to the towne Koshlin, a pretty well build towne, haveing on the van syde a river, and on the other syde a marish, environed with a brick wall, in some places decayed; and, without that, a decayed earthen wall, which might be made with ease strong, and that rather a *fassey bray** than any thing els. This countrey is called Cassubia; and all these townes, except Slagel, are called *ampt* townes, and are Electorall judiciary townes, haveing castells, or rather Electorall houses, where are officers called *ampt-men*, who have inspection and goverment over the townes and lands, as well over the rewenue and contribution as matters of justice. Payed at dinner, for egges, bear, and milk, thirteen grosse.

We came to a little towne, Corlin, a large mylle, lettly burned off, where a castle or Electorall house; and crossing the river Persant, at the mouth whereof Colberg, under the castel and towne, all along the river Krum-water on our left hand, wee traviled two mylles. Here about, in the vil-

* [*Fausse braye,* an outwall, or secondary   enceinte exterior and parallel to the main rampart, and considerably below its level.]

lages on the road, and on both sydes, are many gentlemens houses, plea-
sently situated, the countrey being barren.   Wee dined in a crue, belonging
to the Landrat Colberk, a sea port on the right hand, and Treptow, a
kestor, and head of a district, two mylles on the same hand, and payed here
twelve grosse.   We came from hence to Platt, a small towne, with two
Ducall houses in it, haveing, on the right hand, Griffenberg, and it invironed
with a decayed brick wall, a river running by it with milles on it; and
lodged, a great mylle further, in the village Great Sabow, haveing the
towne Quarkenberg, on our right hand, where payed one floren three
grosse, and to the maid a penny.   Here I turned of from the Stetins road,
agreeing with my fuirman to give him ten reichs dollers more to carry me
to Berlin.

To Neugarten, a small towne, with a decayed brick wall, and a castle March 14.
on the north, environed with a moat, and earthen wall with flanks, being
altogither decayed.   To Marsaw, two myles, a little towne, with a decayed
brick wall, and, in most places, a double earthen wall, belonging to a
Countess; and from thence to Starragard, two mylles, the choicest and best
towne in Pomeren, which is distant from Statin fyfteen mylles, from Berlin
seventeen mylles, and from Posna fyfteen mylles.   This, with Stolp, Slauch,
and Koslin, are governed by a townes counsel, and not by *amptmen*, as
others.   On the north syde, it is exceding strong, haveing a brick wall,
with towers, and without that yet earthen, the river Iena making as it were
a double ditch, and running through the towne also, whereon milles.   On
the other syde is a dry moate.   This river falleth in the Dams Sea, and
that in the Oder.   Wee payed, for dinner and bear, one floren two grosse.
Traviled further, where very many, not great, but churche villages, and
lodged in a crue, two mylles.   Payed here, for bear, five stuivers, and one
to the maide; for fish and milk, five grosse.

Wee went over a marishy passe, which the river Plone maketh, where March 15.
the ruines of two forts; and, crossing the bridges made over the brookes,
wee went to the right hand, to Great Rishau, a village, and so kept to the
right hand of Perits, a little towne, lying in a fertile soyle; the ground
here about being very fruitfull.   This Perits is distant from Stargard three
mylles, and from Bon or Banen, a small towne, two mylles.   Wee came
through many villages to Banen, which hath ane altogither decayed brick
wall, and the signe of a double earthen wall, on the wast syde a lake and

marish.   Wee went a great mylle further to the village Marien Thale, where dyned, and payed eight grosse ; for fish at Banen, four grosse. Passing over the borders of Pomeren, a mylle and ane half, we came into the towne of Klein Konigsberg, in the Mark of Brandeborgh, which is distant from Berlin ten mylles.   This is the chieffe towne of the New Mark, which beginneth a half mylle short of this.   This is a well situated place, environed with a brick wall, ruined in many places.   I payed here a dear discretion* of a reichs doller.

March 16.   Wee traviled three mylles, and dyned by the river Oder in Kustrinken, and payed for fish, bear, seventeen stuivers, and service, eighteen stuivers ; and then along the river, through sandy feilds and a wood, to the ferry, which wee crossed, being a fourth of a mylle, and lodged in Fregenwaldt, a small towne, with stone gates, but no walles, where a healing well, gold and silver mynes, lattly found here.   Wee lodged, and payed for bear, eages, and butter, eighteen stuivers.   It is six mylles from Berlin, and from Kustrin as much.

March 17.   Wee dyned in Waurichen, three great miles, and payed nine stuvers. To Berlin, three miles, where payed for two meal for me and people, a doller, and twelve good grosse ; and to the maide, a floren ; to the barber, two good grosse ; to the Dantzick fuirman, forty eight florens, and two florens drink money ; to bring me out of the towne, two florens.   Here meeting with a Hamburger merchant, comeing from the Frankfurts Misse, or market, he perswaded me that wee should travell together, promising to bring me a day sooner to Hamburg, as by the land coach, and better cheap ; he haveing two servants with him, so that wee were seven persons on a waggon.   I went out of Berlin in the shese which brought me from Dantzick, and being a little without the towne, climmed up into a great open waggon, which was something uneasy for us.

March 18.   Over the river Sprea, two mylles, where bridges and tolle, and rested a mylle further in a krou, where wee payed ten good grosse.

March 19.   To Linum, three mylles, where the Swedes lost a battel to the Brandiburgers, *anno* 1680.   To Haklenberg, and the little towne Ferbelin, where toll is taken, wee crossed a bridge, and a long passe.   A mylle on the right hand, wee came by Rutzen, a gentlemans village, where a vynyard ; and dyned in Manker, a village, which is a mylle from Ferbelin.   Here

* [A gratuity to the collector of the frontier toll or custom. See above, p. 115.]

wee hyred fresh horses, haveing payed for those from Berlin eight dollers. Payed here for dinner, nine good grosse. From a little hill, hard by, can be seen thirty six churches. Wee traviled through the village Wildberg, on a small brook, which hath been fortifyed; and through Canser, another village, where a fort hath been without bulwarks, to Wusterhausen, in all two mylles. This is a decayed towne, and situated in an illand, haveing the remnants of a brick wall. To Kirits, one mylle. Here wee payed for bear, and butter, and bread, six good grosse. Here wee tooke fresh horses, haveing payed for the other, two dollers and a half.

Wee rod all the night, and came to Perlberg, a good considerable towne, March 20. four mylles; where, getting fresh horses, wee rod three mylles, and crossed the river Mean, which is the borders of the Elector of Brandiburg his dominions; and, half a mylle further, dyned in a village called Korlous, where payed fourteen grosse. And, on the left hand, wee crossed the river Elbe by bridges. Wee came to a gentlemans house and village, by the river Elbe, called Benug, and to Tripko, a village, being three mylles; where getting fresh horses, we came to Neuhausen by the river Elbe, a village, two mylles; where, taking fresh horses again, wee passed in the night tyme through a litle towne called Bitsiburg, belonging to the Duks of Saxen Lauenburg, being two mylles; and, by day light, came to Lauenberg, a mylle. This March 21. towne giveth title to a brench of the Saxonian family, who have a palace here. Then, a mylle further, wee changed horses in a village. Wee went three mylles further to a towne called Baredorffe, a little towne belonging to the cityes of Hamburgh and Lubeck, but now the Duk of Luneburgs people had by force taken possession of it, and lived upon free quarter. Here I was stopped untill I had shouen my passe. Then passing thorou, we came to Hamburg, two mylles. In this passage we see many pleasent houzes and gardens belonging to the towne of Hamburg, as also the small fort, where the Duck of Luneburgs people and the Hamburges had lattly a bloody rencounter. This Hamburgh is most pleasantly situated on the river Elbe, most convenient for traffick, as being in the very center of the north parts of Europe, and wanteth no convenience but good neighbours.

This day, a man and a woman, a burger of the towne, being the womans March 22. master, for murthering, were carted from the prisone to the house where the murder was comitted; and there before this house, with hotte pinsers, the flesh was torren out of their armes, and from thence ware carted to the place of justice without the towne, and there broken and layed on wheeles. This evening, I was plentifully feasted by Mr. Nathanael Cambridge, where was the English resident, and the principalle merchants of the English company.

March 23.

Haveing bespok a coach, at the rate of a doller a day, I took coach and rod to Altenaw, and from thence to the river syde, and went aboard of an English ship which was bound for London. I gave to bring me aboard, a mark Lips; and to the seamen drink money, a half a doller. I received letters from my son in law and Mr. Vinius, the first dated from Kyow, and the other, the seventh February, from Mosko. The English resident came after noone and gave me a visitt.

March 24.

Being invited, I supped with the English resident, where ware the principalle merchants of the English company, and ware plentifully entertained. Mr. Cambridge agreed with the skipper, for fraught, meat, drink, and use of his cabben, for me and three persons, to London, for ten pund sterling.

March 25.

Being Annunciation Day, I went by coach to Altenaw, and heard devotion.

March 26.

I did writt to Mosko by post, to the Boyar, Kniaz Vasily Vasiliovitz, to Mr. Vinius, to Mr. Hartman, Collonell von Mengden, and to my wyfe, all under the *coverto* of Mr. von Sowme, addressed to Mr. Vinius. Wrott also to Madame Crawfuird, in a *coverto* to Mr. Gray, addressed to Mr. Adie,* to Dantzick.

March 27.

I supped by Mr. Robert Jolly, and was very kyndly entertained.

March 28.

Being invited, I was at a christning feast by Mr. Foster, where were the English resident and the principalle English men and women. Here was plenty and variety.

March 29.

Being impatient to stay for a faire wind, I resolved to travel by land, and tooke boat in a wery stormy day; and not being able to go downe the river to Blankness, wee went to Harborg, being reckoned a large mylle, and haveing Mr. Jolly in company. I payed to the ferrymen four mark Lipses. Wee hired a waggon to Buckstehude, being three mylles, paying for each mylle a halfe a doller, according to the ordainance in those places, for a vaggon withe two, three, or four, or five persons. This Harburgh is an open towne, yet hath a decayed wall from the land syde, a castle being

---

* [Probably the Alexander Aidy, who had a birth brieve from the baillies of Aberdeen,   in 1670. See the Miscellany of the Spalding Club, vol. v. p. 348.]

by the river, well fortifyed with a wall, bastions, and moats, and belonged to the Duke of Luneborg. Wee traviled through a very barren countrey to Buckstehude, where, at an old monastery without the towne, wee hyred horses to bring us forward, and ware cheated by the fuirman; for he, pretending bad way, said, he could not bring us speadely forward, nor carry us thorow, with one waggon, bot would neads have another, desiring for that only a discration. So wee agreed with him for three dollers and a half to Closter Sewen, being four mylles, whither wee came about eleven aclock at night; haveing payed in the old closter, for bear and eages, ten Lipses shilling. In Sewen, wee had nothing; yet, for sitting be the fyre, I payed for each person a Lips shilling, and to the waggen master here, for each person, two grosse. Here we ware forced to take two waggens, and thereafter at Ottersberg, they drawing the practise of the Buckstehudes fuirman unto a consequens, and so payed double fraught to Bremen, to wit, for each mylle a doller.

A litle befor seven a clock, wee came to Ottersborg, which is three March 30. mylles, and payed there, for wyne, bear, and eages, a mark; and getting fresh horses, wee passed by the castle, which is pretty well fortifyed; and crossing a river by bridge, and a long marish passe, wee came to Bremen, being three mylles, and payed for each of these stages three dollers.

Bremen is a towne very pleasantly situated on the river Weser, and well fortifyed, yet not thriving so well under the Swedish yoke as befor. Here I was kindly entertained in the wyne seller* by Mr. Spense, and then took waggon, and came in the evening to Delmenhorst, being a long mille; for which I payed a doller and a half, according to the ordainance, which is to be seen and read every where in the common innes. This is a little open towne, with a large pallace or castle by it, and belonged formerly to the Dukes of Oldenburg, but now, by hereditary right, is possessed by the King of Danmark. About ten a clock, getting fresh horses, wee traveled all the night, and, about six a clock, wee came to Oldenburg, a towne pretty well fortifyed, on the river Hund; the Dukes pallace being also fortifyed, with a moat and draw bridges. Here I payed for this stage, being four mylles, for four persons, a hundred and sixty grutt, or two doller and sixteen grutte; and to the fuirman, drink money, eight grutte. I payed here, for brackfast, thirty three grutte, which is twenty two Lips shilling. Wee traveled

---

* [The wine cellars, under the ancient town hall, renowned for their old hock.]

through a pretty pleasant countrey, and, baiting half way to Apen, where payed for bear six Lipses shilling, wee came to Apen, being four mylles, and payed the same fraught as at the other stage, and for bear here, four Lipses shilling.   Wee passed by a castle, and, little further, a small fort, being the borders of the Dutchy of Oldeborg; and then came unto East Frease Land, by a little fort, to an open towne, Detteren, being a mylle, for which I payed fraught, a doller, and for bear here, four Lipses shillings.   And then passing by another castle, environed with a moat, and earthen wall without bullwarks, haveing on the east syde a hornwork with a moat; then passing along by the river Ems, through very bad watery way, wee came to the open towne Lier, being a mille, late in the night, and payed fraught, a doller and ten stuivers, where I did meet Mr. Leslie and Mr. Wood.   There I stayed all night, and payed, for two kans of bear and lodging, eighteen stuivers, and two stuivers to the maid; four stuivers to the postmaster.

April 1.   Wee mounted our waggon, and passing along the Eems by the fort Lieroort, where crossing the ferry over the Eems, which is by the fort, and a quarter of mile from Lier, where I gave drink money only, six stuivers, and came to Panda, a mile and a halfe, and then to New Skonse, the first garrison of the Hollanders on that syde, where, by a late inundation, many houses and fields are drowned.   I payed here, for fraught, fyve florens; drink money to the fuirman, three stuivers.   From hence to Winschotten, a Hollands towne, one and a half mile.   Payed fuir, a doller; spent there for bear, six stuivers.   Here wee took boat, and went to Groeningen, being six houres, as they call it here, and payed fraught, for each person, eleven stuivers; for bread, two stuivers; to bring our baggage, on a sledge, through the towne to the other boat, twelve stuivers.   Albeit it was evening, yet wee went into the boat and came to Strowbush, three and a half houres, paying fraught, nine stuivers a man, and for carrying my baggage to the other boat, four stuivers.   From thence to Dockum, four houres, and payed fraught, nine stuivers a peece, and for carrying my baggage to the other boat, a stuiver a man.   Here, and in the night, extra, for drink and cakes, sixteen stuivers.

April 2.   From hence to Leewarden, four miles.   Payed fraught for us fowre, forty stuivers; for transporting baggage, six stuivers; for bread and bier, six stuivers; to the boy, a stuiver.   From hence to Bolswaert, four houres. Payed for bier, two stuiver; for fraught, forty stuiver; for baggage, six

stuiver.   From thence to Workum, four houres, in the common boat.
Payed for fraught, sixteen stuiver.   From hence wee hired a large vesell,
and payed, all of us, ten florens, being the ordinary fraught; my share comeing to three florens fourteen stuivers; drink money, six stuiver; toll for us,
two stuiver each; for bringing my baggage to my lodging, eight stuiver.
Wee came to Amsterdam in the morning early, being twelve houres from April 3.
Workum.   Payed here, for trimming, eight stuiver; and at the Doll, for
seeing pictures and wyne, twelve stuiver; at the Swane, for wyne, thirty
stuiver; for a trunk, seven floren six stuiver; for a lock, nyne stuiver; for
a hatt, three floren eighteen stuiver; for dyet in two dayes, nyne
florens; drink money, twelve stuiver; for washing some linnings, fourteen
stuivers.

    Being Easter, I heard devotion.   After dinner, went and saw the Doll, April 4.
the ships, the Old Church, and the Rhathouse, the principall streets and
buildings of the city.

    I went early to boate, and came to Harlam, Leyden, and to the Hague, April 5.
paying the ordinary fraught; and for supper and breakfast, seven floren
eight stuivers; for coach hire, twenty foure stuiver; wages, twelve stuiver,
in the signe of the Scots Armes.

    I went by boat to Delft and Rotterdam, and lodged in the signe of April 6.
Dundee; fraught to Delft, ten stuiver; to Rotterdam, twenty stuiver.   Here
I did meet with many good ffriends, and stayed two nights.   Bought lace to
kravates and rufles for fyfty foure florens; payed in my lodging, eight florens
twelve stuiver; wages, twelve stuiver; extra, twenty six stuiver; for eleven
bookes, twenty eight stuiver; for wine on the way, a doller; for other provisions and necessaryes, foure florens; for breakfast that day, twenty six April 7.
stuiver; and for fraught, twenty shillings sterling; for bed, fyve shillings;
wages, fyve shillings.

    Wee sailed downe the river Schie, and anchored anent Delft Sluis.   April 8.

    Wee anchored befor the Briell, where, and at the Delft Sluis, it cost me April 9.
twenty eight stuiver.

    Wee weighed anchor, and went out with the morning tyde, with April 10.
April 11.
difficulty getting over the flattes, and then with a pretty gale of wind made
towards the English coast, a sight whereof wee had the next day called
Lands End, which is reckoned to be forty eight leagues.   Aboard this ship
were many passengers, most whereof French, fleeing, as they said, for their

religion.* At night wee cast anchor in the rivers mouth, not farr from Margat.

April 13.

Seeing small hopes of getting up the river in hast, I, with some other gentlemen, caused our selves be put on shoare, and so did go on foot, about three miles to Margat, where, and at putting on shoare, I payed two shillings six pence. Here I hired two horses to Canterbury, paying for them, nyne shillings, and to the boy, six pence, it being fyfteen miles; for wine, six pence; for post horses to Sittingbourne, being twelve miles, eight shillings. At Sittingbourne, an old woman gave me retour horses, for which I payed but fyve shillings, and to the hostler, four pence. I had not ridden four miles, when one of the horses wearyed, so that I had enough ado to gett him driven to Rochester, where I was forced to lodge, paying for lodging, bier, and brandy, sixteen pence; for horse, sixteen pence; drink money, ten pence.

April 14.

I rode away befor day, and with great trouble gott the wearyed horse brought to Gravesend, being from Rochester fyve miles, and from Sitting-bourn, thirteen miles. Payed to a youth, who showed us the way, six pence, and for breakfast, fyfteen pence. I bespoke a paire of oares, and payed for myself, son, and a litle boy, whom I found in the boate, and had nothing to pay, six pence a peece. I went into the Mitre taverne, in Gracious Street,† and, calling for a bottle of wine, and some bread, I sent to seeke Mr. Meverell, and Mr. Wulffe, and Mr. Spence. But none of them was to be found; wherefor, paying sixteen pence, I tooke up my lodging in the same street. All these I sent for came to me in the evening, and my cousin, Alexander Gordon, from whom I had the present transactions. Here I payed for a gazet, one penny; for supper and lodging, eight shillings seven pence; drink money, fyve pence.

April 15.

Mr. Meverell, and my cousin Gordon, comeing to me in the morning, I tooke coach, and road to Yorke Buildings, and tooke my lodging by John Hayes, whom I employed to make a suite of cloaths for me, according to the fashion. Generall Drummond, and other friends, came to visitt me. The Generall told my Lord Melfort,‡ of my being come, who, haveing showne the King thereof, His Sacred Majestie ordered me to be brought to him the next morning, about eight a clock. I furnished my self this day

* [The Edict of Nantes had been revoked six months before.]
† [Gracechurch Street.]
‡ [One of the two principal Secretaries of State for Scotland.]

with severall necessaryes, and having received from Mr. Meverell seventy two punds sterling, I payed for a periwigg, seven punds sterling; for a hatt, two pund ten shillings; for silk stockens, twelve shillings; for shooes, fyve shillings; for a pair of sleeves and handkerchieffe, ten shillings; to a barber for trimming, one shilling; for overgilt buckle, one shilling; for dinner, fyve shillings six pence; for swords, fourteen shillings; for three west belts, six shillings; for one to my self, fyve shillings; for makeing some kravats, ruffles, and small lace to the ruffles, ten shillings; for coach hire, eighteen pence.

About eight a clock, Generall Drummond gave me notice that it was April 16. tyme. I tooke a chaire, and went downe to his lodging, and with him to Court, to my Lord Melforts lodging, who, after halfe a houres stay, introducted me to His Majestie, in the comeing out of his bedchamber, who was pleased to receive me very graciously. And haveing kissed His Majesties hand with the usuall ceremonies, and a short compliment, His Majestie asked many questions concerning the Tzars, the countrey, the state of effaires, the militia and government, as also of my jorney and many other particulars. His Majestie going in to the Queens syde, I had occasion to be welcomed by the Scots nobility who were there; and afterwards, whilst I attended His Majestie, walking in the Parke, he was pleased to tell the Prince Georg* of me, to whom also I was addressed. I dined in a Dutche house in the Pell Mell. Expended this day, drink money to the taylors jorneymen, two shillings six pence; chaire hire, one shilling; coach hire, three shillings; to servants, eight pence.

I tooke a chaire in the morning, and went with Lievetennant Generall April 17. Drummond to Court, and waited upon the King, in the Park, at his walke, as also in the evening, haveing this day payed my respects to some noblemen, at their lodgings. Expended this day, for chaire hire, eighteen pence; for dinner, with wine, four shillings; to my servants, twelve pence; coach hire, eighteen pence.

Being Sunday, I went to St. Jameses, and heard devotion, and dined, April 18. with other gentlemen, at Mrs. Crosses, and payed for dinner and wine, fyve shillings, for myself and son; to servants this day, eighteen pence, and at night a shilling.

It being very inconvenient and expensive to stay in the lodging where April 19.

* [Prince George of Denmark, husband of the Princess Anne.]

I was, because of hireing chaires or coaches to and from the Court, I tooke up a lodging in the Pellmell, at the signe of the Crowne, paying for a dineing room, chamber, and a roome for my servants, eleven shillings a weeke.   Here I had the convenience of a lane and gate into St. James his Parke, which was both pleasant and saveing.   This day I recovered my baggage from the shipp, which cost me in all, eight shillings four pence. Payed also for shoos to Shenka and Daniell, six shillings four pence; for buckles to both, one shilling; to a sick Scotsman, one shilling; for chaire hire, one shilling; for dinner, two shillings; to servants, two pence; tea, four pence.

April 20.   I went to Lincolne Inne Fields, haveing, with Sir James Kenedy,* James Lindesay, and Captaine Seton, hired a coach, to convoy the Duke of Hamilton, Generall Drummond, and Sir Georg Lockart, the President of the Session, who, haveing been sent for by the King, to prepare them for the ensuing Parliament, returned this day.†   We convoyed them to Barnet, being ten miles, and dined there; and, towards evening, returned to London. Expended this day, for trimming, one shilling; to sonne and servants, two shillings six pence; for tea, six pence; coach hire and wages, fyve shillings six pence; dinner, four shillings.

April 21.   Attending His Majestie at his walke in Arlington Gardens, he was pleased, walking up and downe the alley, to speake with me about halfe a houre, enquiring particularly armes, and manner of warring, the business of Czegrin,‡ and many other things.   Expended this day, for dinner, three shillings six pence; to servants, two shillings; at night, fourteen pence.

April 22.   According to my ordinary custome, I went and waited on the King, at his walking in the Parke.   The King caused try the new invention of the pumpe, made by Sir Robert Gordon,§ but some things breaking therein, it

---

* [The Conservator of the Privileges of the Scottish nation, in the Low Countries.]

† [Sir John Lauder notes that on the 26th of March, 1686, 'the Duke of Hamilton, the President of the Session, and Generall Drummond, part for London, being called thither by the King, to receive his commands anent the Parliament, because the first two showed some aversion in the secret committee, to consent to the rescinding the penall laws against Popery; and the Chancellor [the Earl of Perth] had procured their upcalling, to cajole them over their scruples.' They returned to Edinburgh on the 27th of April. [Fountainhall's Historical Notices, vol. ii. pp. 714, 718.]

‡ [Tschigirin, in the defence of which Gordon distinguished himself in 1678.]

§ [Sir Robert Gordon, the grandson of the historian of Sutherland, and the third baronet of Gordonstoun, born in 1647, died in 1704. According to an unprinted account of the family, quoted by Sir Robert Douglas, he 'travelled much into foreign countries for his improvement, was a man of extensive learning and knowledge, and particularly skilled in mechanics and chemistry, which sufficiently appears by the long correspondence by letters he kept with that celebrated philosopher, Mr. Boyle. He contrived a curious machine or pump for raising of water, which was

tooke no effect. Expended this day, for tea, four pence; for dinner, three shillings eight pence; to the servants, with my sonne, two shillings six pence. I went and saw Westminster Abbay, and the monuments in King Hary the Sevenths Chappel.

Being St. Georg his day, wee heard devotion, and a elegant sermon in April 23. St. Jameses. The Queen, being somewhat recovered, walked to Hide Parke, through St. James Parke, in her coach, attended by fyve others, and a troope of guards. Expended this day, for dinner, four shillings four pence; at night, nineteen pence; to my sonne and servants, two shillings six pence, being a shilling to my sonne, and six pence to each servant.

I went by water to London, and spoke with my ffriends upon the Ex- April 24. change, who entertained me with a glasse of wine, in the Ship and Castle. Expended for tea, two pence; for oares, a shilling; for coach hire back againe, eighteen pence; for servants, two shillings; at night, fyve pence; for trimming me, six pence.

Heard devotion at St. Jameses, where was the King and Queen, who April 25. dined publickely this day, with musick, at which I stayed, and was forced to dine alone afterwards, all my ordinary company haveing dined already. Expended this day, for dinner, with sonne and servants, six shillings eight pence; at night, to the servants, a shilling; for my self, fyve pence.

Hearing that the King intended to go to Chattam, I procured a note from April 26. my Lord Melfort to be taken aboard of one of the Kings yachts; and so, accordingly, went in coach to Billings Gate, the King being at dinner in the Towre by my Lord Dartmouth; and, hireing a boate, wee came to Detford, and was received aboard of a yacht, which wee could have done without a note, there being six yachts, and very few attendants, with the King. Being come to Tilberry skonce, over against Gravesand, the King went a shoare, and went round the fortress, takeing a view of every thing, and asked my opinion concerning the fortifications and oppurtenances, which, as reasonable, I extolled. The King made hast to the yacht, and was saluted

---

tried in the fleet and highly approved of, and found far to exceed any thing of that kind then known, both for the facility of working, and the quantity of water it discharged; but, as neither the inventor, nor the present possessor [his son, the fourth baronet, who died in 1772], had ever an offer of any encouragement suitable to the merit and usefulness of the thing, it still remains a secret in the family.' (Douglas' Baronage of Scotland, pp. 8, 9.) An underground chamber at Gordonstoun is shewn as his laboratory, and he lives in the popular traditions of the neighbourhood as a mighty wizard—the Michael Scott of Murray-land.

from the fort by all the cannon, as also from all the ships, comeing downe the river, and the Tower at parting; but the yacht wherein I was being gone farr downe, wee recovered another, and was taken in, and so sailed downe till within some miles of Sherness. This day, expended for breakfast, two shillings six pence; for coach hire, eighteen pence; for oares to the yacht, one shilling; for oares from Tilberry to the yacht, a shilling.

April 27.

About six a clock, the King went ashoare to Shirness, and went round the fortifications, and, being in the top of a tower, asked me what I thought of the fortress? I answered, that it was exceeding well contrived, and well furnished, and that I wondered how the Dutch durst adventure up towards Chattam,* haveing such obstacles in their way. The King said, No, you are mistaken; there was no such thing as this then, only a small skonce, and ill furnished. I replyed, that it gave me greater cause to wonder that such a considerable station for ships should have been, in such a tyme, so ill secured. The King replyed, You say well; indeed, they have learned us witt. And being come into the governours house, and takeing a standing breakfast, he asked me many more things, as what armes we used in Russia? and what discipline? as also what family of the Gordons I was of? if of the Aberdeens family? and many other things. The King made hast aboard, and, our yacht boat being gone, I hired a pair of oares, which, because of the contrar wind, could not gett rowed up to the yachts, who were all under saile; which the King seeing, sent the boat himself was brought aboard in to take me in, which put me aboard of one of the yachts, which cost me fyve shillings. Wee plyed up the river Medway to Chattam, where going ashoare, the King was saluted, as at Shirnesse, by all the cannons from the forts and shipps. The King viewed the shipps which were a building, and then see fyve companies of Collonell Kirks regiment exercized; the Lievetennant Collonell, who exercised them, being on horseback, and the King, with all his attendants, on foot. The King missed six men out of the company of grenadiers, which the Lievetennant Collonell excused. The King, haveing dined here, went aboard of his yacht, which, in coemeing up, had broken her boyersprit on one of the great ships, whereof many lay in this river; and all the forts were now so well furnished with cannon, that neither Dutch nor devil dare adventure againe. I walked on foot to the towne, a

* [In June, 1667.]

litle way, and being four, wee hired a coach for eight shillings to Gravesend, where, after supper, wee haveing hired a boat for six shillings, to London. Expended this day, at Shirness, for the boat, fyve shillings; for breakfast in Chattam, eighteen pence; coach hire to Gravesend, two shillings; where wee tooke coach, six pence; supper in Gravesend, two shillings; oares to London, eighteen pence.

It being a great storme on the river, wee gott to London about four April 28. a clock in the morning. I went immediately to bed, and riseing about nine a clock, went to Court, and waited on the King at Privy Staires, who came in his barge, and landed about eleven a clock. I dined with my ordinary company, and expended this day, for dinner, two shillings two pence; to sonne and servants, with the tyme I had been away, seven shillings; for a booke, two shillings; for makeing of some kravats, lace to ruffles, ten shillings; for a kravat, seventeen shillings; for three travelling kravats, nine shillings; for washing of my sonnes linnens, three shillings. I payed also the taylors bill, being twenty six pund; for house meale* by him, six shillings; for stockens to the page, two shilling; for shooes to him, three shillings. I sent a paire of sables to my Lady Melfort.

I went by water to London, and haveing done my business upon the Ex- April 29. change, I returned about eight a clock at night, and went to Court; and, about ten a clock, meeting with Mr. Marr,† he told me that the shipp wherein my sonne should go to Dunkirk in was gone downe to Gravesend, and that, by four a clock next morning, he must be gone. So that, the tyme being pressing, I came home, and, albeit late, I bought some linnens for him, and made all things ready. Expended this day, for oares to London, six pence; for wyne there, two shillings two pence; for a ken,‡ with hand, nine shillings; for coach hire to returne, eighteen pence; for sonne and servants, two shillings; for two shirts to my sonne, seven shillings.

About four a clock, haveing sent for Mr. Marr, wee went and tooke April 30.

---

*[House rent. Gordon had hired the tailor's lodging for two or three days. See above, pp. 126, 127.]

†[A friend, to whose intimate knowledge of the history of his church in Scotland I have been more than once indebted the Reverend George A. Griffin of New Abbey, informs me that "Mr. Marr" was but another name for Father James Forbes, a member of the Society of Jesus, who was superior of its Scottish mission in 1679, was appointed one of the King's chaplains at Holy-rood in November, 1686, and became Rector of the Scotch College at Douay, after the Revolution of 1688. See Dr. Oliver's Biographical Memoirs of the Society of Jesus, pp. 21, 107; Letters of James, Earl of Perth, to his sister, the Countess of Errol, p. 104.

Mr. Griffin adds that, neither the names of Gordon's sons, John and James, nor the name of his cousin, Alexander, are to be found in the roll of students at Douay.]

‡[A cane.]

oares at Yorke Buildings. I convoyed my sonne neare the bridge, and then returned on foot, being early, and no coach to be had. Expended this day, to James* on the way, fyve pund sterling ; at Gravesend for him, seven shillings ; for two bookes, one shilling ; for dinner, three shillings two pence ; for wine at night, two shillings two pence ; for tea, eight pence ; to servants, two shillings.

May 1.

Haveing promissed to visit my good ffriend Meverell, and his family, at Chersey, I went in coach to Stanes, fifteen miles, and walked from thence to Chersey on foot, being two miles, where I was cordially welcomed. Expended this day, for washing of linnens, three shillings two pence ; for a red trimming, fyve shillings ; for boots and spurrs, seventeen shillings six pence ; for breakfast, eight pence ; for coach hire, for my self and servant, seven shillings ; drink money to the coachman, one shilling ; in Stanes, three pence ; for a guide, six pence ; for trimming, six pence.

May 2.

I passed the tyme in reading and walking, and seeing the great multitudes of sheep which were brought thither to the market, and which was to be there the next day.

May 3.

I bought a horse from Robin Jacobs, for seven pund sterling ; and a jewell, for ten pund sterling ; and a mare, for three pund ten shillings. And giveing drink money, three shillings, after breakfast, I rode to London, intending to take my leave of the King as soone as possible, which I was perswaded to delay, upon the account of nothing being heard from the Scots Parliament.†

May 4.

I dispatched my servants, with such baggage as I had by me (my trunkes from Amsterdam not being come), to the shipp, which was already at Gravesend. This day the English Parliament conveened, and was prorogued to the twenty third of the ensuing November. I went to the citty, and by the way did meet the Scots Batallion, marching through the citty, well cloathed, armed, and disciplined. I tooke my leave of ffriends in the citty, and of Esquyre Hebden in the Fleet, and, returning, saw the tragedy of Hamlet, Prince of Denmark, acted in Whitehall, in the presence of the King, Queen, and all the Court. Expended this day, for fraught and meat

* [His son.]

† [It had met on the 29th of April, but adjourned to the 6th of May, when the debate on toleration of the Roman Catholic religion began. The subject had been touched upon in the interval, as well in a committee appointed to draw up an answer to the King's letter, as in the meeting of the Lords of the Articles.]

for two servants to Scotland, forty shillings; on the way to them, twelve shillings; for my two servants dyet, whilst I was at Chersey, four shillings; for dinner, eight pence; tea and ale, six pence.

I received from Mr. Meverell, money which made up his account to me, May 5. of one hundred and forty five punds sterling. This night, the letters came from Scotland of the Parliaments actions, and how it was scarsely carryed, that, in their answer to the Kings letter, they should call the kings ffriends Roman Catholicks.* I payed this day, for dinner, thirteen and a half pence; for tea, one penny; for wine, two shillings; and visiteing a woman in childbed, it cost me, wages, three shillings. I writt letters to Russia to my ffriends, according to the copies

I began to looke about for furniture, and Maior Dougall bought for me May 6. a sadle, with furniture and sadle cloth, for seventeen shillings ten pence. Gave to a poor widdow, two shillings; to Shenka, four pence; for trimming, six pence; for dinner, with wine, two shillings six pence; to the boy, at night, four pence; for carrying things to the boate, one shilling. I saw the Scots Batallion exercized in the Hide Parke befor the King and Queen, and saw the comedy, Rehearsal,† acted.

I gave to Mr. Marre twenty pund sterling, for my sonnes maintenance May 7. at Doway, and three pund more, for his first suit. Spent for coffy, this day, six pence. I hired another more private lodging, at a brasiers in Pellmell, pay-

---

* [These letters must have referred to what passed in the committee on the King's letter, or among the Lords of the Articles; or must have reported the anticipated result of the division of the 6th of May. "The great debate,' says Sir John Lauder, " arose upon the appellation of koman Catholicks, which the [King's] letter gave the Papists. It was urged, that it was not fit for a Protestant parliament to give them this title, which they assumed to themselves as their due . . . I proposed it might run, 'those commonly called koman Catholiques' . . . The Chancellor [the Earl of Perth] called this a nicknaming of the King; and proposed it might run in general terms, thus: ' as to those subjects your Majesty has recommended.' The Archbishop of Glasgow's overture was: ' That we might call them koman Catholicks, not as acknowledging them to be such, but only as a bare repetition of the King's words.' So it went to the vote, and by the plurality of 37 votes, it carried that these words [koman Catholicks] should stand in the answer."

(Fountainhall's Historical Notices vol. ii. pp. 720, 721) The Scottish Parliament, at that time, numbered about 180 members. The King was so intent on this matter, that, on the 19th of April, he gave orders to his Commissioner, the Earl of Murray, "that no act be touched with the sceptre, or the Royal assent given thereto, till the act concerning the Roman Catholicks be past, except acts of dissolution." Subsequently, on the 12th of May, the King sent additional instructions to the Commissioner, "requiring him, if the Parliament shall refuse to pass the Act relating to the Roman Catholics, to dissolve them immediately, without passing any of the public acts mentioned in his instructions." (Abstracts of the Papers relating to Scotland, which past his Majesty's hand from 9th April, 1686, to 25th Feb , 1686-7, nn. 39, 69, MS)]

† [The well-known farce, written by the Duke of Buckingham, the author of Hudibras, Martin Clifford of the Charter House, and Sprat, the friend and biographer of Cowley. It was first acted in December, 1671.]

ing, for a chamber, fyve shillings six pence a weeke, and a bed for my servant.

May 8.   I removed to my new lodging, paying, for house hyre and some bookes which I bought, two pund eighteen shillings three pence; for dinner, two shillings six pence; for a trunk maile, seven shillings six pence; for two paire of stokens, eight shillings; for candle, six pence.

May 9.   I heard masse and sermon at St. Jameses; and payed for dinner, two shillings three pence, and at night, eight pence. I bought some necessaries, as a cover to a sadle, bosses and rings thereto, foure shillings; for combes and inkhorne, one shilling six pence; for fyre, three pence; for dinner, two shillings two pence.

May 10.   The English Parliament did againe meet, and was againe prorogued to the twenty second of November, by the Lord Chancellour, there being, in the upper house, twenty four, and in the lower, one hundred and thirty members.

May 11.   I spoke to the Secretary of State, that he might informe His Sacred Majestie, that I desired to take my leave, who told me the same day, that the King said, I should have private audience. Befor I went, the King touched many persons diseased with that called the Kings Evill,* in the first chamber of presence. Payed, this day, for coffy, eight pence; for dinner, two shillings; at night, one shilling six pence; to my servant, six pence; for a booke, four pence.

May 12.   I dined in the Dutch house by St. Jameses, and payed, for dinner, one shilling six pence; for a booke, two shillings; for ale, foure pence; and for coffy, three pence. This day, Prince George, with his Princesse and family, went for Windsore, and much of the Kings plenishing or furniture went thither.

May 13.   Newes came from Windsore that the Princess, the evening befor, was

---

* [See, on this subject, the very learned and elaborate paper of Mr E. L Hussey, 'On the Cure of Scrofulous Diseases attributed to the Royal Touch,' in the Archaeological Journal, vol. x pp. 187-211, 337, (Lond. 1853.)

It would appear, from a passage in the Diary of Mr. James Melville, (pp. 657-8), that our Scottish Kings had not been accustomed to touch in their own realm, and that when King James I. became King of England he somewhat unwillingly consented to the rite, for some politick reasons, lest, omitting the ceremony used by the Kings of France, he should thereby lose some of the title which he had to the kingdom and crown of France.'

Even at the end of the last century, it was believed, in the Highlands that certain septs of the great clan of MacDonald were able, by their touch, to cure the *glacagh*, a disease of the lungs or chest, called, also 'the MacDonald's disease,' in the same way as scrofula was called 'the King's Evil.' The MacDonalds, it need scarcely be added, were supposed to be sprung from the Kings of the Isles.]

delivered of a daughter; wherefor, the King, who intended not to have gone thither befor Saturneday, prepared to be gone the same day. I thought to have gott audience, but the suddaine departure of the Kings hindred; wherefor I resolved to ride the next morning to Windsore, where I promised to my self the better convenience.   And haveing this day heard devotion at St. Jameses, and about three a clock attended the King at his departure, I went about my other business, and bought a sadle for eight shillings.   Gave to the servant, six pence ; and at night, eight pence.

I rose early, and haveing payed the ostler for eleven nights, at the rate May 14. of one shilling six pence for each horse *per diem*, and given to the ostler, sixteen pence wages, I mounted and rode to Windsore, through the ordinary roade, it being deep way.   About ten aclock I came thither, and haveing shifted myself, I went to Court, and found the King walking in the Parke, and ready to returne.   His Sacred Majesty was graciously pleased to tell to the Earl of Fewersham what I was, and then asked me if I had ever been there befor, and what I thought of the place?   I answered to His Majesties satisfaction.   In going through the roomes, His Sacred Majesty told me that in the evening he would speake with me.   So haveing heard devotion, and seen the King dine, I went to my lodging and dined, and about four a clock went to the Court againe, and passed the tyme in viewing the large and well decored roomes of the Palace, and went afterwards into the Parke, and viewed all the walkes and conveniences of it ; this being a most de-lightful place, and haveing a most delicate prospect.   About six a clocke, the King, with the Queen, came to walk in the Parke, accompanyed with the Prince Georg, and after ane houres divertissement, returned.   In the evening, about sunsett, the King being in one of the great chambers, called me to a corner of the roome, and entered in a large discourse with me, enquireing where, and how long, I had served abroad, and many other things relating to military effaires ; to all which I answered as well as I could.   He was graciously pleased to tell me, that I should make hast to returne, and that he would have a care of me, and do for me what he could ; which discourse lasted above halfe ane houre, and then dismissing me, about halfe ane houre thereafter, I seeing his Majesty going towards his closet, went, and sitting downe on my knee, His Majesty graciously gave me his hand to kisse.   And haveing not seen any of our Scots nobility, or any acquaintance to address me to the Queen, I begged of His Majesty the honour to kiss the

Queens hand; whereat his Majestie smileing, was pleased to conduct me to the Queen, who was sitting at a table with some ladies at cardes; and the King acquainting her, beckoned to me to come nearer, where I had the honour to kiss Her Majesties hand; which gave occasion of discourse to the nobility and courtiers, some saying, This gentleman hath gott a fine introductor indeed. The King, in passing by, was pleased to say to me, You must not stay long there, and wee shall write to the Tzaars about you. Prince Georg being in the same roome, I went and tooke my leave of his Royall Highness, in a short complement, first in Dutch, and then in English; to the which he made litle answer.* I went to my lodging, and haveing payed for my horses and my self, six shillings six pence, and wages, two groats, and sleeped about foure houres, I tooke horse, and returned to London, and made

May 15. ready to be gone; and the same day tooke my leave of my Lord Me'fort, and diverse other noblemen. Payed for dinner, nineteen pence; for coffy, foure pence; to my servant, six pence, and at night, two shillings.

May 16. I tooke my leave of my Lord Middleton,† and diverse others. I heard devotion at the Venetian Ambassadours, and dined with many ffriends at the Dutch house, by St. Jameses, and were merry, where it cost me eleven shillings. At night, wee did meet with some ffriends at a taverne, and were very merry, where, contrar to expectation, Sir Robert Gordon‡ payed the shott.

May 17. I rose early, and payed in my lodging, for lodging, six shillings; wages, two shillings; for horse meat, nine shillings; for ale, fourteen pence; wages to the ostler, one shilling. And so, takeing leave of the kind people of the house, I, with the Laird of Lochyiell, called Sir Ewin Cameron,§ tooke coach and went to Smithfield, where wee fitted our selves with some small things, for which I payed here, three shillings ten pence; for breakfast with my cousin Alexander, two shillings four pence; and for horse meat, a shilling. About midday, we tooke jorney, and came to Waltham Crosse, twelve miles, where we rested, and payed for our selves and horses, two shillings six pence.

---

* ['I have tried Prince George sober.' said King Charles II., ' and I have tried him drunk; and, drunk or sober, there is nothing in him.']

† [Charles, second Earl of Middleton. in the peerage of Scotland, one of the principal Secretaries of State for England.]

‡ [Of Gordonstoun. See above, p. 128]

§ [Lochiel was at Court on the business of his lands in Lochaber—an old cause of controversy between the Camerons and the Gordons. On this occasion, MacConnel Dhui was backed by the powerful influence of his brother-in-law, Robert Barclay, the author of the Apology for the Quakers. His Jacobite biographer has concealed that Lochiel himself was believed to regard the Friends not without favour, and that one of his daughters was a member of their Society.]

It is needles to make a discription of all the particular places by and through which I passed in this jorney, which can be seen at full and large in printed bookes, as in Cambden* and others. Let it suffice, once for all, that it is a most pleasant and fertile countrey, and scarsely any poverty to be discerned in the meanest cottage, but everywhere plenty and chearful-nes. Wee rode eight miles further to Ware, where wee lodged in the posthouse, and, the next morning, payed for supper, foure shillings six pence; for our three horses, foure shillings six pence; for a pint of sack in the morning, a shilling; wages, eight pence; for stuffing a sadle, eight pence; and for a horse shoe, six pence. Here is the river Lea and Ware.

The morning being somewhat misty, through deep and strait way, May 18. wee came to Roiston, fourteen miles; and then further, through worse way, to a village called Aringtowne, where wee dined. Here I perceived the trunke male had sitt downe upon my horse back, and navelgalled him, for which I could find no remedy, nor a horse to hire; so that, paying for our selves and horses two shillings seven pence, we travelled to Huntingtowne, eleven miles, haveing, near the towne, passed through Godmanchester, a fine towne, with the most industrious inhabitants for husbandry in all England; † and truly here, in passing through, I saw the most, in such a place, hand-some and beautifull women that ever I saw in my lyfe time. The river Ouse runneth here, which wee crossed by a faire stone bridge of four bowes. Wee lodged here, and my horse being spoiled in the back, and Lochyell his horse likely to faile, wee were forced to think of swapping; and, the next day, May 19. many horses being brought to us, but most of them lame, wee were a long tyme befor wee could get condiscended on any bargaine. At last my comerade gave forty shillings, and I three pund one shilling, in boot with our horses, for others by farr not so good as ours when wee brought them from London; but so are travellers preyed upon every where. Wee payed here, for our selves, six shillings two pence; and wages, ten pence; for beer, extra, six pence; for stuffing the pillion and sadle, ten pence; for a iron barr to the pillion, six pence; for horse meat, foure shillings; and I payed

* [Gordon had possessed himself of a copy of the 'Britannia' when at Riga in 1667. See above p. 103]

† ['Godmanchester is flat seated by as fruitfull and flowry meadowes as any this king-dome yeeldeth, and is the most spacious of any one parish in fertile tillage, oft hauing waited on their soueraigne lords with nine score ploughes in a rurall pompe.' (England, Wales, Scotland, and Ireland Described, by John Speed. Lond. 1627.)]

to a coachman, to bring the trunke maile to Duncaster, foure shillings. In the evening, wee rode to Stilton, nyne miles, where lodged, and payed for our selves, twenty pence; for our horses, three shillings six pence; wages, six pence.

The Prince of Denmarkes last borne daughter, christined and named Anna Sophia; the Earle of Fewersham, godfather; the Ladies Roscommon and Churchill, godmothers; christined by the Bishop of Durham.

May 20.

Wee rose early, and came to Stamford, twelve miles, crossing here the river Welland, by a stone bridge, and rode ten miles further, and dined in a village called Kolsfoot, where wee payed for victuals, twenty pence; for horses, fifteen pence; wages to the ostler, two pence. Then wee rode through Grantham, six miles; and, a mile further, wee had a delicate prospect of a fertile valley, with a ancient place, called Beavoir Castle, on our left hand. Wee passed through the valley, and lodged in a large long village, called Great Billingtowne, which is five miles from Grantham, where wee payed for our selves, twenty nine pence; for horses, three shillings six pence; wages, one penny.

May 21.

Wee came to Newarke, fyve miles, where wee passed the river Trent, and, at the ferry, paid six pence. Wee came further, through a low countrey, and dined in Tuxfoord, ten miles from Newarke, where wee had a sight of Lincolne on the right hand. Here wee payed for our selves, thirty two pence; for horses, fifteen pence. From hence wee rode through Shirwood Forrest, the old haunting place of Robin Hood, to Barnby on the Moor, eight miles, and to Skribtree, three miles, where wee lodged, and payed for our selves, two shillings six pence; for horses, three shillings; wages, six pence.

May 22.

Wee came to Doncaster, being six miles, where I received my trunk maile by the Yorke coach. Being afrayed to spoile my mare, as I had done the horse, with the maile, I bought a portmantle or bagge, and put in the linnens, and such other things as could not be the worse of being pressed, and caused fitt the maile pillion better; and, refreshing ourselves, wee payed for our selves, two shillings six pence; for dressing the pillion, one shilling six pence; for foot socks, twelve pence. Here, crossing the river Done, wee came foure miles further to Robin Hoods Well, and, by the old Roman causey way, to Wentbridge, three miles; and to Ferrybridges, three miles, very stony and strait way; and then to Aberfoord, six miles. All this way wee had a sight of Yorke forward on our right hand. Here wee rested, and payed in all thirteen pence; and rideing six miles further, wee passed the river Wherf by a stone bridge, at Wethersby, where wee lodged.

Being Whitsonday, wee rested till midday, passing the tyme in the morning by viewing the pleasant fields and course of the river. Haveing dined, wee payed, for our selves, four shillings six pence; for our horses, two shillings nine pence; and wages, six pence. Wee tooke horse, and rode to Borrowbridges, ten miles, where wee crossed the river Ouse, rested, and payed two shillings six pence in the Red Lyon, and rode four miles further to Topcliffe, where wee lodged, and payed, for ourselves, two shillings one penny; for our horses, three shillings. — *May 23.*

Wee rode eight long miles to Northallertowne, and fyve miles to Smittotowne,* where wee dyned, and payed, for our selves and horses, three shillings four pence. Then to Darneton,† fyve miles, where a great faire; where payed, for a flaggon of ale, foure pence; and rideing foure miles further, to Yakcliffe,‡ where wee rested a litle, and payed thirteen pence; and it being a great raine, wee could gett no further as Ferryhill, being fyve miles, where wee lodged, and payed, for ourselves, thirty two pence; and horses, three shillings; wages, fyve pence. — *May 24.*

Wee came to Durham early, being fyve miles, where great preparations for a faire; and then twelve miles, to Newcastle, where dyned upon good fish, paying, for our selves, two shillings; for our horses, twenty one pence; for rings to a sadle, foure pence; and then twelve miles, to Morpeth, where wee lodged, and payed, for our selves, two shillings two and a half pence; for our horses, three shillings two pence. — *May 25.*

Wee rode to Fermlington, eight miles; and, over a great hill, to Whittinghame, six miles, where dyned, and payed, for ourselves, one shilling two pence; for our horses, nyne pence. Wee lodged this night in a inne called Haugh Head, a mile short of Woller, and payed, for ourselves, thirty three pence; for our horses, six pence; wages, six pence; and, at parting, two and a half pence for brandy. — *May 26.*

To Wuller, a mile; to Newtowne, where a fort, four miles; to the Scots Borders, four miles; to Kelso, where wee crossed Tweed at a foord, foure miles; where wee dyned, and payed, for our selves and horses, foure shillings three pence; wages, six pence. From hence wee rode through the pleasant countrey of the Merse, to Lawder, ten miles, where wee lodged, and payed, for our selves, two shillings six pence; for our horses, two shillings four pence; wages, six pence. — *May 27.*

* [Smeaton.]　　　　† [Darlington.]　　　　‡ [Aycliffe.]

May 28.

Wee rode to Gingle Kirk,* foure miles ; to Sotry,† two miles ; to Falaw, one mile ; to Dalkeith, fyve miles, where dined, and payed, for our selves, two shillings three pence ; for our horses, ten pence ; and wages, two pence. About three a clock afternoone, wee came to Edinborgh, four miles, where I tooke up my lodging in the foot of the Cannongate, at the signe of the Kings Armes.

About two houres after my arrivall, the Duke of Gordon came to see me, and welcomed me very kindly. Afterwards, diverse other particular ffriends gave me the honour of a visitt.

May 29.

I went in the morning and payed my respects to his Grace the Duke of Gordon, who was exceeding kind, and offered to conduct me to his Grace the Lord Commissioner,‡ and to the other grandees, desireing me to make no address by any other person, but himself. So, takeing me into his coach, I went to Court, and was addressed to his Grace the Lord Commissioner, who received me very kindly. After some stay, wee went to the Lord Chancellour,§ who was yet a bed. Afterwards, I went and gave a visitt to the Earle of Aberdeen, and dyned with my cousin, Mr. Thomas Gordon, clerk to the Justice Court.|| Afterwards, wee went to a chamber opposite to the Crosse, and see the ceremonies at the Cross, by the Provost and magistrates, in drinking the Kings health, and remembring the late Kings birth day, and happy restauration, which was followed by some volleyes of shott, and thereafter by many bonefyres all along the streets.¶

* [Channelkirk. The name, anciently written Childenchirch or Childeschirche, is said to have had its origin in an incident of the boy life of St. Cuthbert, in honour of whom the church was dedicated. (Libellus de Ortu Sancti Cuthberti, cap. xxiii.; Liber S. Marie de Dryburgh, p. 131.)]

† [Soltra.]

‡ [Alexander, fourth Earl of Murray. Sir John Lauder notes that the Roman Catholics found a good omen in his nomination to preside in this parliament, 'that as one Earl of Murray made the first penal laws against them in 1567, so another Earl of Murray, his great-grandchild, should take them away: but this presage failed them for this time.' (Fountainhall's Historical Notices, vol. ii. p. 736.)]

§ [The Earl of Perth. He was cousin and brother-in-law of the Duke of Gordon.]

|| ['Honest Thom Gordon,' as he was called, was made clerk of the Court of Justiciary in November, 1682. He was a writer to the signet,

and seems to have been in the confidence of the Scottish Roman Catholics.]

¶ [How the King's birthday was kept in the Scottish capital in these days, may be seen from the following official account of the ceremony in the year 1700:

'In the morning the great flag was put up in the Castle, with the discharge of nine piece of canon, and, at the same time, divers tunes suitable to the occasion were played on the musick bells . . . . . The trained bands of the City, Leith, and the other suburbs, about noon, being drawn up in good order upon the street about the Cross, his Majesty's High Commissioner, being invited by the Lord Provost, who, with the other magistrates, had for that end waited on his Grace in the morning, came attended with a great train of coaches, and the whole troop of Horse Guards, the right honourable the Earl of Argile being on their head, as was likewise the Earl of Crawford, and all their other officers, who sat on horseback during the

Being invited to devotion and dinner, by my Lord Chancellour, I went May 30.
thither in the morning with the Duke.   At dinner, were the Duke, the
Earles of Erroll,* Airly,† Dumferling,‡ with some ladyes and gentlemen.
After dinner, I went with the Earls of Erroll and Dumferling, and had,
with some more company, a merry collation.

I visited the Dukes of Hamilton and Queensbury, and the Marquess of June 1.
Athole, being brought to them by the Duke.   I went, along with the Duke,
and waited upon the Lord High Commissioner, and then, with the Duke, in
his coach, went to the Parliament House,§ and satt at the foot of the throne,
below the Duke; and afterwards dined in company with the Duke, and many
noblemen, in Krombies,‖ and went downe the street with the Duke, in his
coach.   I received the visits of many noblemen and gentlemen, and had
notice that my trunks from Dantzick were come to Lieth.   I sent my horses

solemnity. His Grace, being alighted from his coach, went to the Laigh Session House, and the Lord Provost having sent to know if his Grace was in readiness to go to the solemnity, and the messenger being returned, his Lordship, with the baillies and the rest of the council in their robes, the city music playing, and city regalia being carried before them, came to the outer gate of the Session House, where they waited till his Grace, attended by his Grace the Duke of Hamilton, the Marquis of Athol, and most of the principal nobility, came out, and then they marched on before his Grace the Lord High Chancellor, with a good number of persons of quality following after, to the theatre erected at the Cross, on which stood a large table with divers piramids and boxes of sweet meats and confections, at the upper end of which was a little table raised about a foot above the other, on which was laid a velvet cushion, and a chair of state, set on a pedestal raised as much above the floor of the theatre, for his Grace to repose himself in. The nobility and magistrates having taken their places about the table, the Lord Provost proposed his Majesty's health, and divers other healths to his Grace, which, going round, they threw the glasses and confections among the crowd; the great guns being in the mean time discharged round the Castle, and trumpets and hoboys playing upon the Cross, from whence divers pipes did run with wine. His Majesty's health being drunk, and the confections thrown amongst the people, the Commissioner his Grace returned to the Session House, from whence he went to the Palace, attended by most of the Members of Parliament, whom he splendidly entertained, together with the ma-

gistrates, at dinner; and in the evening, gave a fine ball to a great number of persons of quality of both sexes. In the evening, the magistrates, with the captains of the trained bands, with the city music playing before them, went to wait upon the Commissioner his Grace, who being attended by divers persons of quality, entertained them by drinking his Majesty's health at a bonfire in the Palace Close, where a battalion of the foot guards were drawn up in good order, and, by three salvoes of small shot, assisted at the solemnity. The evening concluded with ringing of bells, firing of guns and illuminations, which were very numerous on this occasion, no manner of disturbance being made by throwing of stones at windows, as has been formerly too frequent on the like occasions.' (The Edinburgh Gazette, no. 178, 7 Nov. 1700.) Cf. Arnot's History of Edinburgh, p. 607 'for a description of the celebration of the birthday,' in the year 1665.]

* [John, twelfth Earl of Erroll, was the Chancellor's brother-in-law.]

† [James, second Earl of Airly, was the husband of the Dowager Marchioness of Huntly, mother of the Duke of Gordon, of the Countess of Perth, and of the Countess of Dunfermline.]

‡ [James, fourth Earl of Dunfermline, was brother-in-law of the Duke of Gordon, and of the Earl of Perth.]

§ [Gordon must have mistaken the date of this visit to the Scotch Parliament. It met upon the second, but not upon the first of June. (Acts of the Parliaments of Scotland, vol viii., p 591; Fountainhall's Historical Notices, vol. ii, pp. 727, 728.)]

‖ [A tavern kept by Alexander Crombie.]

to be fed in the Parke. I did writt to the Earle of Middleton, the Viscount of Melfort, to the Paters Dumbar* and Marr, and to Alexander Gordon.

June 2.

I received some visitts in the morning, and dined in my lodging. After noone, I gave a visitt to the Earle of Aberdeen, and had much discourse with him, concerning my owne particular. I agreed with my landlady to pay for three servants dyet, eighteen pence a day. I did writt to my brother to send me some papers to Edinburgh, and the necessary charters, of the business betwixt my Lord Erroll and me.

June 3.

I was in the Parliament,† and dined in Blaires,‡ with some noblemen. In the afternoone, I payed some visitts to the noblemen who had done me the honour. In the evening, meeting with some noblemen, wee went and tooke a merry collation.

June 4.

I dined in my lodging, and, after noone, went and visitt my cousin, Mr. Thomas, where I received letters from my sonne, James, from Doway, dated   .   .   . May.

June 5.

I dined in my lodging, and, after noone, went into the Parke to walke. I gott up my trunks from Lieth, which came from Dantzick, and found all safe.

June 6.

Haveing been invited by my Lord Chancellour to dinner, I went and heard devotion, after which, in my Lord Chancellours packet, came, in a *coverto* of Mr. Cambridge of Hamburg, a letter from our chieffe Minister of State,§ acknowledging the reseat of some of myne on the way, and giveing me power, in their Majesties name, to bring along some officers of inferiour quality, as also some engeniers, fireworkers, and minirers, and to promise them yearly pay, according to their quality, and liberty to go out of the countrey when their occasions required. After noone, I went downe to Lieth with the Earles of Airly and Dumferling.

June 7.

I sent in the morning some cavear, and forty ermines, to the Duke of

---

* [Father William Dunbar, a member of the Society of Jesus. In November, 1686, he was appointed Almoner in Scotland to the King, with a pension of £100 a year. (Abstracts of the Records of the Secretary's Office, 1686-7, no. 393, MS.)

The Reverend Mr. Griffin of New Abbey informs me that the papers of the Douay College describe him as born 'ex parentibus Domino Alexandro [Dunbar] de Berwick, et Domina Margarita Abercromby nobilibus.' Father Dunbar was alive at Douay in 1714.]

† [Here again Gordon's reckoning is wrong. The Parliament met upon the second and the fourth, but not upon the third of June.]

‡ [A tavern of note. A kinsman writes from Edinburgh to the Countess of Erroll, in November, 1688: 'I am overjoyed to be confirmed of my Lord's final transaction with the town of Edinburgh, which was performed on Thursday last in Blair's, where my Lord Chancellor was with my Lord [Erroll], and where both were treated by the town.' (Miscellany of the Spalding Club, vol. ii. p. 294.)]

§ [Golizyn.]

Gordon, and as much to the Lord Chancellour. I dined in the towne with some noblemen; and, in the afternoone, did writt letters to Russia, London, and Hamburg.

I dated and dispatched my letters to our chieffe Minister of State, to my *June 8.* wyfe, Mr. Vinius, Mr. Cambridge in Hamburgh, my cousin, Mr. Meverell, and Maior Dowgall, in London.

I payed some visitts to those I had not seen, and, intending to have *June 9.* gone north, I was, by my cousine, perswaded to stay untill my writeings should come.

The Duke of Gordon tooke me up to the Castle, and show me all the *June 10.* places worth the seeing therein. I gave two dollers to the keeper of the magazine, and four dollers to the guards. From thence I gave a visitt to the Lady Marquess of Huntley.*

I dined in my lodging, and, in the afternoone, passed the tyme in the Parke. *June 11.*

Father Lesly† came to me in the morning, and gave me a letter from *June 12.* my sonne, James, and another from the Rector of the Colledge of Doway, called Gilbert Inglis.‡ I dined in the towne with some noblemen, and was in company this evening. Our dinner costed us ordinarily about halfe a crowne, and our collations, two or three shillings a peece.

I heard devotion in Lady Lucy Hamiltons,§ and, being invited, dined *June 13.* with the Earle of Airly; and, after noone, went to Lieth, and passed the tyme there. In the evening, the Duke came by me, to whom I gave a Turkish cimiter. Then wee went and walked in the Parke.

* [Mary, daughter of Sir James Grant of Freuchie, widow of Louis, third Marquis of Huntly, and now wife of James, second Earl of Airly.]

† [William Aloysius Lesley was a son of the house of Balquhain. He was born in Aberdeenshire in 1641, and, in 1666, became a member of the Society of Jesus. He was Superior of the Scottish College at Rome, from 1674 to 1683. He returned to Scotland in 1685, and continued to labour as a missionary there until his death in 1704. (Dr. Oliver's Biography of Members of the Society of Jesus, p. 28)
Father Lesley is believed to be the author of the ' Laurus Lesliana Explicata, sive clarior enumeratio personarum utriusque sexus cognominis Leslie. (Graecii 1692.' fol. To him also is ascribed the Italian Life of St. Margaret, Queen of Scotland, printed at Rome in 1675. (Vitae Antiquae Sanctorum Scotiae, p. 308.)]

‡ [The Reverend Mr. Griffin informs me that Father Gilbert Inglis, a native of Aberdeen, was more than once Rector of Douay. He is mentioned in Dr. Oliver's Biography of Members of the Society of Jesus, p. 24.]

§ [Lady Lucy Hamilton, third daughter of the first Earl of Abercorn, was affianced, before 1627, to Randal Lord Dunluce, afterwards Marquis of Antrim, who refusing to complete the marriage, was ordered to pay £3000 to the lady. (Secretary Stirling's Register, MS.) She had a pension from the Crown, which had fallen into arrear in January, 1686-7, when King James II. ordered the Lords of the Scottish Treasury to see it paid. (Abstracts of the Records of the Secretary's Office, no. 478, 15 January, 1686-7, MS.) Her house in Edinburgh, with those of other Romanists, was plundered by a mob at the Revolution in 1688. Count Anthony Hamilton, the author of the Memoires du Comte de Gramont, was her nephew.]

June 14   I was in the towne at dinner with diverse noblemen, where the Earle of Eglintowne desired me to take his sonne, Mr. John,* along with me to Russia.

June 15.   Diverse acts were ratifyed in the Parliament. I went and saw Heriots Worke, and, in the evening, were very merry, with the Earles of Erroll and Marshall, and the Lord Collington ;† haveing dined this day by Generall Drummond.

The Parliament being adjourned to the seventeenth of August next, the Lord Commissioner made preparations to be gone.

June 16.   I dined in towne, sent my trunks a ship board, with my servant Daniell, and, in the evening, past the tyme with Sir Thomas Dalyell.‡   The Earle of Aberdeen went north.

June 17.   The Lord High Commissioner went from Edinburgh, being convoyed by most of the nobility, and with many volleyes of great and small shot. He lodged in Haddingtowne all night, and I tooke up my lodging with the Viscount Kenmoir.§

June 18.   In the morning, I went and visited the Duke of Lawderdale his tombe,‖ and afterwards waited on the Duke, from whome I went and tooke my leave of my Lord Commissioner, who gave me a very high complement. After breakfast, wee returned and visited the Pallace of Seaton, and were merry in Preston, and came in good tyme to Edinburgh.

June 19.   I tooke my leave of the Dukes of Hamilton and Queensbury, the Marquesse of Athole, and other noblemen. I dined at home, and in the evening were merry with some noblemen.

June 20.   I dined by the Lord Chancellour, and tooke my leave of his Lordship, and then made a progresse in takeing my leave of other noblemen and

* [John Montgomery, third son of Alexander eighth Earl of Eglinton. His projected journey to Russia was never made. He entered the army at home, and had risen to the rank of major, when he died unmarried.]

† [Sir James Foulis of Colinton, a Lord of Session from 1661 to 1684, and Lord Justice Clerk from February, 1684, till his death in January, 1688. His son, Sir James Foulis of Colinton, appointed a Lord of Session, in 1674, seems to have been known during his father's lifetime as Lord Reidfurd. He was afterwards styled Lord Colinton]

‡ [The eldest of five sons and three daughters born by various concubines to Gordon's old friend, General Dalyell. He had letters of legitimation in 1682, and was made a baronet in November, 1685]

§ [Alexander Gordon, fifth Viscount of Kenmure. After the Revolution, he followed the fallen King to St. Germains. His son— the 'Kenmure's on an' awa' of Jacobite song —lost his life on the scaffold for his share in the insurrection of 1715.]

‖ [In an aisle of the parish church at Haddington. The inscription is printed in Crawfurd's Peerage of Scotland.]

ffriends; and in the evening, were merry with my Lord Dumferling, Lievetennant Collonell Buchan,* and Coxstowne.†

I went early and tooke my leave of the Duke, who excused his not June 21. convoying me to Lieth as he intended, by reason of his indisposition. And so takeing coach, I was convoyed by many ffriends to Lieth, where breack-fasting, and takeing leave of ffriends, I tooke boat, and crossed to Burnt Illand, where, hyreing a horse for one of my servants, with a guide, I rode to Dagatie,‡ four miles, and there tooke my leave of the Lady Dumferling,§ who tooke me exceeding kindly. I rode from thence to Kirkaldy, where I had notice that the ship wherein my trunks were had this day weighed ankor from the roade. I lodged in Kennoway.

I came to Cowper in a very rainy day, and crossed the ferry at Dundee, June 22. where I made no great stay, haveing dined on the other syde, and came to Ardbroath, where I rested and baited the horses. At the Redhouse, Sir Georg Skeen‖ and Baily Adie¶ overtook me, and wee lodged together in Montrose.

Wee crossed the Northwater,** and through Bervy by Steenhave, and June 23. dined in Cowy, it being all the tyme a deluge of raine. At the Bridge of Dee, wee drank a glasse of wine, and about four a clock, came to Aberdeen, and lodged in the Katherine Raes. Many ffriends came to see me. I dispatched a post for my sonne.

My unkle,†† brother John, and my sonne, came, and many ffriends in June 24. the towne came to see me.

---

* [Thomas Buchan, a younger son of the house of Auchmacoy, in Aberdeenshire, was born about the middle of the seventeenth century. After serving in France and Holland, he was appointed a lieutenant-colonel by King Charles II., in 1682. By King James II., he was made colonel in 1686, and major-general in 1689. In the following year, after the death of Dundee at Killiecrankie. and the repulse of General Cannon at Dunkeld, he was des-patched from Ireland to take command of the Jacobite forces in Scotland; but within a few weeks after his arrival, was surprised and de-feated by Sir Thomas Livingstone. He sur-vived the year 1721, and died at Ardlogie, on the banks of his native Ythan. There is a portrait of him at Auchmacoy.]

† [Alexander Innes of Coxtoun. He was one of the representatives of the shire of Elgin, and a Lord of the Articles, in the Parliament of 1686.]

‡ [Delgaty.]

§ [Lady Jean Gordon, daughter of the third Marquis of Huntly, and sister of the first Duke of Gordon.]

‖ [Sir George Skene of Fintray, for many years Lord Provost of Aberdeen, and repre-sentative of the city in Parliament He was knighted by the Duke of York, at Holyrood, in 1681.]

¶ [Sir John Lauder says that Bailie Ady, in Aberdeen, was conspicuous, along with Mr. Thomas Gordon, and Sir William Paterson, for importunity in soliciting members of Parliament to support the bill for repealing the penal laws against the Roman Catholics (Fountainhall's Historical Notices, pp. 735, 737; Cf. Miscellany of the Spalding Club, vol. ii., p. 295.)]

** [The North Esk]

†† [His father's brother, James Gordon of the Eastside of the Westertown of Auchleuch-ries. He was afterwards entrusted, by General Patrick Gordon, with the charge of his affairs in Scotland.]

June 25.   Haveing dyned, and hearing my trunks were come from Edinburgh, I tooke horse and rod to Kelly,* where I was kindly welcomed by the Earle of Aberdeen, and the Lord Haddo, his sonne. Wee had large discourses of many things, and spoke at length of my owne particular ; and haveing perused the charters and writeings of the lands of Achluichries, wee found it convenient not to sell it, it being both well holden and well worth the keeping.

June 26.   After breakfast, I tooke horse and passed Ithan water by boat ; and it being a very great raine, I made a visitt to the Laird of Shivees,† and then to the Milne of Drumwhendill, where the river Ebry being greatly encreassed and overflowing the banks, I was forced to stay at the Milne about three houres, untill the water did fall a litle, and then rode the fuird with great hazard and danger.‡   In *passanto*, I made a visitt at Coldwells,§ and another at Dudwick,‖ and takeing a standing drink at the Bony Wyfes, in the evening, I came to my brother John his habitation.¶

June 27.   I rose up early, and walked up to the Kairne, and to the Karny Winke, and then downe to my unkle, and about some part of the fields thereabout, which I beheld to my great satisfaction and contentment, and dined by my unkle.   After dinner, my sister, with her husband and diverse ffriends, came to see me.   Towards evening, wee went over and supped by my brother John.

June 28.   Nethermuir** being come, wee consulted and spoke with my brother John about his accompts.   He gave in a long reckoning of expenses for my children and effaires, wherewith I was no wise satisfyed ; so being to go downe to Crowdan, wee deferr'd all to the next day.   Haveing visitted diverse gentlemen in the parish, I dined with my sister, and was very merry ; and afterwards visiteing others, I returned at night to my brothers.

* [Now called Haddo House.]

† [George Gray. The house of Schivas still kept by the old religion : hence, perhaps, its motto, ' Faith is an anchor ']

‡ [' The Ebrie, in its ordinary volume, is of no great account ; but in heavy rains, owing to the unusual declivity of the banks along its course, it swells into an imposing torrent : the occasional fury of its passage has worn deep holes in the channel, so that, from a harmless-looking stream, it sometimes proves a dangerous pit-fall.' (Buchan, by the Rev. John B. Pratt, p. 243. Aberd. 1858)]

§[The seat of a family which gave birth to Dr. John Gordon, consecrated Bishop of Galloway in 1688. Following the fortunes of King James VII, after the Revolution, he was, by that prince, made chancellor of the diocese of Dublin. Some years afterwards, he formally abjured the Reformed faith, by a writing which is printed in Le Quien's Nullitè des Ordinations Anglicanes, t. ii. p. 313. Paris, 1725. He died at Rome in 1726, at the age of eighty two.]

‖ [Then possessed by the Fullertons, the first of whom, a colonel in the French service, was of the ancient faith. In the previous generation, Dudwick belonged to General James King, a soldier who distinguished himself in the Thirty Years' War, and was created Lord Eythin or Ythan, by King Charles I., in 1642.]

¶ [Westertown of Auchleuchries.]

** [John Gordon.]

In the morning, I walked and tooke a view of some places which I had not seen; and after long discussing with my brother about his accompts, wee scarsely came to ane agreement, and some ffriends being come to see me, wee tooke breakfast, and afterwards horse, and rode to New Deer parish, some ffriends meeting me by the way. I first touched at Barak,* then Knavin,* and so Achmunyell,* and befor evening, I came to Dalgaty, where I found my Lord† but newly come home. He made me very welkome. Wee supped merrily with good company.

Haveing walked untill about nyne a clock, afterwards wee did fall upon our particular,‡ and after litle scruples and difficulty, wee gott an end, my Lord very nobly condiscending to all we desired. Wee dined with my Lord verry merrily, among the most excellent discourses of a compleet, well bred lady ;§ and, indeed, all the civilities imaginable were showed me by both those worthy persons. Haveing, with great satisfaction, taken my leave, I made a visitt at Achry,‖ who was in company with us in Dalgatie, and being nobly entertained, I rode to Achmunyell,¶ Achridy,¶ and Nethermuir,¶ where I made short visitts, and came to Barak,¶ where I lodged.

After breakfast, I rode to Ellon, some ffriends haveing mett me by the way, so that wee were about thirty horse. Here I spoke with the Lairds of Rothemay ** and Watertowne †† about my owne particulars, the last whereof I visited in his house; and being returned to Ellon, I, by a notar,

---

* [All three dwelling places of Gordons.]
† [The Earl of Erroll.]
‡ | The lands of Auchleuchries were held by Gordon in feu-ferme, of the Earl of Erroll, for a yearly rent of twelve pounds Scots. His 'particular' with the Earl was doubtless the arrangement of some question in their relation of lord and vassal.]
§ [Lady Anne Drummond, countess of Erroll, only daughter of James, third earl of Perth. She is understood to be the authoress of 'An Account of Buchan, and what is remarkable therein,' printed in the Collections for a History of the Shires of Aberdeen and Banff, pp. 94-97. A few letters written to her by her brother, in his exile, have been printed for the Camden Society, in the Correspondence of James, Earl of Perth, Lord Chancellor of Scotland, Lond. 1845. Four of her own letters are preserved in the Miscellany of the Spalding Club, vol. v., pp. 193-200. It appears from these that she was in correspondence with Bishop Burnet, and with Dr. Turner, the deprived bishop of Ely. Some letters, addressed to her, are published in the Miscellany of the Spalding Club, vol. ii., pp. 293-296.

One of these shows that the new town of Edinburgh was projected so early as the year 1693: 'they design to build on the other syd of the Nore Loch, and to cast a bridge of stone over it, and to enclose that new tane in ground with a wall.']
‖ [William Cuming, first of that name, laird of Auchry, had a Gordon for his first wife. The lands of Auchry were of old the patrimony of the Roman Catholic family of Conn, whose expatriated representatives appear to have lived at Paris till about the beginning of the eighteenth century. The tomb of a son of this house, the author of the 'De Duplici Statu Religionis apud Scotos,' who died in 1640, when about to be made a Cardinal, is still to be seen in the Church of San Lorenzo in Damaso, at Rome. His portrait is at Gordon Castle.]
¶ [All seats of Gordons]
** [John Gordon.]
†† [Thomas Forbes, son of Sir John Forbes of Watertown, and nephew of the Earl of Aberdeen. He claimed the office of Constable of Aberdeen, as an appurtenance of his lands of Carmucks, the old inheritance of the Kennedys.]

gave him a warning concerning the wedsett of the Muirtacke,* against which he protested. After some large discourses, and received the visitts of very many gentlemen, who were here at a meeting, and at our going from hence, drinking the Kings health at the Towstone or Tollstone, and being convoyed a part of the way by many ffriends, I came in the evening to Aberdeen, where I received letters from the Duke of Gordon and from my cousin, Mr. Thomas, with ane enclosed from Mr. Meverell.

July 2.   Businesse being not well accorded with my brother, in reference to his accompts, albeit I condiscended to all and more by farr as was reasonable or exspected, I was forced to writt to my unkle, desireing him to come in and help to conclude the businesse.

July 3.   I received some visitts, and in the evening my unkle came. The skipper told me that it would be Wednesday or Thursday next befor he could gett out for nipping, whereat I was not well pleased, seing I could have spent the tyme better in the countrey, makeing visitts to my ffriends, and ordering my business in greater solitude.

July 4.   After devotion, I dined with my ffriends, and, in the afternoone, made a visitt to my Lady of Aberdeen,† and afterwards to the Lady Wartle.‡

July 5.   This day, ffriends were very busy concludeing business with my brother, and at last brought it to a period, he giveing me a bond for four hundred merks, and ane assidation for three hundred merks a year, for the Westsyde of Westertowne, I haveing allowed him a large sallary, all the expences he could pretend, and my childrens maintenance to the rigour.

July 6.   I caused draw up a register or list of all the charters and papers I have on the lands of Achluichries, beginning from A.D. 1423, to this present year, of forty five peeces, besides small. I was at the buriall of Old Craige,§ who was buryed in the Snow Kirke, ‖ in the Old Towne. The magistrates and many gentlemen convoyed him. From thence, wee went to the master of the musick schoole his house, and with excellent musick, and many ffriends, were very merry.

---

* [A small outlying farm, or 'pendicle' as it was called, of the estate of Auchleuchries.]

† [The Countess of Aberdeen, Anne, daughter of George Lockhart of Torbrecks.]

‡ [Either Anna Gordon, wife of Alexander Elphinstone of Meikle Wartle; or Elizabeth Gordon, daughter of Patrick Gordon of Badenscoth, wife of Alexander Leslie of Little Wartle.]

§ [Francis Gordon of Craig. He succeeded to the family estate on the death of his father about 1650, and married Elizabeth, a daughter of Sir Gilbert Menzies of Pitfoddels. He was of the church of Rome.]

‖ [The church of Our Lady of Snow—for a short while the parish church of St. Machar—appears to have fallen into ruin at the Reformation. Its deserted area soon afterwards became a frequent place of burial with Roman Catholics.]

I went and see the Colledge in the Old Towne, and was very well *July 7.* received, and showed all worth the seeing there. I went to the Linkes afterwards. In the evening, the Earle of Aberdeen came, to whom I payed a visitt.

I was invited to a collation by the Lord Provost and Magistrates, where, *July 8.* with my ffriends, I was heartily entertained, and all my relations who were there made burgesses.* My sister and sisters in law being come into the towne to see me, wee made very merry with good musick.

I did writt to the Duke of Gordon, and to some ffriends in Edinburgh, *July 9.* and mad some visitts in the towne. My ffriends tooke their leave, and went home. In the morning, I went over Dee, and to St. Fiacres Church.†

The Laird of Watertowne being come to towne, wee did fall to talke of *July 10.* a composition concerning the Muirtake, he desireing a tollerance of mosse for his lyfe tyme, and I, being perswaded by Aberdeen, promised it for seven yeares; whereof he not allowing, wee broke of.

This afternoone, I made some visitts, and walked in the evening, and at *July 11.* night passed the tyme with the Earle of Aberdeen.

The Earle of Aberdeen, with my Lady, went from hence. In the *July 12.* evening, the Earle Marshall‡ came to towne, whom I visitted, he comeing over to my lodging, where supped, and were merry.

In the morning, I tooke my leave of the Earle Marshall, who went *July 13.* north. In the afternoone, Nethermuir, older and yonger, went from hence, I haveing given a factory for my effaires to my unkle, and the yonger

* [The burgh register places this event on the *seventh* of July:—

'Eodem die, in presentia Prepositi, Balivorum, Decani Gilde, et Thesaurarii dicti burgi, Joannes Gordon in Westertoun [de] Achlouchries, Joannes Gordon filius natu maximus excellentis viri Domini Patricii Gordon de Achlouchries, Generalis Locumtenentis sub Emperatoribus Russie, et Jacobus Gordon filius secundo genitus Joannis Gordon in Westertoune de Achlouchries [recepti fuerunt in burgenses gilde burgi de Aberdeen.']

The cost of the collation appears from the Guildry Accounts:—

'Item of the expenssis of wax and parchment for the burges actis of John Gordone of Auchleuchries, John Gordone, sone to Livetennant Generall Gordone, and of James Gordone, sone to Auchleuchries, £1 4s 0d.

'Item of the expenssis of wyne, etc. debursed with the magistrats and utheris with them, at making them burgessis of the toune, £31 12s. 6d.']

† [The parish church of Nigg, on the south bank of the Dee, was dedicated to St. Fithak, Fiack, or Fiacre, an Irish recluse of the seventh century, long held in great veneration in France. In 1641, Anne of Austria made a pilgrimage on foot to his shrine in the cathedral of Meaux; and the eloquent Bossuet invoked his protection for Louis XIV., when undergoing a surgical operation. The French hackney coach received its name of *fiacre*, from an image of the saint, hung up for a sign by one Nicolas Sauvage, who was the first in Paris to hire out carriages by the hour or day. So lately as the year 1630, the kirk session of Aberdeen ordained that any one repairing to St. Fiacke's well, in the bay of Nigg, 'in a superstitious manner, seeking health to themselves or bairns,' should be punished with the punishment due to fornication]

‡ [George, eighth Earl Marischal, succeeded his brother in 1661, and died in 1694 He had served in the French army, and distinguished himself in the battle of Worcester in 1651]

Nethermuir. I went thereafter to the Links, and passed the tyme with inexpressible contentment.

July 14.

I went with some ffriends to the Bridge of Dee, and dined in a taverne upon excellent fresh salmon. Returning, wee see our ship gone over the barr. I went and took my leave of these neerest ffriends I had reserved till last. In the evening, I received letters from London, and from the Duke of Gordon ; in the letters from London was the copy of the Kings letter which was to be sent in my favours, and was written so :

James the Seventh, by the grace of God, King of Scotland, England, France, and Ireland, Defender of the Faith, *etc.* to the most heigh, most potent, and most serene, our most dear brothers, the Great Lords, Czaars, and Great Dukes, Ivan Alexeowich, Peter Alexeowich, of all the Greater, Lesser, and White Russia Self Upholders, Czaars of Moscovia, Kiovia, Volodomiria, Novogardia, Czaars of Casan, Czaars of Astrachan, Czaars of Siberia, Lords of Plesko, and Great Dukes of Smollensko, Tweria, Ugoria, Permia, Vatkia, Bolgaria, and others, Lords and Great Dukes of Novogardia, of the Lower Countreyes, of Czernichow, Rezan, Rostow, Yaroslaw, Beloozersky, Adorsky, Obdorsky, Condinsky, and Commanders of all the Northern Coasts, Lords of the lands of Tveria and Grudzinia, Czaars of the lands of Cabardinia, Czirkassia, and the Dukes of the Mountaines, and of many other dominions and countreyes, east, west, and north, from father and grandfather Heirs, Lords and Conquerours ; sendeth greeting, and wisheth all happiness and prosperity : Whereas wee are informed that our trusty and wellbeloved subject, Patrick Gordon, hath served your Imperiall Majesties many yeares, and now serveth in the quality of Lievtennant Generall ; who now, by the deceass of his father, is to inherit lands, for which he is to performe personell service unto us ; and wee haveing use for the service of such of our subjects as have been bred up in military employments, wee do, therefor, desire of your Imperiall Majesties that you would dismiss the said Patrick Gordon, with his wyfe, children, family, and effects, out of your dominions, which wee rather desire, because wee know that your great vertue hath procured from God the blessing of an universall peace with all your neighbours. The doing this, will be an encouragement for men of honour to repaire to your service, whenever you shall have occasion for them ; and whenever the opportunity is given us of doing you the lyke

pleasure, wee shall heartily embrace it.   And so wee pray God to have your
Imperiall Majesties into His holy protection.   Given at our Court at Windsor
the twenty ninth day of May, one thowsand six hundred eighty six yeares,
in the second year of our reigne.

Your affectionate brother,

Melfort.   JAMES R.*

With the letters from the Duke of Gordon, was a letter from his Grace
to Kniaz Vasily Vasiliovits Golitzin, chieffe minister of state in Russia,
the copy whereof followeth :

Illustrissime ac Excellentissime Domine,

Diuulgata per orbem Excellentiae
tuae perillustris fama atque singularis omnium de tuis animi dotibus
existimatio, praecipue vero illa tua praeclara gesta mihi a cognato meo
vice praefecto Gordon relata, amicitiae tuae me cupidissimum reddiderunt.
Dicti autem vice praefecti tanta ad Excellentiam tuam redeundi, atque
honoris et amicitiae, quam et dignatus es illi tribuere, friendi cupido, quae
de tua Excellentia disseruerit, quam maxime confirmat.   Cum itaque Regi
nostro Serenissimo notus atque ab illo in honore habitus sit, nec non ab aliis,
qui non mediocrem animi illius magnitudinem integritatem atque fortitu-
dinem mirandum in modum suspiciunt, eundem cognatum meum tutelae
tuae, fidei, amori et benevolentiae non verebor commendare.   Si qua occasio
se offerret praestandi in his borealibus mundi plagis, quod tuae Excellentiae
gratum acceptumque foret, avide arriperem.   Dum interea temporis, Excellentissime Domine, tot ac tanta Imperii Russiae negotia tibi commissa
ac demandata sustines, his successum maxime prosperum tuaeque Excel-
entiae summum honorem atque faelicitatem peroptat

Excellentiae vestrae,

Gordon Castle,   GEO: DUX DE GORDON.
    12 Julii, 1686.

Superscriptio :

Serenissimorum Dei gratia Potentissimorum Dominorum Imperatorum

---

* [The letter is noted in the 'Abstract of Papers relating to Scotland, which past his Majesty's hand, from 9th April, 1686, to 25th February, 1686-7' (no. 108) :—
'The Kings letter to the Emperour of Russia, desiring him to dismiss Lievtennant Generall Patrick Gordon from his service, His Majestie having occasion for him in Scotland. Dated at Windsor, 29th May, 1686.   Melfort.   JAMES R.']

et Magnorum Ducum Johannis Alexiades, Petri Alexiades, totius Majoris, Minoris et Albae Russiae Autocratorum, multorum dominiorum et terrarrum orientalium, occidentalium et septentrionalium Dominorum, Haeredum, Successorum, Imperatorum et Possessorum, Imperialis eorum Majestatis proximo Bojaro, Duci Basilio Basilidis Golitzin, augustioris Imperii sigilli custodi et supremo magnarum legationum et rerum Imperii Directori, et Nouogrodiensi Locumtenenti.

July 15.
I rose early, and tooke my ordinary walke in the Links, and takeing my leave of these pleasing places, I returned, and, haveing heard devotion, dined sooner as ordinary. The magistrates, about twelve a clock, came to me, and called me. They convoyed me to the boat, where I tooke my leave of them, and others my ffriends, and with my sonne, brother, and Walter and William Gordon, went aboard our ship. The skipper and merchant comeing, our ffriends tooke leave, and wee hoised saile, and with a fresh gale of wind, held on our course. Yet wee keeped sight of Scotland till neer night, and with sadd hearts, bidd it farewell. I went immediately to bed, being not well by reason of the great tossing, which continued all night, the next and third day, and the fourth, litle better, albeit wee entred by the Jutshe Riffe, and passed the illands of Lesow, Anout, and the dangerous rock called the Trindle. The shipp was called the Christin, of Borrowstowness; skipper, Robert Cumming.

July 19.
By day light, wee had a sight of the Kole, but, by contrary winds, were kept farr to the north of it, so that wee passed this whole day laboreing, till, in the evening, haveing reached the point, and the wind more favourable, and pilots comeing aboard, wee sailed forward, and, a litle after midnight, let our anchors fall in the road befor Elsonure.

July 20.
Wee went ashoare very early, and called at Mr. Melvills, where haveing bespoke our dinner, wee walked out into the ffields. Here, I received a letter from Mr. Cambridge, and returned ane answer thereto. Haveing dinned, I payed our skipper, Mr. Cumming, for fraught for my self, and foure more, twenty dollers; it cost me lykewise, drink money and other expences here, and on the ship, foure dollers. And haveing notice of an English ship going for Riga, wee bespoke him, and though he would not come to ane agreement with us for our fraught and victualls, yet about two a clock afternoone, wee went aboard of him, haveing first taken our leave of

our kind Scots ffriends. Wee hoysed saile, and, with a moderate gale, came so farr as the road of Copenhaven, where, being a great calme, wee anchored. This shipp, called the Paradis; the skipper, William Buck, belonging to Yarmouth.

By day light, wee weighed anchors and set forward, and with a ordinary July 21 wind passed by the illands Amach and . . . being in company with some other ships, who were bound to diverse places. Befor evening, wee passed by Falsterboom.

Haveing a pretty gale, wee passed by the illands Borne and Erdholme; but in the evening, the wind proveing easterly, wee were forced to hold over to the Pomers coast, and so continued some dayes, laboreing too and againe without any memorable accident, untill the . . . when wee had July 26. a sight of land which, by calculation, wee judged to be the sands by east of the Memell, and the place called Pologna and Heiligen Aa.

Wee labored up along the coast of Churland, without being certaine July 27. how farr wee were.

Wee had a sight of land which wee thought to be Wendaw, but towards July 28. night found it to have been Libaw.

Wee passed by the Wendaw, and so in by the Domesness, with a good July 29. gale, haveing Oesel on our left hand, and so holding within the Riffe, wee unadvisedly turned of to the right hand, and so in a bought of land were becalmed all the next day.   July 30

With a slow wind wee made towards the road, and about one a clock August 1 gott into the harbour within the river. Wee went ashoar, and gave account what wee were, which was needles, and better wee should have exspected aboard their asking of us. Wee went along up the river with a slow gale, and, in the evenıng, anchored within a large halfe mile of Riga.

At sunriseing, wee tooke boate, and landed at Riga, going in at the August. 2 Water Gate. I came to my former lodging without being questioned by the watch, which was, I think, because my servants had the same livery, blew and yellow, as the Sweds have. With halfe an houre, an officer came to my quarters enquireing what I was, and what gate I came in, whereof haveing received satisfaction, he departed. I payed for dyet and victualls to the skipper at the rate of twenty shillings sterling for each person, masters and servants.

I did writt to the Earle of Perth and Viscount Melfort in a *coverto* to August 4.

Alexander Gordon, to the Earle of Middleton and Esquire Cooke, all in a *coverto* to Mr. Meverall, by Mr. Philes convoyance *per mare*. Writt also to the Duke of Gordon, the Earles of Aberdeen and Erroll, and to Nethermuir, in a *coverto* to William Gordon in Aberdeen, to my unkle, brother, and Mr. Thomas, all by my nephew, James Gordon.

August 5. I did writt to my wyfe, Collonell von Mengden, and Mr. Vinius, per post, Robert Gordon,* James Adie, and Bayly Adie in Dantzick per post, as also to Madam Crawfuird. And not thinking it fitt to take my nephew into Russia, I sent him back by sea to Scotland. This night I supped by Mr. Holst, and was entertained most magnificently.

August 7. I did writt to Mittaw, to *Patri Ernesto Sturmio residentiae superiori*.

August 8. I dined by Mr. Frazer, and was nobly entertained.

August 9. I supped by Mr. Watson, and was kindly entertained; and the rest of my tyme I passed every day almost with walking and shooting. I payed for dyet for my self and another, a doller, and for foure servants at the rate of tenpence for each, with lodging.

August 12. I did writt to the Earle of Middleton and Mr. Meverell per post; and, haveing hired two Rigish fuirmen, for eight dollers a peece, with two horses and two waggons of retour of a Russe, with one horse at fyve dollers for both, I tooke jorney, and being convoyed in a coach a large halfe mile without the towne with kind ffriends, wee made merry with good liquor, which the ffriends brought along with them; and at New Mills,† crossing the river . . . and the river Aa, wee lodged in a inne, hardly being foure miles from Riga.

August 13. Wee jorneyed three miles, and dined in Rosembems krow, and, going two and a half miles further, wee lodged in a krow, by a morass.

August 14. Wee dined a mile short of Wolmar, and passing that towne, and three miles further, haveing passed over the river Bresla by a bridge, and by the two castles, Great and Litle Ropen, betwixt which the forsaid river runneth, lodging in a krow or inne, within a wood.

August 15. Wee passed foure miles, and dined in a small village; and this afternoone, the way being better, wee came six miles further, and lodged in a pleasant village in a inne, by the Black River. From Wolmar, wee had nine miles all wood.

* [Perhaps the founder of Robert Gordon's Hospital at Aberdeen. He is understood to have been a trader in Dantzic about this time.]
† [Neuermuhlen.]

Crossing the Black River on a float, wee came through a litle more August 16.
pleasant countrey foure and a half miles, and dined in Roughs krue, where a
litle church.   Then a countrey full of little pleasant hills, about foure miles.
Wee lodged in a inne, a mile and a halfe short of Niewhausen.

Wee passed by Niewhausen unquestioned, and dined in the towne August 17.
Petshure, being foure miles, and lodged in Peshky, foure miles.

We came to Plesko, foure miles, about eight a clock, and gave the August 18.
Governour immediately notice of my comeing, who excused himself from
seeing me this day; the Governours name, Kniaz Michael Gregoriovits
Romodanofsky, my old acquaintance.

I dined by the Woywod, and, haveing gott posthorses and provisions August 19.
from my old ffriend, the Chancellour, about fyve a clock wee tooke jorney;
and about fyfteen verst wee supped in a small village, and, travelling all
night, wee came in the morning early to Zagoria.

Getting fresh horses, wee marched and dined, twenty fyve verst further, August 20.
in a village called Putilowa, and, travelling twelve verst further, wee supped
in the fields; and then, travelling the whole night about fyfteen verst, wee
crossed the river Shibna.

Wee came fyfteen verst further, and dined in Soltsee; and, in the even- August 21.
ing, comeing to Mpsiaga, fyfteen verst, wee went by boat downe the river
Mpsiaga, and, in the night tyme, had an extraordinary great storme, so
that with much ado wee could gett into a creek, where wee stayed about
fyve houres, untill, being calmer, wee lanched out againe; and so, with a August 22.
pretty gale, sailed in the lake, and, in the evening, came to the monastery
of St. Georg, where wee lodged.   This monastery hath ane abbot, and
seven hundred pawres* to maintaine him and his monkes.   Here, hard by,
is the bottomless pitt called Pierun, which was in the heathenish tyme the
tutelar God of this place, and was, by the Christians conjured into this pitt;
wherein they now cast malefactors, who are lost in it without any notice
what becomes of them; yet when great raines are, there is water to be seen
in it.   By Novogrodt is a monastery, called Pierunsky Monastery, where
the chieffe temple of this tutelar god did stand.   This lake is called Ilmien,
into which seventy rivers fall, being in breadth in some places twenty to
thirty verst, and in length forty, and at last maketh the river Volcha, which
runneth by Novogrod.

* [Boors.]

August 23.   In the morning, I came to Novogrod, and gave immediately notice to the Governour, who promised my dispatch without delay. I dined by the translator Hutner, and, in the afternoone, visited the governour Peter Vasiliovits Seremetuf, who gave present orders for my dispatch. And so, getting another boat, in the evening wee set forwards up the river Msta.

August 24.   And being all night on the river, wee came, about sunriseing, to the village Brunets, being thirty verst from Novogrodt by water; and, getting horses, wee went from hence about eleven a clock, and comeing fyve verst further, wee crossed the river Nissia, which runneth to the south and falleth in the lake Ilmien. Then through woods, the most part of the way being bridged, ten verst, to the village Krasny Stanky; then to the village Podlitovia, and to Sayontskowa, where hath been formerly a stage. Here wee supped, and about midnight set forward, and by day light wee crossed the river Moshna, haveing fed the horses; and then haveing the river Chotilewa on our left hand all the way, the way likewise haveing been most bridged, wee came

August 25.   in the morning to the village Kresty;* where, dineing and getting fresh horses, wee travelled in better way through a pleasant countrey, and, crossing the river Cholowa diverse tymes, to the village Rekin, and through woods with lakes on each syde. Wee fedd the horses by the river Poluma, which crossing, wee passed through the village Yosselbitza in the twilight; and travelling the whole night, befor day wee passed through the village Balday,† where most Littavers live. Here, in a lake, is a monastery called Iversky, which hath large lands in this tract belonging to it.

August 26.   About three verst further, wee came to Ziemna Gora, where getting fresh horses, and paying for each . . . about sunriseing, wee set forward, and came through a hilly stony countrey, to a lake called Shidorowa, with a village of the same name; then twelve verst further, to the village and river Beroosa, where dineing, and crossing the river by a bridge, where a litle chappell, wee came twenty fyve verst further, to the village Cholilowa, which hath been formerly a stage; and ten verst further, wee fed the horses in the fields, by the village Columna, here haveing rested the most part of the night.

August 27.   Wee travelled twenty verst, and crossed the river Slino, by the village Brosda; and fyve verst further, wee crossed the river Tzna, by Visnogo

* [Krestelskoi-jam.]   † [Walday.]

Vloizka,* where wee dined, and gott fresh horses, paying for each . . . Wee came ten verst further, and by a litle monastery, dedicated to St. Nicolaus, wee crossed the river Twerets† the first tyme, through woods the most part of the way, being bridged to the village Cholocholka, through which runneth a brooke of the same name; and haveing the river Twerets on our left hand, wee went foure verst further, and baited in the fields, and six verst further, wee crossed the Twerets againe, by the village Widropusk, which belongeth to the Iversky Monastery. Here is the border of the Dukedome of Novogrodt, and beginneth the Novo Torsky district. Wee travelled all night.

About seven aclock, wee came to Torshok, where wee dined. This is a August 28. very pleasant countrey. Wee had excellent way, seventeen verst, to the river Logovisha, which wee crossed at the village Marina; and thirteen verst further, wee crossed the river Twerets the third tyme, at the village Medna, where wee supped. Here endeth the Novo Torsky district, and beginneth the Dukedome of Twere. Wee tooke jorney about midnight, and befor day, fed our horses by a monastery, fyve verst short of Twere, and twenty fyve from Medna.

About sunriseing, wee came to the ferry, and crossing the river Volga, August 29. wee breakfast in the Yempsky Slobod, where getting fresh horses, and with good weather, came and baited by the village Gorodisha, which is from Twere . . . verst. Here hath been a fort for preserving the passages on the river Volga, which wee had here all along on our left hand. Fyfteen verst further, wee crossed on a float the river Moskna, by a village of the same name, and fyfteen verst further, to the village Zavidova, and about fyve verst further, fed the horses in the fields.

By day light, wee set forward by the village Spass, and dined by the August 30. river Zamoga, and then to Klin, which is ninety of the old verst from Mosko, and of the new but thirty nine. Here wee crossed the river Sustra; and through very badd way, and crossing the same river againe, three verst further, wee came to Moshna, a village, twelve verst, and so on to Peshky, where wee rested till midnight.

Being good weather, and indifferent way, wee set forward, and dined August 31. fyve verst short of Czirkishowa; and so on came to the Stranger Sloboda,‡ about fyve a clock afternoone.

* [Wyschnij Wolotschok.]	†'[Twerza.]	‡ [Of Moscow.]

September 1.   Being the Russes Newyeares day, I went into the towne, was very kindly welcomed by the Boyar Kniaz Vasily Vasiliovits Golitzin, and afterwards see the eldest Czaar, and the procession. I convoyed the Boyar home, and wished him a good year, and dined in the Slobod, received some visitts, and went to another quarter.

September 2.   I stayed, and put my house in some order, and did writt to my wyfe per post.

September 3.   Being in towne, I dyned by Kniaz Vasily Vasiliovits Golitzin, made hast home, and received visitts.

September 4.   Haveing gott some stitches, and a sort of a bastard pleurisy, I gott some ease by letting of blood.

September 5.   I tooke in some spirit of hartshorne, about thirty drops, and yet gott no sweat.

September 6.   I tooke in a strong dose of pills, which had ordinary operation.

Sept. 7 and 8.   At home.

September 9.   I was in towne, and made some visitts to the neerest Boyars.

September 10.   I went to Czarny Grasse, to the Boyar Knias Vasily Vasiolivitz Golitzin, dined with him, and after dinner, had much discourse, yet nothing of carrying on the warr, only of my jorney, and my effaires. Wee went to hunting afterwards, and I tooke my leave in the fields.

Sept. 11 and 12.   At home.

September 13.   I was in towne, and should have been at the Emperours hand, to which end I stayed long above.* Being come home, Mr. Munter brought me the Kings letter to the Czaars in my favours.

September 14.   The Kings letter was delivered by the Hollands Resident, Mr. Van Keller, to whom it was recommended by the Hollands Ambassador, Mr. Citters, in London. I was at the Czaars hands, who only asked me of my health by a Boyar. Being brought to the Princess hand, she said, God reward thee for keeping thy word.

September 15.   The Kings letter was interpreted by a Dutchman, who understood but litle English.

October 24.   I dyned by Major Generall Bilts.

October 25.   I made ready a larger remonstrance, wherein I put many things not written in my former. I received letters from Riga, and dined by Commissary Van Korke.

* [That is, at court, in the Kremlin.]

My remonstrance, given in the twenty third, being translated, and read October 26. above,* received no answer.

I did writt to my wyfe, to Collonell Levingston, and to my sone in law, October 28. per post.

Haveing had notice from Riga that my things, sent from England, were October 29. forwarded to Plesko, I did writt thither that they should be sent forward to Mosko.

I gott Eustachius to translate my remonstrance in the Slavonian October 30. language.

I stayed at home, and heard devotion, and afternoone made some visitts. November 1.

I did writt to my wyfe per post. November 4.

I spooke to the Boyar† about sending for my wyfe, who gave me a November 5. dubious answer.

I, notwithstanding, resolved to send for my wyfe; and so did fall to November 6. writeing of letters.

I stayed my servants going, in hopes of getting Major Van Bockhoven November 8. to go along.

I dispatched my servants to Kyow for my wyfe, giveing them three November 9. horses along, and to four persons three rubles on the way.

I agreed for cutt dry birch wood, at halfe a ruble the fathom. November 10.

I did writt to my wyfe by a surgeon, who went to Baturin to the November 12. Hetman.

I dyned by Collonell Wibergh, where were a whole housefull of November 14. company.

The Russes began to forme their regiments, and joyned some of the November 15. Streletses regiments two in one.

I was told by some Russes, who pretended to be my ffriends, that if I November 16. did not petition for favour or grace, some severe methods were resolving on, as to send me, with my family, in some remote place of their empire.

I was by the Hollands Resident, who altogether declined to medle in November 17. my business, telling me that the Russes had from the avisoes conceived an evill opinion of our King, as favouring the Turkes too much.

I was by some of the great persons, some whereof told me that the November 18. Princess was very much incensed against me for my obstinacy, as it had

* [At court, or in council] † [Golizyn.]

been represented to her, and that she was enclined to have a harder sentence put upon me.

November 19.   I made another remonstrance ready, which I gott rectifyed by M. V.

November 20.   I gott the remonstrance written over by another hand.

November 21.   I was advertised by diverse ffriends, that if I did not, by confessing my fault, and craving their Majesties pardon, make hast, suddaine sentence was to be executed upon me; wherefor they advised me to make what hast I could to prevent the ruine of my self and family, which, if prolonged, their teares could not be able to help me. The thoughts of this so perplexed my mynd, that I could not gett sleeped the whole night; and the worst was, I had no body whom I durst trust with my mynd, all being ballanced by interrest, or careless of another mans state, or then not capable of affoording any help or counsell.

November 22.   The Emperour* and Princess being in Ismailow, I went thither in the morning early, and to the Boyars† lodging, where, after a whiles stay, the Boyar did fall out in great passion against me; and because I vindicated my self the best way I could, and had the great advantage of reason upon my syde, he was the more incensed, so that in great heat he ordered me to be writt in for an ensigne, and sent away the next day. Some noblemen comeing in, and hearing the contest, did fall all to the Boyars syde; and in his favour, though even against reason, and their owne judgement, began to lay a great deale of blame upon me, and urged me to take other measures. The Boyar also, with very high words, and threats, and reasoning, without all reason, or the least show of uprightnes, or valuing, or considering, any thing I said, insisted still that I should acknowledge my error, and crave pardon, and promise to serve in future. So that, knowing his power, and that all things were caryed according to will, and not to reason, or justice, and fearing the ruine of my family, I, with much reluctancy, consented to what they would have me; and so caused writt a very circumspect petition, acknowledging that, seeing by my petitioning to be out of the countrey, I had offended their Majesties, I desired pardon, and promised to serve as formerly. This petition being read above, was not thought sufficient, as not being penned in humble enough tearmes; so that, being forced, and threatened to be sent, with my family, to the remotest places of their empire, I told them they should sett downe, or give, a copy of such a one as

* [Ivan, the elder of the two Czars.]   [Golizyn.]

they desired; and so parting, I came to the Slobod, haveing seen in the way the glasse hutts.

I stayed these two dayes at home, being much grieved at the great in- Nov. 23 & 24. justice and wrong done to me.

I went to the towne, where, in the office, the Dumny Diack Yemelian November 25. Ignatjewitsch Ukraintzuf gave me the copy of a petition, which I should cause transcribe and subscrive. Haveing read it, I found some things in it not fitt, whereof blotting out these, I caused writt it over, and put my hand to it, albeit it was conceived in as submissive tearmes and expressions as could be done to God Almighty. When it was read above, there was a great silence, neither did the Princess say any thing, all knowing it to be forced from me by threats and compulsion.

Haveing ane occasion, I gave notice of what I had done to my ffriends November 26. in Shewsky.

I did give the same notice to my ffriends in Smollensko.   November 27.

I did writt to Collonell Hamilton in Shewsky at large.   November 28.

I received, by post, a letter from the Earle of Middleton, one of his November 29. Sacred Majesties of Great Brittaine principall Secretaries of State for England, the copy whereof is this:

Whitehall, 25 October, 1686.

Sir,

I have the favour of your letters of the twelfth of August, from Riga, and of the seventeenth of September, from Moskowe. I would have sooner acknowledged the first, had I been sooner instructed with the Kings pleasure thereupon; which I am now to tell you, is, That his Majestie thinks fitt to honour your self with the character of his Envoy Extraordinary to their Czaarish Majesties, and to that end your credentialls and instructions shall be forthwith prepared, and sent to you to Riga, where I hope this may meet you, and where you are to stay till your dispatches do arrive. In case you be further advanced towards us, I hope you will give me notice of it, that I may know whither to write you. I am,

Sir,
Your most faithfull humble servant,
MIDDLETON.

With this letter I was very much surprised. I went and consulted with the Hollands Resident, and the Chancellour Vinius, who gave me dubious and uncertaine advice.

November 30.   I went early to the Dumny Diack, Iemelian Ignatjewitsch Ukraintzuf, and told him, and gave him the letter.   Wee went together to the Boyar,* who told me, that I should translate it into Latin, and give it into the office to be translated into Russe; and this because they had no English translator. I gave in also a particular remonstrance with the letter, which was also translated.

December 1.   The Emperours and Princess went to the countrey in pilgrimage.   The Chieffe Minister of State* went along, and promised to make relation of my business.

December 3.   I did returne an answer to the Earle of Middleton, which I sent in a *coverto* to Mr. Samuel Meverell, and that to Mr. Frazer in Riga, desireing him to address it to Sir Peter Wyche, his Sacred Majesties resident in Hamburgh, under whose *coverto* it had come to him.   From Mosko, it went in Mr. John Sparvenfelts *coverto*.   The copy hereof is in my other booke.

December 4.   By vexation and grieving, I contracted a sicknes, which turned to a ague; whereby I was forced to keep my bed for the most part for some dayes.

December 8.   Their Majesties returned from their progress in the countrey.

December 9.   The Earle of Middletons letter, and my remonstrance, being read above, had no other effect but a confirmed deniall of letting me go.   The order was written so: The Czaars and Princess, with the Boyars, have heard these writeings above in the Privy Chamber, and have ordered that Livetennant Generall Patrick Gordon cannot be Extraordinary Envoy from the King to the Tzaars, because he is to be in the great army in this expedition against the Turks and Tartars; and that he, Patrick Gordon, shall writt to the Earle of Middleton, that if the King, to maintaine the brotherly love and amity with the Czaars, will send any ambassadour or envoy, he shall be received graciously, and with favour.

December 10.   I was called for, but was not in towne, not being able to come.

December 11.   Being in towne, I was sent for to the Boyars* house, who told me that the Czaars had graced me, and had remitted my fault, and ordered me to be in my former charge.   And so thus ended this stage play.   The justice

* [Golizyn.]

and equity which I had on my syde, may appear from the many remonstrances which I gave in; which, because they could not answer, they passed all over, and told only all were tales or fables. The copyes of all my remonstrances are apart.

I insisted to have a copy of the order on the Earle of Middletons letter, December 13. and my remonstrance, pretending not to understand the true sense of their words, saying that I would send the copy of their order, and fearing that if I wrote any thing of my self, it might disagree with their Majesties order.   But the incongruity of a word or two in the order letted that they would not give me a copy of it, and with much ado I recovered the originall of the Earle of Middletons letter.

The Boyar being at his village, I went and insisted for the copy of the December 16. order, which he promised me.   I came late home.

I did writt to Collonels Hamilton, Ronaer, and Menezes, and informed December 18. them of the progress of my effaires.

I received letters from the Earle of Melfort, Mr. Cooke, Mr. Meverell, December 20. and another letter from the Earle of Middleton to the same purpose, as also from my cousin Alexander, and my sonnes from Doway.

I returned answer to my sonnes letter, ordering James to stay there as December 24. he had been ordered before, and telling John, that seeing he had no mind to learne, I had ordered his going to Edinburgh to stay at the . . . some tyme to gett some knowledge in the lawes.

Being Christmasse, Fetka Mieln* came and told me of my wyfe being December 25. on the way, and that she would be here on Moonday.

I went and did meet my wyfe and children in Semenofsky, and came to December 27. the Slobod with them about midday.

I got orders to writt to the Earle of Middleton, and to show it in the December 29. pricase or office first.

I show the letter into the office in Latin, which being translated was December 30. approved of, and I ordered to send it by the first post.

I sent the forsaid letter, a copy whereof in my other copy booke of December 31. letters, by post, in a *coverto* to Mr. Frazer.

---

* [His servant.]

[A.D. 1687.

In a book quoted by the German editors—Korb's *Diarium Itineris in Moscoviam*, page 316—it is said that Gordon was not merely threatened with degradation, but that he was actually reduced to the lowest rank. But this statement seems to have been hazarded without sufficient grounds. Nor is it true, as the same writer affirms, that Gordon did not regain his former

January 2.   dignity until the fall of Golizyn. On the contrary, so early as January, 1687, he was formally apprised that, by order of the Czars, he was to command the select regiments of the second division, in a war against the Tartars of the Crimea. He lost no time in drilling his soldiers, and after a month's diligent exercise, was able to begin his march on the twenty-

February 22.   second of February.

To Gordon, as quartermaster-general, it fell to find the means of transport, to reconnoitre the line of advance, to make the roads and bridges, and to determine where the camp should be pitched for the night. The route was over steppes swarming with the light horse of the Tartars, so that the Muscovites had to march in dense columns, flanked on either hand by rows

May 8.   of waggons, to break the charge of the enemy. It is noted that, on the eighth of May, when the expedition set out from the neighbourhood of Kiew, the string of waggons, twenty thousand in number, was a thousand fathoms long, and five hundred and fifty-seven fathoms broad. By

June.   the middle of June, the army had reached the lower steppes of the Dnieper, when the grass having been set on fire by the Tartars, or, as was suspected, by the Cossack allies of the invading force, dearth of forage for the horses compelled a retreat. The troops were soon afterwards disbanded; thanks and more substantial rewards being bestowed upon the officers. Gordon's

September 11. services were recompensed by promotion to the rank of General.

A.D. 1688.

He spent the next year quietly at Moscow. He records that the Boyars, Peter Alexeiewitsch

January 8.   Golizyn, and Boris Feodorowitsch Dolgoruky, dined at his table in the beginning of January. A new city was to be built where the Samara flows into the Volga, and of the plans which were called for, Gordon's was chiefly followed. But he was not without his detractors. At a great council, the Patriarch spoke bitterly against him, saying that the Muscovite arms could not hope to prosper so long as a heretic commanded the best troops of the empire. But the Boyars only laughed at this display of orthodox zeal. From his Butirki regiment—so called from the place where it was quartered in the neighbourhood of Moscow—trained soldiers and drummers were drafted to Kolomenski, at that time the residence of the younger of the two Emperors; and this, it would seem, was the beginning of his intercourse with that remarkable man. Henceforth, the name of the Czar Peter becomes more and more frequent in the Diary.

January 25.   Thus, on the twenty-fifth of January, it is noted that a privy council was held, at which the Princess Sophia and both the Czars were present, the younger for the first time.

January 27   Two days afterwards, being the anniversary of the Czar Alexei Michaelowitsch of blessed memory, the younger Czar went to all the prikases, gave money to some prisoners, and set others free.

On the twentieth of February, at Woskresenskoje, there was firing of cannon and burning February 20. of fireworks in presence of the younger Czar.

On the twenty-eighth of June, there was service in the cathedral in honour of the birthday June 28. of the younger Czar. The Boyars and other great people got brandy from his Majesty, and a cup of wine from his mother, the Empress Dowager.

On the thirtieth of August, Gordon writes, 'I was in Kolomensk and dined by the Boyar, August 30. when the Boyar said to me: Wee could agree well enough with your Kings father and brother, but we cannot come to right with this; he is prowd beyond all measure. I, makeing as if I understood only his not sending any hither, answered, That the King, because of his great troubles in his owne dominions, had not leasure to think of business lying so farr off, as I thought. He said, moreover, That the English could not subsist without their commodities, as leather, hempe, potash, tallow, and masts; to the which I gave a dubious complying answer.'

On the second of September, eight soldiers were selected from Gordon's regiment to serve September 2. as grooms to the younger Czar.

On the seventh of September, the Czar Peter sent an express for five fifers and as many September 7. drummers from Gordon's regiment. The Boyar Golizyn was highly displeased that they should have been despatched without his knowledge. The Czar soon sent for more drummers, and Gordon gave him five.

On the eighth of September, the Czar sent to the Boyar for more drummers and fifers, and September 8. the Boyar complied with the demand, although much against his will.

On the twenty-third of September, the younger Czar sent for a drunken serjeant, or clerk of September 23. a company, and inquired if the serjeants or clerks had any distinctive rank and pay. He asked questions about other small matters. This was not well taken.

On the fourteenth of October, Gordon celebrated the King of England's birthday in company October 14. with several of his countrymen. They were all very merry, and at parting, the Dutch resident remarked that His Majesty was happy in having subjects who observed his birthday so joyfully at such a distance from his dominions.

On the thirteenth of November, all the drummers of Gordon's regiment were called away by November 13. the Czar Peter, along with ten soldiers, to serve as grooms.

On the twenty-second of November, Gordon had a conversation with 'the second favourite,' November 22. Feodor Leontjewitsch Schaklowitoj, and with other persons in authority, on the designs of the Dutch against England.

On the ninth of December, Gordon received tidings from Riga that the Prince of Orange December 9. had landed at Torbay on the fifth of November. It was not until the thirteenth of January that he heard of King James' flight from England.

A.D. 1689.

On the twentieth of January, the Czar Peter, now in his seventeenth year, was married to January 20. Eudoxia Feodorowna Lapuchin. The marriage festivities were held at court on the seventh of February.

The renewal of the war against the Crim Tartars was now resolved upon; and, in February, Gordon received orders to hold himself in readiness. But he was required first to furnish plans for the military lines of defence on the Dnieper, and to make some other arrangements. All these having been performed to the great satisfaction of the court, Gordon set out with the

May

army, acting as before in the capacity of quartermaster-general. By the end of May, he had conducted it as far as Perekop, when the enterprise being thought too hazardous, the troops were again ordered back. Rewards were once more distributed among the officers, but not without strong opposition from the younger Czar. Besides a share in such common gifts as a piece of velvet, and a glass of brandy from the Emperor's hand, Gordon had the special privilege accorded to him of being addressed for the future in the third person, whether in speech or in writing, and of being styled Ivanowitsch, that is, the son of John (his father's name.)

July 24.

He notes, in his Diary, on the twenty fourth of July, that the younger Czar refused for a time to sanction what he considered the excessive rewards given to the officers. Three days

July 2 .

afterwards he was persuaded to give his consent, but he would not receive the officers when they went to Preobraschenskoje to thank him. They had thus, as Gordon expresses it in his country's proverb, ' to take the bitt and the buffet with it.' Every body saw that a storm was brewing at court.

August 6.

On the sixth of August, there were 'rumours unsafe to be uttered.'

August 7.

The next day, the tempest broke. At midnight, tidings reached the Czar Peter that the Strelitzes and soldiers of the guard had received orders from the Kremlin to march upon Preobraschenskoje, and to put certain persons to death. He instantly sprang from his bed, and without waiting to pull on his boots, ran to the stables, and flinging himself upon a horse, galloped to the nearest wood. Here he remained till his clothes were brought him, when, accompanied by a few attendants, he renewed his flight, and riding in hot haste, reached the monastery of Troitzka (the Holy Trinity,) about forty miles from the capital, by six o'clock in the morning. Throwing himself upon a bed, he burst into tears, and telling what had happened, besought the protection and help of the abbot.

It was now an open struggle between the young Czar and the Princess Sophia. Peter summoned the Strelitzes and other troops in Moscow to join him at Troitzka. The Princess forbade their march. The Czar renewed his command in a written order, addressed to the foreign officers, stating that there was a conspiracy against his life. Gordon undertook to show the writing to Golizyn, and to ask what was to be done. The minister tried to dissemble his alarm, and said he would consult the elder Czar and the Princess Sophia. Gordon answered that if he and his brother officers were to disobey, their heads would be in danger. Golizyn assured him that he should have an answer before night, and desired that Gordon's son-in-law, Colonel Strasburg, might be left behind to carry it. This seems to have decided Gordon. He went home, and immediately began to prepare for marching. When the other officers came to him, he told them that, whatever order might come from the Kremlin, he had resolved to set out for Troitzka that night. They avowed themselves ready to follow his example, and the next day saw them all at the gates of the monastery. The young Czar was at his mid-day dinner when their arrival was announced. Gordon was at once admitted to His Majesty's presence, and ordered to keep by his side, while the other officers remained with their regiments outside the monastery.

Four days after, Peter entered Moscow in triumph, and the trial of the conspirators began. Schaklowitoj, the second favourite, as Gordon calls him, was tortured and beheaded along with many others; the Czar's reluctance to shed blood having been overcome by the Patriarch. Golizyn himself was banished, and his estates confiscated, his life being spared through the intercession of his kinsman, who was Peter's chief adviser. The Princess Sophia was sent to a convent, where she died after a seclusion of fifteen years. And the imbecile Ivan agreed that the sole rule of the empire should be in the hands of his younger and more energetic brother. The revolution was complete, and Gordon, who had done so much to bring it about, enjoyed a fair share of its advantages.

A.D. 1690.

On the eighth of January, the Governor of Terki, Andrei Besobraszow, who had employed *January 8.* magic to regain the favour of the Czar, whom he had displeased, was put to death; and two others, whom he had instigated to bewitch the Czar, were burned. Ten of his servants were beaten with the knout, and sent to Siberia. One of the culprits being asked at his trial what means of witchcraft he used, answered, that placing himself to windward of the person whom he wished to propitiate, he made a wind blow which gained the end desired.

It is noted, on the tenth of January, that the mother in-law of the Boyar, Andrei Iwanowitsch *January 10.* Golizyn, having spoken against the government of the Czar and his friends, in the hearing of the Boyar and others, the Boyar and his friends were banished, their property confiscated, and some of their servants knouted.

The next day, Gordon was at the Kremlin, and saw the Czar, who was making ready *January 11.* fireworks.

On the sixteenth of January, Gordon dined at the Kremlin. The fireworks were set off, and *January 16.* were successful.

Three days afterwards, Gordon was again at court, and accompanied the Czar to the country *January 19.* house of a Boyar, where they were entertained at a sumptuous noon-day meal. They next went to a summer residence of the Czar, where they set off fireworks, and returning to the Boyar's house, had another sumptuous banquet.

The entry in next day's journal is that he was ill of the last night's debauch, and had to keep *January 20.* his bed till afternoon.

He dined at the Kremlin on the twenty-first of January, and was there again next day, when *January 21,22.* his son-in-law burned his face in making fireworks.

On the twenty-third of January, he was at the funeral of Colonel Bockhoven's wife. He *January 23.* went into the city next day, but did not go to the Kremlin, as it is not permitted to appear *January 24.* before the Czar for three days after being at a burial or seeing a corpse.

January 28.   The twenty-eighth of January was spent in writing to Scotland, to his son John, to the Earl of Erroll, and to the Earl of Aberdeen. This last letter follows:

TO THE EARLE OF ABERDEEN.

Mosco, 28 January, 1690.

May it please your Lordship,

     I doubt not but myne of the fyrst February last yeare is come to your hands, for I had notice of the receit thereof at London. I am perplexed that I have heard nothing from thence in two yeares, for which I blame the negligence of my sonne very much; for albeit by the troubles there, the passage by the way of London might have been uncertain, yet I doubt not but ships have come from Aberdeen to Dantzick, by which he might have written.

     I am very much grieved for the troubles, divisions, and the distracted condition of that our poor country. I pray God to grant peace and quietness, for there is nothing more, as to my owne particular, which I desire in this world, as to come home and end my lyfe, where I received it, in tranquillity. I have written to Nethermuir, and my sonne, concerning the particulars of my affaires, so that I only most earnestly recommend to your Lordship's care and protection my sonne and effaires there. So takeing leave, I remaine

        Your Lordship's most humble and devoted servant,

              P. GORDON.

January 31.   On the thirty-first of January, the Czar gave orders that Gordon's wine and other things should pass free of duty.

February 4, 5.   On the fourth and fifth of February, he was in the city, and had long conversations with the Czar. This is an entry which now falls to be frequently repeated.

February 19.   On the nineteenth of February, he was in the city. When the Czar returned from church, he gave Gordon a glass of brandy with his own hand. Gordon was again summoned to the Kremlin in the evening, and had to stay there all night.

February 2?   On the twenty-third of February, the troops repaired to the Kremlin to congratulate the Czar on the birth of a son. Gordon, in name of the regiments which he commanded, made the following speech:—'God grant that thou, Great Czar, and Grand Duke Peter Alexeiewitsch, Autocrat of all Great, Little, and White Russia, and Lord, Heir, and Ruler, though father and grandfather, of many lordships and lands in east, west, and north, with your Majesty's new born heir and our lord the most Serene Prince and Grand Duke Alexei Petrowitsch, of Great, Little, and White Russia, may be preserved in health many years.' Gordon then drew up his regiments in line three deep, the first rank kneeling, the second stooping, the third standing. In this position they fired all at once, while their drums were beat, and banners waved. The Czar was so delighted with all this, that he ordered it to be repeated again and again.

On the twenty-fourth, and, again on the twenty-sixth, of February, there were displays of Feb. 24, 26. fireworks, under direction of the Czar. A five-pound rocket went wrong, and carried off the head of a Boyar. Gordon did not get home till morning.

Two days afterwards, Gordon should have dined at the Kremlin, but the Patriarch protested February 28. against the presence of a foreigner.

The next day, the Czar made him be invited to a country house, where His Majesty and March 1. Gordon dined at a table by themselves. Peter kept talking to him all the way home. Gordon confesses that next day he was not very well.

Towards the middle of March, he notes the receipt of his half year's pay, amounting to 271 March 10. rubles, 6 alten, 4 dangi.

On the thirtieth of April, the Czar, with the Boyars and chief men of the court, supped with April 30. Gordon, and were well satisfied .

In the beginning of May, he writes to the Earl of Melfort: ' We have had a change at court. May 8. The Princess and her favourites were overthrown, and the younger Czar and his party assumed the government. The elder Czar remains as formerly. I have got this court to own still his Sacred Majesty, and not to hear of any other.'

There was a great feast in honour of the Czar's birthday, on the thirtieth of May. After May 30. dinner, the Czar himself handed a glass of brandy to each guest.

At a mock assault, on the second of June, a fire pot, as it is called, burst close by the Czar June 2. and burned his face. Gordon and other bystanders were slightly wounded.

On the twentieth of July, there was a division among the clergy regarding the election of a June 20. Patriarch. The higher clergy, with the Czar Peter, were for one Marcellus, but he was opposed by the inferior clergy, and the dowager Czarina, because, as they said, he had too much knowledge, and would, they feared, favour the Roman Catholics and other sectaries.

Along with the Czar, Gordon rode to Troitzka on the twenty-fourth of July, and dined with July 24. the Boyar Boris Alexeiewitsch Golizyn, where there was the greatest abundance of everything.

The next morning Gordon had a severe colic, which lasted for four hours, with violent July 25. vomiting and diarrhœa. The Czar himself came into Gordon's room, and promised, as soon as he got back to Kolomenskoje, to send him medicine. It came about one o'clock, and gave him such relief, that two hours afterwards he was able to ride to Kolomenskoje, a distance of fourteen versts.

On the fourteenth of August, Gordon dined with the Czar at the house of a Boyar.   August 14.

The Czar and others made very merry in Gordon's house on the twenty-second of August.   August 22.

The election of a Patriarch was made on the next day. Marcellus was not chosen. The August 23. Czar wished him, but he was hated by the old Boyars and the generality of the clergy for his learning and other good qualities.

On the morrow, there was a great feast, with fireworks in the evening. The Czar was so August 27.

delighted that he made the Boyars, counsellors, and officers stay with him and carouse all night in the great hall. During the debauch, he took offence at something which was said, and was not pacified but with the greatest difficulty.

September 23.   Gordon's daughter, Mary, was married to Captain Daniel Crawfurd on the twenty-third of September, and the Czar graced the nuptials with his presence.

October 25.   On the twenty-fifth of October, the Czar dined with General Le Fort, Gordon being one of the party.

November 15.   On the fifteenth of November, he wrote to the Duke of Gordon at Paris, and to the Earl of Melfort at Rome.]

FOR HIS GRACE THE DUKE OF GORDON.

Mosco, Novembris 15, 1690.

May it please your Grace,

The sad revolution in our countrey, and the Kings misfortunes, wherein your Grace hath a large share, hath occasioned inexpressible grieffe to me, which brought me in a sicknesse and even almost to deaths doore. Had I been in a place where I could have been serviceable to his Majestie, I should have vented my passion another way. I perceived even when I was there, that the Kings too great goodnes and credulity in intrusting dissaffected and ill principled persons in high charges, could not but prove fatall. Notwithstanding all that hath fallen out, I am sorry from my heart that his Majestie did not, when I was in Scotland, lay his commands upon me to stay there, albeit without employment. Then might I have had occasion, at this tyme, to have given proofs of my loyalty and what I can do. Wee have nothing from our countrey but what wee have from the Hollands Gazets, from which, though partiall, wee may collect that the want of good conduct and vigilancy are partly the causes why his Majesties effaires and armes have so bad success there. If there were any likelyhood of doing any good, and that I had a commission, I am ready still to hazard lyfe and all I have in his Majesties service, and for the maintaining of his just right, and that in any place where his Majestie shall command, and in whatsoever quality I may be thought capable of. I may have some difficulty in getting of from hence, yet being so near the Tzaar as I am now (for I have access to his Majestie every day), I doubt not but to obtaine licence, if it be but for a tyme. I have gott this court still to owne his Sacred Majestie, and not to heare of any other. If their friendship could signify any thing to the effaires of his Majestie or the Most Christian Kings, it may (notwithstanding former disgusts) be obtained by a message from the

Most Christian King, which, perhaps, he will not send because he will not seeme to be seeking. Yet it might breed great ombragies and jealousies in our neighbours, albeit it were but a complement. I shall think myself much honoured by receiveing a line from your Grace. The way of Polland is not the best, because of the suspicions and jealousies ariseing betwixt these nations. So, committing your Grace to the protection of the Omnipotent, I desire still to be esteemed

Your Graces most humble servant,
P. GORDON.

Pray cause forward the enclosed.

FOR HIS EXCELLENCY THE EARLE OF MELFORT, AT ROME.

Mosco, 15 Novembris, 1690.

May it please your Excellency,

I find myself honoured with your acceptable of the fyfthe of August, some posts ago. I am glad to heare of the least hopes or appearance of any good in his Majesties effaires, and am sorry that in Irland things have gone so cross. Wee have nothing here but what wee learne from the Hollands Gazetts, from which, though partiall, wee may gather that all does not go in our countreyes according to Orange his wishes; so that it may be hoped that by tyme a strong partie may appear, and act vigorously for his Majesties restauration. I wonder how they can endure so long such slavery and oppressions by forreigne forces, and intollerable taxations. I looke upon that revolution as another conquest by a medley of forreigne nations. I am sorry that I must, in such a tyme, be a looker on, and not capacitated to serve his Majestie with any thing but prayers, wishes, and goodwill. Wee have not here been in a condition to act any thing this summer, but are resolving of doing some thing the next, to please our allyes. I have nothing else now, but still desire to be esteemed

Your Excellencys most humble servant,
P. GORDON.

[He wrote to his son John at the same time. On Christmas Eve, he notes in his Diary :]

In towne. The copy of the letter from the pretended King of England, December 24. calling himself William the Third, and dated the third of June, interpreted, and no further notice taken of it, upon pretension that the Hollands Resident his name was not in it, it being sent to him to be delivered publikely and solemnly. Another had been sent befor, dated in Aprill, but not haveing the full titles, was returned by the Resident, and this sent; so that it seemes they must have a third, and then a question if that shall be received, for diverse reasons.

[To this year, apparently, must be referred the following memorial of Gordon's services in Russia. It is written by his own hand:]

P. I. Gordon, by birth a Scottishman, came in the quality of Major to Mosko, in the yeare 7169th [A.D. 1661], and was sent out of the ambassy into the stranger office; and in the yeare 7171 [A.D. 1663] in September, was preferred, for his comeing into the countrey, to be Lievetennent Colonell; and was in the yeare 7172 and 3 [A.D. 1664-5] at his Maiesties service in Smolensko; and in the yeare 7173 [A.D. 1665], the 11th of February, he was preferred, for his services, to be Colonell. In the yeare 7174 [A.D. 1666] he was sent on his Maiesties affaires to England. In the yeare 7176 [A.D. 1668], he was at service in Trubschefsky, Branskoy, and other Ukrainish townes. In the yeare 7179 [A.D. 1671] he was at Novoskol against the rebellious Cosakes; and from that yeare to the 7185th yeare [A.D. 1677], he was at service in Skewsky, and from Shewsky in the 7182, 7183, 7184 yeares [A.D. 1674—A.D. 1679], he was at service at Kaniow, Pereaslaw, and at Czegrin at the takeing of Doroschenko; and in the 7185th yeare [A.D. 1677], at the seige of Czegrin. And in the 7186th yeare [A.D. 1678], he was in Czegrin at the siege or beleaguering of [it], in which yeare, the 20th of August, for his service at Czegrin, he was preferred to be Major Generall, and was at the marching of from Czegrin, until the army was dismissed the 11th of September, in the 7187 etc. [A.D. 1679]. From this yeare to the 7191 [A.D. 1683], he was at service in Kyow, in which yeare, he was, for his service, preferred to be Livetennent Generall, and was thereafter in Kyow to the 7195 yeare [A.D. 1687], in which yeare, he received the command of the Moskowish Selected Regiments of Sojours, and the same yeare, was at service in the Crimish expedition. In the 7196th yeare [A.D. 1688], the 11th of September, he was, for his services, preferred to be Generall. In the 7197th yeare [A.D. 1689], he was at service in the Crimish expedition; and in the 7198th yeare [A.D. 1690], in the expedition to the Monastery of the Holy Trinity of Serge.

[A.D. 1691.

On the second of January, Gordon was at Preobraschenskoje, and, when taking leave, was January 2. ordered by the Czar to make ready dinner and supper for his Majesty and the court next day.

The Czar came about ten o'clock in the morning, and immediately sat down to table. He January 3. was accompanied by eighty-five persons of distinction, with about a hundred servants. They were all very merry, both at dinner and at supper, and spent the night as if in camp.

On the fourth of January, his Majesty and the whole company dined with Lefort.   January 4.

Gordon notes, on the nineteenth of January, that 'the Hollands Resident was prevailed upon January 19. to receive the pretended King William his letter to their Tzaarish Majesties;' and, five days after- January 24. wards, that 'the Hollands Resident gave up the letter from the Prince of Orange, giveing notice of his being advanced to the crowne of Great Britaine.'

On the sixth of March, the Czar made Gordon a gift of silver plate and other confiscated March 6. property, worth in all a thousand rubles.

Towards the end of May, he again wrote to the Duke of Gordon.]   May 22.

FOR HIS GRACE THE DUKE OF GORDON.

Mosco, 22 Maij, 1691.

May it please your Grace,

I received, by the last ordinary, your Graces most kind and obligeing letter, dated at London the twelfth April, *anno* 1690, being sent from Varsow by Harie Gordon. Haveing heard of your Grace being in Paris, I did writt to your Grace the fyfteenth of November last yeare, with an enclosed, being a returne to the Earle of Melfort. I shall be glad to hear your Grace hath received it. Your Graces behaviour all along is highly commendable, and in myne opinion, and all honest mens, you have done very wysely. Wee have nothing here but as represented to us by the Dutch and Hollands Gazettes, which are partiall; yet wee may collect that Orange is not so setled but he may be removed. For I cannot imagine but that, when the English see their purses emptyed, their trade ruined, and their necks bowing under a forreigne yoke, and small hopes of prevailing against the Most Christian King, a sense of loyalty and generosity, at least of their owne ruine and slavery, may prevaill so as to move the most generous of them to take other measures. There is nothing here more highly commended in the Most Christian King, as his generous and most Christian resolution, not to give eare to any peace untill his Sacred Majestie, our gracious King, be restored.   As for Harie Gordon,* he is in Varsow in Polland, exspecting my advice, which I have sent him by this post.   I have showne him the conveniencies and inconveniencyes of this countrey, so that, if he resolve to come in hither, I shall not be wanting in any thing that lyes in my power to do for him.   By our change at court, I am in a better condition as formerly to help myself and others, haveing the favour of the yongest Czaar in a large measure, and dayly accesse to him.   Here is an *internuncius* from the Roman Emperour, sent hither to move us to divert the Tartars, but lyke to prevail litle, wee neither being in a capacity, nor resolved, to do any more as intended befor his comeing, which is to defend oure borders.

I shall, from my heart, wish to hear of hopes of his Sacred Majesties restauration, and that your Grace may enjoy your owne in tranquillity, to the which, if I knew a way to contribute any thing, I would most willingly hazard my lyfe and fortunes.   I long to hear if your Grace approve of what I wrote in my former.   In the meane tyme, I confort my self very much with the thoughts that your Grace is pleased to give me a place in your remembrance and favour, the continuance whereof I humbly crave, and shall, as in duty obliged, remaine

Your Graces most humble and totally devoted servant

whilst I breath,

P. GORDON.

[Gordon's son-in-law, Colonel Strasburg, after repeated injuries from the Czar's fireworks, of which he seems to have taken the chief charge, was, in January of this year, burned almost to death by an explosion which killed three others outright.   He lingered on till December, when becoming worse, the Czar visited him nearly every day until his death on the fourth of January, 1692.   His widow received a pension of three hundred rubles.

A.D. 1692.

The beginning of this year found Gordon occupied with settlements of his Scotch affairs, for the approaching marriage of his eldest son with Elizabeth Grant, eldest daughter of the Laird of Crichie.]

* [Probably the gentleman of the same name who, two years before, served under the Duke of Gordon as one of the garrison of Edinburgh Castle.—(Siege of the Castle of Edinburgh in 1689, pp. 36, 58, 60, 75.)

The German editors inform us that Captain Harry Gordon arrived at Moscow in the year 1691, and was well received, being promoted to the rank of major in the following year, through the influence of General Patrick Gordon. That officer writes in his Diary on the eighth of November, 1694: 'This afternoon took place the betrothal or Major Harry Gordon with the second daughter of the late Colonel Roonaer.   I lent the Colonel's widow 7½ rubles.   Major Roonaer paid me 3 rubles, 20 alten, and remained still 2 rubles in my debt.'   Harry Gordon is last heard of at Archangel, in the year 1698, when he was in correspondence with General Patrick Gordon.]

TO HIS SON JOHN.

Mosco, January 11, 1692.

Loveing Son,

My last to you was the eighth August, by Captain William Gordon, since which I have yours of the third of July; as also, a joint letter from my unkle and Nethermuir, which I answered the next post after I received it, viz., the twelfth past, and gave notice of my resolution. But now to the particulars of yours. You tell me of many letters you have written, but how addressed, nothing; and if there be any miscarriage, it is betwixt that and London or Dantzick, for Mr. Meverell in the first, and Patrick Forbes in the last, are very carefull, to whom you should writt, and enclose that to me in theirs. You tell me of paying postage from Mosco to Aberdeen, for a packet dated the sixteenth of February last, which is a great abuse, and I would gladly know where it lyeth, for I sent that packet by a ffriend, one Mr. Brest, to Amsterdam, enclosing it in a letter to Mr. James Gordon, merchant in Roterdam, who gave me notice that he had forwarded it, but whether by ffriend or post he gave me no notice, so that at the most you have but payed postage from Amsterdam to Aberdeen, after which you may enquire. As to the business of the wedsett of the Mains,* you may use the ordinary course and diligence, as also in the business with Watertowne. I wonder to hear of a backbond given to my brother John by my father concerning the Muirtake. It was great injustice in him to conceale it when I was there, and even malice now to detaine it. If I had knowne any thing of it, I had not ordered his bond of four hundred merks to be given to him befor he had restored that. How he hath dealt with me, it is well knowne. It was great injustice in him, if not worse (if worse can be), first to move my father to give him an heretable right to the Muirtake, which could not be either justly or lawfully done, my father haveing disposed the heretable right of the whole to me befor that; and then to take a bond of our father for three hundred merks, and hereupon to serve himself executor creditor, thereby to defraude me and the rest of the moveables and any thing left by our parents. But, *transeat;* I never see men useing un-

* [The Mains of Auchleuchries.]

just wages thrive.   I think he may be summoned, and constrained to deliver that bond.   The Earle of Aberdeen, to whom I entrusted the inspection of my effaires, by whose advise, at lest consent, it was done, and who assuredly promised to me, at my last being in Scotland, that I should have my owne againe, should be sollicited to gett his nephew* to do me justice.   At Captain Gordons going from hence, he and I made up our accounts, and he remained owing to me only three hundred merks, with the annuall rent for eight yeares, which amounteth to nynety six punds Scottish ; and two hundred merks, with the annuall rent for fyve yeares, which amounteth to forty punds Scottish ; in all four hundred and sixty nine punds Scottish, six shillings eight pence, which strive to recover, and put it out upon bond, bearing annuall rent in my name, to some responsable person ; which bond must be given in custody to my unkle, Nethermuir, or to any other whom they and the Earle of Aberdeen shall advise.   As for the things I did writt for, send them when you have a sure occasion to Dantzick or London.   I left the notice of the things left in Edinburgh with you, and send it twice since, and now againe under my hand.   See to recover them ; but to make a jorney to Edinburgh, without haveing other business, will be expensive.

I am sorry for the death of my brother James, but more for the poor condition he hath left his family in.

As for London James, I hope, at his displenishing, you have recovered all is due from him, being very sorry for his inconstancy.

I have not received a letter from you since that, by your brother James, of A.D. 1690.   Letters of the fyfth May, not received, were sent to Dantzick, so that your Aberdeens merchants are negligent, it seemes.   My letters writt last yeare are of the second January and sixteenth February, which you say you have received.   The others are of the fyfth of May, per post to London, and of the eighth of August, by Captain Gordon.   As to the last, but of greatest consequence, I have sent a disposition of the heretable right of the lands of Achluichries to you, reserving only for my self and my wyfe, during our lives, the summe of three hundred merks yearly ; and my wyfe, for security, to be infeft in the two pleughs of Easter Achluichries (free of publick dues and burthens, as it was in the tyme of Gawn Cruikshanks wedsett) ; as also two thousand punds Scottish as a portion for one of my other sons, but not to beare annuall rent untill he comes thither himself to setle.

* [Thomas Forbes of Waterton.]

I do this upon my unkles recommendation and advice, albeit I know that this Laird of Pitfoddels his father marryed twice, and gott considerable portions, without being infeft in a furr of land so long as his father lived, and diverse others too long here to mention.

Thus you see how punctually I have answered every particular of your letter, which you but litle observe in answering of myne, and leaves out the maine thing, which is the accounts of the rents of the lands, and how disposed. And now you haveing for your owne proper use so much of the lands, I expect hereafter a more exact account of what I have reserved for myself, which may move me not to forgett you when I dy.

This yeare of my age hath been a sad and unfortunate yeare to me, haveing lost both my sons in law; the eldest whereof, Collonell Strasburg, was buryed but fyve dayes ago, the other in May last; two of the compleetest and best qualifyed men in this countrey. Collonell Strasburg hath left a son and two daughters, and Major Crawfuird a posthumous son.

[In a letter, of the same date, to his uncle, James Gordon of Westertown, he forwarded conveyances of the lands of Auchleuchries, to his son John.]

COPY OF THE DISPOSITION GIVEN TO MY SON JOHN, OF MY LANDS OF ACHLUICHRIES IN SCOTLAND.

Be it knowne to all men by thir presents, that I, Patrick Gordon of Achluichries, Generall over the Selected Regiments of his Imperiall Majesty of All Russia, do hereby fully and freely dispose and give over the heritable right of all the lands of Achluichries, lying within the parish of Crowdan, in the shire of Aberdeen, in Scotland, to my oldest son, John Gordon; reserving only for me and my wyfe our lyferents of the two pleughs of Easter Achluichries, and that free from all publick dues and burthens or any the least other particular duty or acknowledgment to any person whatsomever; as also, two thousand punds Scottish as a portion for one of my sons who may come to Scotland and setle there, and to whom it shall be assigned; yet this summe of two thousand punds Scottish to beare no annuall rent untill the first Whitsunday after he shall come to Scotland, and then the aforesaid summe to be delivered to him, or assignes, or to be left upon annuall rent as he pleaseth. I will also that my said son John be countable to me for the yearly rents of the said two pleughs of Easter Achluichries, and that free of all publick dues and burthens; and the said money to be given out to responsable persons upon bonds bearing annuall rents, and the said bonds written in my name, and to be given in keeping to my uncle, James Gordon of Westertowne, and my cousin, John Gordon of Nethermuir, or to any other to whom they shall advise and agree to be given unto. And because, in this countrey, wee are ignorant of the formes and termes of law in Scotland, so have I subscrived foure sheets of paper battered together, both on the margins at the glewing or battering, and at the bottome, befor the same witnesses that this is subscrived, to witt, Maior Generall Pawl Menezes, Colonell Alexander Liviston, and Maior Hary Gordon, desireing that the said blank sheets be filled up, conforme to the Scottish formes, with the contents hereof, being a full and free disposition of the heritable rights of all the lands of Achluichries to my son, John Gordon, reserving only for my and my wifes liferent the two pleughs of Easter Achluichries and two thousand punds Scottish in manner as above, and that a bond of provision, and such other instruments requisite and usuall in law be made and taken and delivered into the custody of my unkle, James Gordon of Westertowne, and John Gordon of Nethermuir, or in any others hands in whose they shall advise and agree with the Earle of Aberdeen : constituteing for my proctors, James Gordon of Westertowne, John Gordon of Nethermuir, Patrick Gordon of Cults, these or any two of them ; and the bond of provision and the writeing for the three hundred merks to be registrate. So given at Mosco, the eleventh of January, in the yeare of our redemption 1692.

THE EXACT COPY OF THE DISPOSITION SENT TO SCOTLAND.

Be it knowne to all men by thir presents, that I, Patrick Gordon of Achluichries, Generall over the Selected Regiments of their Imperiall Majesties of All Russia, do hereby fully and freely dispone, and give over, to my eldest son, John Gordon, the hereditary right of all the lands of Achluichries, lying within the parish of Crowden, in the shire of Aberdeen, in Scotland ; reserving for me and my wife, dureing our naturall lives, the summe of three hundred merks Scottish money yearly ; and for the more security thereof, my wyfe, Elisabeth Born Roonaer, to be infeft in the lands of the two pleughs of Easter Achluichries : which summe of three hundred merks yearly, is to be payed at the terme of Whitesunday next, and so, yearly, so long as I and my wyfe liveth ; and to be punctually delivered to my uncle, James Gordon of Westertowne, John Gordon of Nethermuir, and

Patrick Gordon of Cults, and they, or any two of them their discharges, to be sufficient acquittances, I haveing entrusted my effaires there to them; reserving also, as a portion for one of my other sons, to whom I shall assigne it, the summe of two thousand punds Scottish, which summe of two thousand punds is not to beare annuall rent untill the first Whitesunday after he to whom it shall be assigned shall come to Scotland, and produce the assignation or attested copy of my testament; and for the more security hereof, a bond of provision to be made up, and that, as well as the infiofment, to be registrate according to our Scottish formes, and these bonds and writeings to be delivered to the custody of my above mentioned ffriends, whom, also, for this and other purposes, I constitute my proctors; and because, in this remote place, wee are ignorant of the Scottish formes of such dispositions and other writeings, so have I subscrived foure sheets of paper battered together, subscrived on the margine at the battering or glewing, and at the bottome, to be filled up according to the Scottish formes, befor the same witnesses that this is subscrived, to witt, Major Generall Pawll Menezes, Collonell Alexander Leviston, and Major Hary Gordon.   So done at Mosko, A.D. 1692, the eleventh of January.

TO THE EARLE OF ABERDEEN.

Mosco, 11 January, 1692.

May it please your Lordship,

My last was the eighth of August, by Rothemayes brother. By this I have sent a disposition of the heretable right of the lands of Achluichries to my eldest son, John, reserving two hundred punds Scottish yearly for me and my wyfe, during our lives; as also two thousand punds Scottish, a portion for one of my other sons.   For security of the first, I desire that my wyfe be infeft in the two pleughs of Easter Achluichries, and for the other, a bond of provision to be made, which writeings, and a bond for the money, to be gott from Rothemay, and any other writeings, I desire to be given in custody to any whom your Lordship shall advise; for it is dangerous tyme now, and the old proverb proveth but too oft true:

Non pater a filio, non hospes ab hospite tutus,
Non socer a genero, fratrum quoque gratia rara est.

And to say the truth, I have reserved that rather to keep my son in duty, and to make him frugall, than that I have any hopes of ever comeing to that countrey. I entreat you to gett Watertowne to do me justice. I rely upon your Lordships word, that I should have my owne againe. As in this, so in all my other concernes there, I rely on your Lordships protection. I was moved to send the disposition upon the account of my sons intending to marry. I have nothing else, but the tenor of humble and due respect, *etc.*

TO THE DUKE OF GORDON.

Mosco, 12 January, 1692.

May it please your Grace,

My last was the twenty second of May last yeare, since which I have the honour of your Graces most acceptable of the twenty second July, which made me grieved, and, in some measure, contented. I am exceedingly grieved to heare of your Graces great losses, and that you must live so farr and so long from your owne; and am thereby surprized to hear of the large measure of hard usage you had in such a tyme, when loyall persons should have been cherished and courted by all who loved the King and governement. It seemes they had forgott the maxime of King James the Sixthe in his Basilicon Doron, that loyalty runneth in a race or lyne. Whom should they have trusted, or who was able to have maintained the Kings authority and their interest, if not your Grace? I remember King Charles the First, by evill counsell, upon the account of lessening the greatnes of your house, tooke away the hereditary sherifdomes of Aberdeen and Inverness from your predecessour, as his great grandmother did the earledomes of Marr and Murray, which albeit it did not make them recede from their loyalty, yet it made them less capable of serving their Majesties in their need.

I have seen your Apologeticall Relation, and have heard by Harry Gordon and others, passages which may justly eternize your memory for your loyalty and sufferings, and raise both joy and compassion in all loyall hearts. As for my owne part, I am sorry that I had not the honour and happines to have been entertained in his Majesties service, and at such a tyme to have had occasion to have signalized my loyalty. I am very sensible of your Graces favour and endeavors to that purpose, and you were even then but too true a prophet. I am infinitely obliged to your Grace for your gracious expressions, and the esteeme you are pleased to have for my unworthines. Wee live here in peace, neither can the perswasions and pressings of the allyes move us to enter upon any great action in hast. I am still in a cumbersome court lyfe.   In the meane tyme, I am heartily rejoiced to heare that your Grace is in good health, and that you are, as all the world, satis-fyed with your owne behaviour and actions, and shall be exceeding glad to heare, from tyme to tyme, how your Grace disposeth of yourself, of whose wellfare and prosperity none can be a greater well wisher, as

Your Graces most devoted and humble servant,

P. GORDON.

[A.D. 1693.

The first entry in the Diary of this year, is, on the first of January: 'God grant us all a January 1. happy new year. I waited on his Majesty, and told him that the mortars had been examined, and found fit for use'

The Czar set out on his first journey to Archangel, on the fourth of June, and returned on June 4. the first of October.

The next day, Gordon notes, 'His Majesty and his company came to supper with me, and October 2. were very happy.'

On the eighth of November, 'His Majesty was so gracious as to come to my house, and take November 8. from me three books on artillery.'

Again, on the twenty-eighth of December, 'His Majesty honoured me with a visit. The December 28. English presented his Majesty with a gold watch, worth sixty-five pounds sterling, and with a box of instruments worth thirty-five pounds sterling. His Majesty graciously handed each a cup of wine.'

A.D. 1694.

The beginning of this year found Gordon again making arrangements as to his affairs in Scotland]

COPY OF THE FACTORY SENT TO JOHN GORDON OF NETHERMUIR, AND PATRICK GORDON OF CULTS.

Be it knowne to all men by these present letters, wee General Patrick Gordon of Achluichries, forasmuch as I being engaged in the service of his Imperiall Majestie of Russia, so that I cannot be present in Scotland to manage my effaires in my own person, and haveing certain experience of the fidelity, ability, and dilligence of my cousins, John Gordon of Nether-muir, and Patrick Gordon of Cults: Witt yee me, therefor, the said Generall Patrick Gordon, to have made, constitute, and ordained, and by the tenor hereof, makes, constitutes, and ordains the said John and Patrick

Gordons my lawfull, undoubted, and irrevocable procurators, actors, and factors, to the effect underwritten; giveing, granting, and committing to them (they acting allwayes in my effaires by the especiall advice of the noble Georg, Earle of Aberdeen,) my full power, commission, and warrand to receive from my oldest son, John, in Scotland, the summe of two hundred punds Scottisch yearly, dureing the naturall lives of me and my wyfe, beginning at the terme of Whitsunday nexte; to which effect in my prescriptions to the disposition of the heretable right of my lands of Achluichries, I have ordained my wyfe, Elisabeth, to be infeft in the lands of Easter Achluichries; as also to keep and dispose of the bond of three thousand merks Scottish, according to my order in the said disposition; and also receive any summes of money which I may remitt to Scotland, or are due to me there, especially the debt due to me by J. Gordon, Laird of Rothemay, upon his brother William his account; and also to uptake, lift, and recover the rents, profits, and duties of any lands, summes of money, and annuall rents, which may accrew to me hereafter; as also to satisfy and pay all debts due by me to whatsumever persons or person, whither by personall or reall security, and to obtaine discharges and acquittances thereupon, or such other conveyances of the samme as shall be thought most expedient for my behoofe, with lyke power to sue, call, and persue all and every person whomsomever, who are or may be due or indebted to me, to obtaine sentences and decreets therein, and put them in due execution, compone, transact, and agree thereanent, acquittances and discharges to give thereupon, and generally all and sundry other things requisite and necessary to do, use, and exerce anent the haill premisses, and anent all my effaires, business, and concernments, within the Kingdom of Scotland, that I might do myself if I were personally present; which I shall hold firme and valid, without revocation; declaring hereby that my said factors shall be bound and obliged, by the acceptance hereof, to make just accompt and reckoning and payment to me, my heirs, or assignes, of all such summes of money and things whatsumever, which they shall uplift and receive by vertue of this present factory, they haveing allwayes allowed to them such summes of money and debts as they shall satisfy for me, with such charges and expenses as they shall happen to disburse and give accompt anent the premisses; and I, the said Generall Patrick Gordon, bynd and obliges me, my aires, executors, and successors, to warrand the above written factory good, valid, and effectuall, at the hands

of all deadly; consenting thir presents to be registrate in the books of
Counsell and Session, within the said Kingdom of Scotland, Sheriffe or
Commissary court books of Aberdeen, therein to remaine *ad futuram rei
memoriam*, and constitutes   my lawfull
procurators: In witnesse whereof, I have written and subscribed this, with
my owne hand, befor these witnesses, Major Generall Paul Menezes, and
Collonell Alexander Leviston: So done in the Strangers Suburb of
Mosco, A.D. 1694, the twelfth of January, old stile.

[On the twenty-fifth of January, Gordon notes that the Czar was in great grief at the death January 25.
of his mother.

On the twenty-ninth of April, His Majesty set out on his second visit to Archangel, which April 29.
he reached on the eighteenth of May. He was accompanied by Gordon, who acted as Rear-
Admiral of the fleet, Peter himself being 'the Great Skipper.'

Two days after their arrival, a ship was launched. 'We dined on board,' says Gordon, 'and May 20.
enjoyed ourselves much, and came home late. Archangel lies in N. lat. 64° 30'.'

On the twenty-sixth of May, 'the Great Skipper dined at my son-in-law's'—Colonel Snivius May 26.
of the Strelitz regiment stationed at Archangel.

In the beginning of June, the Czar sailed in his yacht for a fortnight's cruise, Gordon June.
remaining on shore. During the interval, two English ships arrived.

On the fourteenth of June, says Gordon, 'I was with His Majesty on board the English ships, June 14.
where we were well entertained by both captains, and neither drink nor powder was spared.
On coming away, I gave thirty dollars for drink money.'

On the twenty-ninth of June, Gordon notes that he 'received his Majesty on board the new June 29.
ship, and congratulated him. After receiving a cup of brandy and another of sack from the
generalissimo or admiral, we landed and dined at John Grims, where we were entertained to
excess.'

On the first of July, 'His Majesty, with the whole company, had the kindness to dine with July 1.
me. We enjoyed ourselves, and sat late.'

On the twenty-second of July, the English ship Perry and Lane, of twenty-six guns, com- July 22.
manded by Captain Roddes, came to anchor off Archangel.

'His Majesty'—Gordon writes on the thirty-first of July—'came to me in the evening, and July 31.
gave me the order of sailing, or signals to be observed at sea, written in Russe, requiring me to
have the paper translated into English, and copies made for the English captains. Before going
to sleep, I translated the writing, and gave the translation to Mr. Wulffe to copy.' The signals
were for a cruise along the west coast of the White Sea, as far as Swjatoi-nos, or Cape Sviatoi, on
the north. The vice-admiral's ship went first; then came four Dutch ships; the admiral's ship
followed; after that came four English ships; the yacht, in which Gordon sailed, being last of
all. At Swjatoi-nos the fleet parted company with the foreign vessels, and then made its way
back to Archangel.

September 22.   On the twenty-second of September, the Czar commanded Gordon to order 15,000 arschin of English cloth according to pattern, one-third of it azure, another third dark blue, and the rest raspberry colour.

A.D. 1695.

March.   War against the Turks having been resolved upon, Gordon was ordered to march upon Azof. He came in sight of the city upon the twenty-seventh of March, and, two days afterwards, the army was joined by the Czar and the commander-in-chief of the expedition, Alexei Simono-

June.   witsch Schein. It was the middle of June, however, before the place could be invested. One of two forts, called Callanshaes, having been stormed by Colonel James Gordon, the other was

July.   evacuated during the night following. About the middle of July, the besieged made a sally on General Patrick Gordon's division, but were repulsed. During the following night, a German en-gineer went over to the Turks, and betrayed to them the weak points of the Muscovite lines. The next sally was, in consequence, directed against Lefort's quarter, and was so nearly successful that the division was saved from destruction only by the opportune interposition of Gordon. The Czar scolded and threatened the Strelitzes for failing to do their duty.

August 4.   In the beginning of August, Peter determined to assault the town. It was in vain that Gordon remonstrated; the attack was made, and failed, as he had foretold. 'Such,' he writes, 'was the unfortunate result of this ill-timed and rash undertaking, urged on, as I might say, by Rehoboam's councillors. Of the four regiments, fifteen hundred men were killed, besides officers. About nine o'clock, his Majesty sent for me and the other officers. There was nothing to be seen but angry looks and sad countenances.'

October.   A second assault, towards the end of August, was equally fruitless; and in a few days after-wards the siege was raised. The Czar. with his generals, returned to Moscow about the end of October.

November 15.   On the fifteenth of November, Gordon writes, 'I drove with his Majesty to the iron works. where I hammered a broad plate.'

A.D. 1696.

In January of this year, Gordon is found in correspondence with one of the two Scottish Archbishops, Dr. John Paterson, who, when parson of Ellon, more than thirty years before, was no distant neighbour of the family at Auchleuchries. He had been sent to the Castle of Edinburgh in 1692, on a charge of being in communication with King James.]

TO HIS GRACE THE ARCHBISHOP OF GLASGOW.

January 29, 1696.

May it please your Grace,

I find my self both honoured and obliged by yours of the second July. I am exceeding sorry for your sufferings, but cannot but rejoyce hearing of your constant loyalty, and Christian patience. Suffering for a just cause is meritt, and will be rewarded either in this or the other world. I wish that my bearing a share of your grieffe might procure you ease; then should you, in a large measure, find allay.

I found myself very much concerned at the misfortunes of the loyall party, and especially yours for many respects, which moved me, hearing of your stay at Leyden, to desire these ffriends, who travelled from hence, to present my due respects to you.

The gentleman, your goodfellow, whom you are pleased to recommend, shall, upon your account, receive all the kindness and assistance I am capable of, not doubting but he is a well qualifyed and deserving person.

I shall take it for a great kindnes now and then to have a line from you, when occasion offers, which shall alwayes find a joyfull acceptance, and a returne. I entreat you freely to command,

May it please your Grace,

Your Graces most humble servant,

P. GORDON.

[By March, Gordon was again advancing upon Azof at the head of about fifteen thousand March. infantry. He was at Woronesh on the nineteenth of April, when he records his presence ' at a April 19. feast by Generall le Fort, where, with great solemnity, was drank the Usurpator of Great Brittaine his health, which I refused, and, in place thereof, drank King James his good health.'

The second siege of Azof began in June. The share which Gordon had in it may be told in June. the words of an eye-witness, his son-in-law, Alexander Gordon of Auchintoul. ' The Czar,' says this writer, ' considering the great loss of time he had sustained the preceding year, called a council of war to know the opinion of the generals about the safest and most expeditious method of becoming masters of the place. Most of them delivered their sentiments in the common way, by carrying on attacks, making of great breaches, with mines and batteries; which (they said) would infallibly oblige the Governor to capitulate in the terms of war, or expect the worst. Then General [Patrick] Gordon, as the oldest general, gave his opinion that the safest and most expeditious way to become masters of the town, would be to carry on before them a whole rampart of earth along the front of the town, which, as they advanced, would hourly increase. By having ten or twelve thousand men night and day at work, said he, we shall carry and roll as much earth before us, as will not only be sufficient to fill up the fosse, but will have more over and above than will exceed the height of the town walls; by which means, in a few weeks, we shall oblige the enemy to surrender, or we shall bury them alive. The Czar preferred this opinion, and told them to do as he proposed. So to work they went with such cheerfulness, that, within the space of five weeks, the fosse was actually full, and the earth above the height of the ramparts rolling in over them; which obliged the Governor to put out the white flag. Though this seems to be a very extraordinary and uncommon method of taking towns, yet here it proved very successful and safe, the loss of men during the siege not amounting to above three hundred. According to General Gordon's plan, there were constantly twelve thousand men at work, who threw the earth from hand to hand, like so many steps of a stair. The greatest danger was at the top, the earth being so loose, especially as they advanced nearer the town, that the enemy's small shot killed and wounded several; for which cause, they were relieved every half hour, the uppermost rank falling down and becoming the lowermost, and so on. There were strong guards kept on the right and left, as also in the rear. About the twentieth of June, a body of ten thousand Turks and Tartars, by break of day, endeavoured to pierce the lines and force their way into the town, but were repulsed with considerable loss, and so closely pursued by the Russian cavalry, Cossacks and Calmucks, that most of them were cut to pieces. The only officer of distinction the Czar lost during this siege was one Colonel Stevenson, a Scots gentleman. He was shot in the mouth, being a little too curious, and raising himself too high on the top of the loose earth to observe the enemy. He died of hunger, the eleventh day after he received the wound, not being able to swallow any kind of nourishment. He was a good officer, and much regretted by the Czar, who caused bury him with all the honours of war. On the twenty-eighth of June, the Governor demanded to capitulate. . . . They marched out of the town about six thousand persons, whereof three thousand and six hundred were armed men.'*

October 19   The Muscovite army returned in triumph to Moscow on the ninth of October. Rewards were bestowed on the victorious generals, and Gordon received a medal worth six ducats, a gold cup, a costly robe of sables, and an estate with ninety serfs.

A.D. 1697.

It was in this year that the Czar set out on his travels through Western Europe, leaving Gordon as second to the General-in-Chief, Schein, in the charge of the military affairs of the

---

* History of Peter the Great, vol. i., pp. 107-110. Aberdeen, 1755.

Gordon's engineering device is described by an earlier writer: 'The garrison finding themselves wholly disappointed of their hopes of relief, and the siege having been vigorously carried on, chiefly under the conduct of General Gordon, a worthy and ingenious North Briton, who, on this occasion, to facilitate his approaches, had kept rolling forwards a great fence, or bank, of earth, at several places, of that height that the same looked into the town over the fortifications; so that no man could stir in the day-time but they shot him down from behind the top of these banks; which they began first, and raised at some distance from the walls of the town, out of the reach of the enemies' fire from their small-arms; and by great numbers of men, which the Russes relieved every four hours, and employed as thick as they could stand, without being in one another's way, they shovelled the earth quite from the bottom on the outside, or off-side of the said fence, or bank, and kept throwing it over at the top, to that side next the town, where it rolled and tumbled still inwards; so that, by this method, in little more than a fortnight's time, they advanced these banks or walls of earth (which were much higher than the enemies' bastions) within half musket-shot of the walls of the town, until the cannon from the several batteries at other places had continued playing, and made several breaches in the walls of the town. The enemy finding themselves thus every way distressed by the most surprising and vigorous behaviour of the Czar and his army, and no prospect of the relief which they had expected by their fleet, they were obliged to surrender.' —(The State of Russia, under the present Czar, by Captain John Perry, pp. 148, 149. Lond 1716.)

empire.* In this capacity he marched with a considerable force to Asof, the fortifications of which it was desirable to restore and strengthen as speedily as possible. From Asof he proceeded to Taganrog, where the Czar had resolved, in the previous year, to have a strong fortress. His presence put a stop to a meditated attack by the Tartars upon the cities of the Ukraine; and finding no further occupation for his arms, he began to march back towards Moscow, where he arrived in November.

A.D. 1698.

In the end of February, Gordon notes the receipt of a letter from the Czar, written at London February 27. in the middle of January.

A few weeks afterwards his journal begins to be occupied with that mutiny of the Strelitzes, which, but for him, would, in all probability, have issued in the dethronement of the Czar.

'This afternoon came the greater part of the Strelitz petitioners, and about a hundred others, April 3. who had seceded from the corps of Prince Michael Grigorjewitsch Romodanowski, to the house of their Boyar, Prince Iwan Borissowitsch Trojekurow, and begged to be heard. They were told to send in four, the most influential, of their number; who accordingly came and declared that they could not take the field by such a bad road; and they begged for delay, representing that they had suffered great privations, and were still suffering. They exaggerated everything excessively. But the Boyar interrupted them, and ordered them to go to their duty, and march off immediately. As they declined to do so, he ordered them to be arrested and taken to prison. But their comrades, seeing this, rescued them from the guard that was conducting them, and set them at liberty. This occasioned great consternation among the high authorities. The generalissimo Prince Fedor Jurjewitsch (Romodanowski) sent in great haste for me. When he had told me all the circumstances, with considerable exaggeration, I was of opinion that, considering the weakness of the party, and that they were without leaders, it was hardly worth while to take the matter so seriously, or anticipate great danger. I went, however, to Butirki to obviate all danger, and be ready in case of any tumult or meeting. I made see that all the soldiers were in their quarters, and finding all right, I lay down to get some rest, as it was now late. First, however, I had sent word to the authorities how matters stood.

'On the fourth, at daybreak, I sent to learn how things were in the city. Learning that all April 4. was quiet, I repaired to Generals Alexei Semenowitsch and Prince Fedor Jurjewitsch (Romodanowski), who had been attending an imperial council. I found every body in anxiety about the impending danger, which I tried to allay. But many persons, who are inclined by nature to anticipate dangers, have, in such cases, yet another object; they magnify the circumstances in order that their own zeal and services may appear the more signal in quelling the dangers, and

---

* 'His Majesty appointed an army of 12,000 soldiers, of which most of the officers were foreigners, to be quartered in the suburbs of Mosco, to keep the city in awe, commanded by General Gordon, who had entered in the Russian service in the time of his father, and who, by his extraordinary behaviour and success, had acquired both the love of the army and the esteem of the whole nation.'—(Captain John Perry's State of Russia under the present Czar, p. 156.)

that they may thus extract merit and consideration from them.   After calling at my own house, I went back to Butirki.   Having had all the officers present at the exercising of the regiment, I dismissed two-thirds of them, and with the other part remained all night at Butirki, in deference to the alarm of the other Generals.   Some hundred men of the Semonow regiment were sent to expedite the march of the Strelitzes.   These made no resistance, but marched off at midnight, after delivering up the ringleaders of the insurrection.

April 8.

'On the eighth, I wrote to his Majesty, giving him an account of the occurrences of the last week.'

These were the first distant mutterings of the tempest.   There was to be a lull of two months before it broke.

June 8.

' A report spread that the four Strelitz regiments at Toropetz were disposed to insurrection and disobedience.   An equerry was, therefore, sent to get information of their doings.

June 9.

'An order was issued to detach four officers and forty men of the Butirki regiment, to be sent against the Strelitz regiments; the same numbers were detached from the other regiments in Moscow.   One hundred and forty Strelitz deserters were ordered to be arrested, and sent to the cities of the Ukraine.

June 10.

' Accounts were received of the four Strelitz regiments that had been stationed in the camp at Welikije Luki, and were then in Toropetz, that they were discontented at the dismissal of the rest of the army, and the orders given to them to go to various towns, and were inclined to disturbance.

June 11.

' Two captains returned from Toropetz, and reported that the Strelitzes, after repeated secret consultations, had resolved not to march to the stations appointed for them, but to go straight to Moscow, and that they had required their officers to lead them thither.   On their refusing, they had deposed them, and had chosen four men from every regiment to lead them; they were firmly resolved on coming to Moscow.   This news caused no little consternation among the high authorities.   In a council hastily called together, it was resolved to send against them an army corps composed both of infantry and cavalry; and I was to go before with the infantry, till the cavalry were collected.   I was, therefore, sent for and informed of the matter.   After it had been fixed that five hundred men of my regiment, and a like number of each of the three regiments stationed in Moscow, should go, I selected the officers and men that should be used.

June 12.

' I attended a sitting of council at court, in which the former resolutions were affirmed.   There were no more news of the insurrectionists.   I dined with the Polish Ambassador, in company with the other Ambassadors, and a number of friends.   Twenty-seven equerries were sent to me, to be used in carrying orders and despatches to Moscow.

June 13.

' Another council was held, and I received orders to march with the infantry and artillery for the river Chodinka, and there wait further orders.   After making the soldiers get a month's pay, sending on five cannon to Butirki, and getting a hundred and fifty waggons, I set out from the Sloboda in the afternoon.   After an hour's stay in Butirki, I marched out and pitched camp on the little river Chodinka.   The other three regiments arrived at midnight.

June 14.

' The Polish Ambassador came to the camp.   I sent and received several messengers, but no further accounts of any certainty.

' I broke up in the morning, and pitched camp again on the Swidnja, a verst from Tuschina. June 16. At midnight, the Boyar came, and brought the orders on all the points that we had laid before the council to have instruction and full authority upon.

' On Friday, at six o'clock, I marched with the infantry, and came to Tschernewa, ten versts. June 17. Here I found a nobleman's servant, who said that he had spent the previous night with the Strelitzes, and that they were marching with all speed to reach the convent of Woskressensk that night. This news made me hasten on to get there before them. After advancing five versts farther, I rested a little, and sent a report to the Boyar, requesting him, at the same time, to send me some cavalry. I then crossed the river, and, lest the mutineers should reach the convent before me, I pushed on before with what horsemen I could muster. Two versts from the convent, the scouts brought to me four Strelitzes, who said that they were sent, one man from each regiment, to take a petition to the Boyar. Reading it, I found in it nothing but a catalogue of their services, with exaggeration of their grievances, and a prayer for leave to come to Moscow to visit their homes, wives, and children, as well as to petition for their necessities. I sent them on to the Generalissimo; and having learned from these deputies that the Strelitzes were still fifteen versts off, and could not reach the convent that night, I gave orders to mark off a camp near the convent, as the most convenient place. I arrived at the place fixed upon about sunset, and immediately received information from my scouts that the Strelitzes had reached the river, and were crossing at a shallow place. Hearing this, I hastened thither with what horsemen I had with me. I spoke to them in a calm tone, and advised them to return across the river, and encamp on the other side. Not heeding this, they turned into a line, and remained stationed on a meadow beside the river, outside the village. I returned as quickly as possible to bring up our infantry. I made the first two regiments march through the village, and take post in the best position, while the other two were stationed on the fields by the Moscow road. I then rode down to the Strelitzes, and had a conversation with them; but I found them very refractory in all that we required of them. However, I persuaded them to send two other deputies to the Generalissimo, which they did. After a mutual promise that no movement should take place that night, they returned to their camp, leaving a strong guard in the lane. I made a battalion keep guard not far from them, and stationed another near for relief. I then went to the other regiments, and ordered strong guards and detachments in various places in sight of their camp, to observe them. Having reconnoitred their camp at a little distance, and found no stirring among them, and having also visited our own guards, I went back to the camp at the time of reveille, which I did not allow to be beat, and rested an hour. After which I went to the Generalissimo, and consulted with him what was to be done. After mature deliberation, it was resolved that I should repair to their camp and intimate to them: 1, That they should turn back and repair to the places assigned them; 2, That they should give up one hundred and forty deserters who had run away from Welikije Luki to Moscow, as well as the ringleaders of the present insurrection, and disobedience to the commands of his Majesty; 3, That in the appointed places his Majesty should give them the usual pay, and either bread or money, according to the local prices; 4, That the present fault should be forgiven them; and, 5, That even the others, who were more guilty, should not suffer severe punishment.

' Taking the six deputies with me, I went to their camp, where I communicated the orders to assemble and hear the gracious concessions of his Majesty. When about two hundred had come together, I let the deputies communicate the orders given, and then employed all the rhetoric I was master of to induce them to return to obedience, and give in a petition, confessing their guilt in having transgressed his Majesty's orders. But they answered that they were all determined to die or else go to Moscow, though it were only for eight or three days; after that they would go wherever his Majesty should order. When I told them that they would not be permitted to go to Moscow, and that they must not think of it, they replied that they would rather die than not get to Moscow. With that began two old fellows among them to aggravate their privations, and half a dozen confirmed what they said, and kept up the disturbance. I advised that each regiment should hold a consultation apart, and that they should consider well what they did, and what they were refusing. But they rejected all advice, and declared that they were all of one mind. I then intimated that I would withdraw from the camp and wait an answer outside, adding the threat, that if they did not embrace the gracious offers of his Majesty now, they needed not expect such conditions again, when once we should be obliged to use compulsion to bring them to obedience. But to all this they paid no heed. I then rode out of their camp, and waited at some distance for a quarter of an hour; after which I sent to ask their final answer. Finding no alteration of their mind, I took my departure with an indication of sorrow. After inspecting the best approaches to the rebels, and holding a consultation with the Generalissimo and others, it was resolved to draw up the army, and plant the cannon, and use force. I brought up the infantry and twenty-five cannon to a fit position, surrounded their camp on the other side with cavalry, and then sent an officer to summon and exhort them once more to submit. As they again declined, I sent yet another to demand a categorical decision. But they rejected all proposals of compromise, and boasted that they were as ready to defend themselves by force as we were to attack. Seeing that all hope of their submission was vain, I made a round of the cannon be fired. But as we fired over their heads, this only emboldened them more, so that they began to wave their colours and throw up their caps, and prepare for resistance. At the next discharge of the cannon, however, seeing their comrades fall on all sides, they began to waver. Out of despair, or to protect themselves from the cannon, they made a sally by a lane, which, however, we had occupied with a strong body. To make yet surer, I brought up several detachments to the spot, so as to command the hollow way along which they were issuing. Seeing this, they returned to their camp, and some of them betook themselves to the barns and outhouses of the adjoining village. At the third discharge of the guns, many of them rushed out of the camp towards the infantry and cavalry. After the fourth round of fire, very few of them remained in their waggon rampart; and I moved down with two battalions to their camp, and posted guards round it. During this affair, which lasted about an hour, a few of our men were wounded. The rebels had twenty-two killed on the spot, and about forty wounded, mostly mortally. We had all the prisoners brought to the convent, and shut up in vaulted houses and other places. A list of their horses was then made, and orders given not to touch their property ; only the ammunition and the regimental waggons were brought to head quarters, and an account of them taken. The next thing was to send an officer to Moscow with an account of the business. The whole afternoon we were occupied collecting the arms scattered about on the camp and fields.

'Information having been got as to a few of the ringleaders, from some who thought to gain June 19. favour for themselves, several influential individuals were called up and examined. One of the regiments was then mustered. The greater part of the influential men and others being examined, it was frankly confessed that some had been the ringleaders and guilty rebels. Those that were found good we put on the one side, and the bad on the other. In the afternoon, another regiment was proceeded with in the same way.

'We removed our camp to beside the convent, to be out of the dust of the field where we were. June 20.

'We mustered another regiment of the Strelitzes, and examined various individuals, putting June 21. them to the torture; whereon they confessed the wicked designs they had meant to carry out when they got to Moscow. Word was despatched to Moscow twice or thrice of all that was going on.

'Twenty-four individuals were found guilty, on their own confession, of the most shocking June 22. crimes, and of having designed, when they got to Moscow, to massacre certain Boyars, and to extort an increase of pay, and a new regulation of their services. On these we pronounced sentence of death, to consist in beheading. They were confined apart, and directed to confess, receive the eucharist, and prepare for death.

'Those condemned yesterday were beheaded. The fourth regiment was mustered in the June 23. same way.

'I wrote to his Majesty, giving a short account of the previous events. June 24.

'On this and following days, we were engaged from morning to night in hearing cases; many June 25. were put to the torture, of whom a few confessed.

'An order arrived to send the less guilty Strelitzes to the various convents, and there keep June 27. them closely imprisoned.

'Some Strelitzes that had confessed themselves guilty were hanged. June 28.

'His Majesty's birthday was celebrated, first by divine service, and then by a feast, at which June 29. his health was drunk, with discharge of cannon. A great many Strelitzes were sent under strong guard to various convents.

'Many rebels of the regiment of Colonel Hundertmark were interrogated and put to the tor- June 30. ture; but none would confess himself guiltier than the others. They were therefore informed that they must cast lots, as the tenth man must die, which they did. About two hundred persons were knouted in the afternoon.

'Forty-five men of Hundertmark's regiment, on whom the lot had fallen, were brought out. July 1. They were told that if they would only name the ringleaders of the rising, the rest should go free. After a pause, they began to mutter and to name one or two, who, being tortured, without much ado pled guilty; three or four more were then named, who were also tortured, and confessed after a few strokes. They were then set apart and bid prepare for death; and the others, on whom the lot had fallen, were set free.

July 2.   'To-day, seventy men were hanged by fives and threes on one gallows. Numbers more were sent away to confinement.

July 3.   'An order came for the army to be dismissed. We were all thanked for our services. Three regiments went off immediately. The Generalissimo and we, his assessors or aids, with the Butirki regiment, remained all night.

July 4.   ' In the morning, the four Strelitzes condemned last Saturday were brought out and beheaded. With few exceptions, all those executed submitted to their fate with great indifference, without saying a word, only crossing themselves; some took leave of the lookers-on, One hundred and thirty had been executed, about seventy had been killed in the engagement or died of their wounds, eighteen hundred and forty-five been sent to various convents and prisons, and twenty-five remained in this convent.

July 6.   ' This day, after devotion, I, with many more, were confirmed by the Archbishop of Anura [Ancyra], called Petrus Paulus de St. Joseph, of the Carmelite order; I takeing the name of Leopoldus, and my son Theodorus that of Joseph.

July 19.   ' I was called to Preobraschensk. The gracious letter of his Majesty was read, in which our services were commended. The same was read to the soldiers, who were promised a ruble a piece, besides that they were all to be treated at his Majesty's table. We also were sumptuously treated, especially in drink.

August 23.   'Gott this account of my mother's father. The Laird of Petlurg maryed Janet Ogilby, daughter to the Laird of Cullen, and was soone after killed at the battel of Pinky, leaving him who succeeded unborne, or in the cradle. She was afterwards maryed to one Olgilby of Blarak, her cousin, a cadet of the house of Cullen, and of 3000 merks in the Boyne. By him she had a son called James, brother uterine to Sir John Gordon of Petlurge, and unkle to Mr Robert. This James marryed Marjery Gordon, daughter to Georg Gordon of Coclaraghy. These were my grandfather and grandmother.'

July.   The tidings of the formidable revolt of the Strelitzes reached the Czar at Vienna, towards the end of July, and hastened his journey homewards.

September 2. On the second of September, Gordon, who had gone, with his eldest son and his family, to visit his estate in the country, writes: ' I received a letter saying that the Czar had arrived in Moscow, and had been at my house to enquire for me.' Gordon returned in a few days, and was immediately sent for by the Czar, who received him very graciously, and thanked him in the heartiest way for his faithful services, and the great things he had done.

September 17. 'Many Strelitzes were brought up and put to the torture, his Majesty being desirous to institute a stricter examination than ours.

September 19. ' I was unwell and kept the house. A sharp enquiry was made into the Strelitz business.

September 20. '.More Strelitzes put to the question. A number were directed to prepare for death.

September 23. ' In the afternoon, I went to Preobraschensk, but in vain: every body about the court was engaged in arresting more of the adherents of the Princess Sophia, and putting the Zarina* in the convent.

          * [The widow of the late Czar Ivan, Pro-   vived her husband twenty-seven years, dying
skovia, daughter of Feodor Soltykof. She sur-   in 1723.]

'A number of Strelitzes were executed.　　September 30.

'I was at Preobraschensk, and saw the crocodile, swordfish, and other curiosities, which his October 3. Majesty had brought from England and Holland.

'Orders were issued not to give support to any of the wives or children of the executed November 14. Strelitzes.'

The Diary closes on the last day of this year, with these devout aspirations :—'Almighty December 31. God be praised for his gracious long suffering towards me in sparing my life so long. Grant, gracious God, that I may make a good use of the time that thou mayest be pleased yet to grant me for repentance. This year I have felt a sensible decrease of health and strength. Yet thy will be done, gracious God!'

These were the last words that Gordon was to enter in his journal of many years. His strength was now fast failing, and during the following summer he became so weak that he was unable to leave his bed. He died at seven o'clock in the morning of the twenty-ninth of November, 1699. The Czar, who had visited him five times in his illness, and had been twice with him during the night, stood weeping by his bed as he drew his last breath; and the eyes of him who had left Scotland a poor unfriended wanderer, were closed by the hands of an Emperor.

Peter himself ordered the funeral procession, and took his place in its long line, accompanied by all the pomp of his empire, and followed by the representatives of most of the great powers of Europe. The body was carried on the shoulders of twenty-eight colonels; two generals supported the footsteps of his widow, and twenty ladies, the wives of high Muscovite dignitaries, walked in her train. The religious obsequies were performed by the priests of the church which he loved, in the first chapel of stone which the Roman Catholics were suffered to raise in Moscow. It was built chiefly by his bounty, and his tomb was dug before its high altar, in a vault, where this inscription may still be read :

SACRAE TZAREAE MAJESTATIS MILITIAE GENERALIS

PATRICIUS LEOPOLDUS GORDON

NATUS ANNO DOMINI 1635 DIE 31 MARTII

DENATUS ANNO DOMINI 1699 DIE 29 NOVEMBRIS

REQUIESCAT IN PACE

APPENDIX.

APPENDIX.

AUCHLEUCHRIES CHARTERS.

When in Scotland in July, 1686, Gordon records that he ' caused draw up a register or list of all the charters and papers he had on the lands of Achluichries, beginning from A.D. 1423 to this present year, of forty five peeces, besides small.' This register has not been recovered; but in the following pages an attempt is made to supply its place from the public records and other sources—room being made also for a few charters which show the earlier generations of the family of Pitlurg, from which Gordon drew his lineage.

Confirmacio carte Domini Walteri Moygne de terra de Ochluchry.—(A.D. 1370. *From the Registrum Magni Sigilli,* lib. i., no. 272.)

1 Dauid Dei gracia Rex Scottorum . . . Sciatis nos approbasse . . . donacionem illam et vendicionem quas Johannes de Bona Villa de Balhelvy fecit Waltero Moygne militi de terra sua de Ochluchry cum pertinenciis iacente infra dominium de Ardendracht in vicecomitatu de Abirdene . . . Apud Perth xxiij^{cio} die Octobris anno regni nostri quadragesimo primo .

Confirmacio carte Johannis Fraser de terris de Balhelvy Boneville cum tenandia de Achlochery. —(A.D. 1389 et A.D. 1400. *From Collections on the Shires of Aberdeen and Banff,* pp. 289, 290.)

2 Robertus Dei gracia Rex Scotorum . . . Sciatis nos quandam cartam Johannis Bonvile filii et heredis quondam Johannis Bonvile de Balhelvy Bonvile factam . . . dilecto nostro et fideli Johanni Fraser de Forglen . . . inspexisse ad plenum in hec verba OMNIBUS hanc cartam visuris uel audituris Johannes de Boneville filius et heres quondam Johannis de Boneville de Balhelvy Boneville eternam in Domino salutem / Vestra nouerit vniuersitas me dedisse . . . nobili viro Johanni Fraser domino de Forglen omnes terras meas de Balhelvy Boneville Colynstoun et duas villas de Ardendrachtys vna cum tenandiis suis de Blaretoun de Many et de Achlochery cum pertinenciis in vicecomitatu de Aberdene pro quadam summa pecunie michi . . . persoluta / Tenendas et habendas . . . de domino de Balhelvy Berclay domino superiori dictarum terrarum et tenandiarum in feodo et hereditate a me et heredibus meis . . . Faciendo inde annuatim . . . tres sectas curie ad tria placita capitalia tenenda apud Balhelvy Berclay cum seruicio forinseco domini nostri Regis . . . In cuius rei testimonium presenti carte mee sigillum meum apposui . et pro maiori securitate et euidencia sigilla nobilium Willelmi de Berclay domini de Tolly et Thome Fraser domini de Corntoun cum instancia presentibus apponi procuraui . Hiis testibus Dominis Thoma de Haya constabulario Scocie . Jacobo Fraser domino

de Ferendracht . Alexandro Fraser domino de Fillortht vicecomite de Abirdene . Johanne de Keth domino de Inuerogy . Alexandro Berclay domino de Kercow . Andrea de Turyne domino de Fovern . Thoma de Lask domino eiusdem cum multis aliis . Datum apud Forglen octauo die mensis Januarii anno Domini millesimo trecentesimo octogesimo octauo . QUAMQUIDEM cartam . . . imperpetuum confirmamus . . . Apud Lithqu quarto die mensis Junii anno gracie millesimo quadringentesimo et regni nostri vndecimo .

Resignacio terrarum de Ardendracht et Achleuchrys.—(A.D. 1440. *From Collections on the Shires of Aberdeen and Banff*, pp. 381, 382.)

3 Nobili et potenti domino Patricio domino de Glamys et domino baronie de Balheluie militi domino suo metuendo . vestra humilis Margareta Fraser domina de Ardendracht et Auchleuchry reuerencias omnimodas et honores . In manus vestras ego predicta Margareta in mea pura viduitate constituta . . . predictas terras de Ardendracht et Achleuchrys cum pertinencijs quas de vobis teneo in capite per fustem et baculum sursum reddo . . . In cujus rei testimonium sigillum meum presentibus est appensum . Apud Slainis decimo sexto die mensis Decembris anno Domini millesimo quadringentesimo quadragesimo .

Preceptum saisine terrarum de Ardendracht et Achleuchry.—(Circa A.D. 1470. *From Collections on the Shires of Aberdeen and Banff*, p. 380.)

4 Elisabeth domina baronie de Balheluy de consensu et assensu Gilberti domini de Kennedi mariti mei dilecti / maro et baliuis meis . . . Quia mihi nuper presentatum est tanquam baroni baronie de Balhelwy quoddam breue sasine ex parte dilecti consanguinei mei Willelmi Hay filii et heredis quondam Alexandri Hay de Dronlaw de capella supremi domini nostri Regis super sasina concedenda prefato Willelmo de terris de Ardendracht et Achleuchry modo existentibus in manibus nostris tanquam domine superioris earundem per decessum dicti quondam Alexandri . . . Vobis igitur . . . precipimus . . . quatenus . . . deliberari faciatis prefato Willelmo . . . saisinam et possessionem dictarum terrarum . . . In cuius rei testimonium sigillum meum vna cum sigillo predicti domini et mariti mei est appensum . apud Cassilis anno Domini mᵒ cccc . . .

Service of Gilbert Hay as heir to Ardendraught and Auchleuchries.—(A.D. 1503. *From the MS. Inventory of the Erroll Papers at Slaines.*)

5 Retour of Gilbert Hay as heir to William Hay in the lands of Ardendraught and Auchleuchrics in the barony of Belhelvie. 26 April, 1503.

Carta confirmacionis Johannis Gordoune de Auchluchre super terris de Lumgar et Hiltounc.— (A.D. 1487 et A.D. 1489. *From the Registrum Magni Sigilli*, lib. xii., no. 85.)

6 Jacobus Dei gracia Rex Scotorum . . . Sciatis nos quandam cartam dilecti nostri Alexandri Glastir de Glak factam . . . dilecto nostro Johanni Gordoun de Auchluchre . . . ad plenum intellexisse sub hac forma / OMNIBUS hanc cartam visuris vel audituris Alexander Glastir de Glak eternam in Domino salutem Noueritis me . . . vendidisse . . . honorabili viro Johanni

Gordoune de Auchluchre totas et integras terras meas de Lumger et Hiltoun cum pertinenciis jacentes infra vicecomitatum de Kincardin . . . Tenendas et habendas . . . de supremo domino nostro Rege et successoribus suis a me heredibus meis in feodo et hereditate imperpetuum . . . Faciendo inde . . . seruicium debitum et consuetum et saluis . . . wardis et releuiis . . . In cuius rei testimonium presenti carte mee sigillum meum est appensum apud Abirdene decimo-octauo die mensis Marcij anno Domini jᵐ iiijᵒ lxxxvjᵒ coram honorabilibus viris Roberto Blinsele Jacobo Gordone Thoma Prat Andrea Newton burgensibus de Abirdene Patricio Duncansone et Domino Johanne Striuelin presbitero ac notario publico cum multis aliis QUAMQUIDEM cartam . . . pro perpetuo confirmamus Saluis . . . juribus et seruiciis . . . debitis et consuetis In cuius rei testimonium presenti carte nostre confirmacionis magnum sigillum nostrum apponi precepimus . . . Apud Are vicesimo sexto die mensis Marcii anno Domini jᵐ . iiijᵒ . lxxxixᵐᵒ et regni nostri primo .

Declaratio Alexandri Glaster de Glak super carta per ipsum concessa Johanni Gordoune de Auchluchry.—(7 June, 1493. *From the Acta Dominorum Auditorum,* p. 172.)

7 Anno etc. lxxxxiijᵒ . . . in presentia Dominorum Auditorum Causarum et Querelarum Parliamenti ac Domini Cancellarij constitutus honorabilis vir Alexander Glaster de Glak . . . pro perpetuo confirmauit illas donationem concessionem et venditionem alias per ipsum factas Johannj Gordoune de Auchluchry super terris de Hiltoune Crombiny terris de Litle Warthill et terris de Harelaw . . . Et insuper idem Alexander in suo animo declarauit quod donatio per ipsum facta per cartam et preceptum sasine prefato Johanni Gordoune super terris de Crombiny cum pertinentiis fuit per ipsum ex sua libera voluntate . . . sigillata et dicto Johanni deliberata per spatium vnius anni aut magis antequam prefatus Alexander aliqualem habuit communicacionem cum domino de Innys aut cum Jacobo Dowglas penes prefatas terras .

Decreitt for Johne of Gordoune of Auchinluchry.—(9 July, 1494. *From the Acta Dominorum Concilii,* p. 366.)

8 The Lordis of Consale decrettis . . . that . . . Alexander Fergussone in Litill Ardach dois wrang in the occupacioun and manuring of the landis of Bothmagoak and tharfore ordinis tham to decist and cess tharfra to be broikit and manurit be Johne of Gordoune of Auchinluchry efter the forme of the instrument of sesing gevin to him tharapoun schewin and producit before the Lordis . . .

Decrett aganis Johnne Gordoune of Auchinluchre.—(10 December, 1494. *From the Acta Dominorum Auditorum,* p. 197.)

9 The Lordis Auditouris decrettis . . . that Johnne Gordoune of Auchinluchre sall . . . owrgiff to William Gray of Kyndrocht all richt and claime . . . with all charteris and evidentis that he has of the ferd parte of the tounne of Kyndrocht with the pertinentis liand in the barony of Kynedwart within the schirefdome of Abirdene becaus the said Williame Gray has lauchfully redemit and qwitout the sammyn landis efter the tenour of the reuersioun maid to him be the said Johnne tharapone And ordinis the said Johne of Gordoune to ressaue the somme of five skore of markis vsuall money of Scotland laid in the handis of Maister Archibald Lindesay chantour of Abirdene for the redemyng and outqwitting of the saidis landis according to the said reuersione . . .

Carta confirmacionis Johannis Gordoune de Lungar super terris de Kynmundeis.—(A.D. 1506. *From the Registrum Magni Sigilli*, lib. xiv., no. 197.)

10 Jacobus Dei gracia Rex Scotorum . . . Sciatis nos quandam cartam vendicionis . . . factam per dilectum nostrum Alexandrum Setoune de Touchfraser militem dilecto nostro Johanni Gordoune de Lungar . . . ad plenum intellexisse sub hac forma OMNIBUS hanc cartam visuris vel audituris Alexander Setoune de Touchefraser miles et dominus terrarum de Kynmundeis salutem in Domino sempiternam / Noueritis me . . . vendidisse . . . honorabili viro Johanni Gordoune de Lungar omnes et singulas terras meas de Kynmundeis cum suis pertinentiis videlicet villam de Kynmundy le Myllhill le Myllbrekis Pettymercus et Kynknokky cum singulis suis pendiculis et annexis jacentes infra vicecomitatum de Abirdene . . . Tenendas et habendas . . . a me heredibus meis et assignatis de supremo domino nostro Rege et suis successoribus in feodo et hereditate imperpetuum . . . Reddendo inde . . . seruicium debitum et consuetum . . . In cuius rei testimonium sigillum meum huic presenti carte mee est appensum apud Edinburgh decimosexto die mensis Aprilis anno Domini millesimo quingentesimo sexto   Coram hiis testibus Willelmo Scot de Balwery milite Roberto Innes de Inuermerky Jacobo Gordoune de Auchmyliny Johanne Setoune Johanne Innes Willelmo Pantoune et Johanne Gray notario publico cum multis aliis QUAMQUIDEM cartam . . . pro perpetuo confirmamus . . . Saluis . . . juribus et seruiciis . . . debitis et consuetis . . . In cuius rei testimonium presenti carte nostre magnum sigillum nostrum apponi precepimus . . . apud Edinburgh [*cetera desunt.*]

Instrument on the recognition of the lands of Auchleuchries.—(A.D. 1523. *From the MS. Inventory of the Erroll Papers at Slaines.*)

11 Instrument taken by John Stevenson as procurator for Alexander Hay of Delgatty, superior of the lands of Auchleuchries, bearing that the said lands were recognosced by John, lord Glammis, and doom of forfeiture given thereupon to remain with him in property ; wherefore he required John of Gordon, pretended tenant of Auchleuchries, to compear at Ardendraught against a certain day to shew the writs and evidents of the said lands, and see a gift granted thereof. February, 1522.

Charter and sasine of the shadow half of Ardendraught and superiority of Auchleuchries.— (A.D. 1540 et A.D. 1550. *From the MS. Inventory of the Erroll Papers at Slaines.*)

12 Charter by John, lord Glammis, to Alexander Hay of Delgatty, of the shadow half of the lands of Ardendraught, with the tower and fortalice thereof, the lands of Brodmuir, and the fishing upon the water of Cruden called Peris, with the ward thereof, and the superiority of the lands of Auchleuchries. 25 March, 1540. Sasine following thereon. 29 March, 1549.

Carta confirmacionis Johannis Gordoun de Lungar super dimedietate terrarum de Kindrocht. —(A.D. 1531. *From the Registrum Magni Sigilli*, lib. xxiv., no. 153.)

13 Jacobus Dei gracia Rex Scotorum . . . Sciatis nos quandam cartam . . . venditionis factam per Franciscum Gordoune partionarium terrarum de Kindraucht et Sathlee Johanni Gordoune de Lungar suo fratri germano . . . ad plenum intellexisse sub hac forma OMNIBUS hanc cartam

visuris vel audituris Franciscus Gordoune partionarius de Kindrocht et Sathlee eternam in
Domino salutem Noueritis me . . . alienasse . . . honorabili viro ac fratri meo germano
Johanni Gordoune de Lungar heredibus suis et suis assignatis omnes et singulas dimedietates
partes terrarum de Kindrocht cum earum pertinenciis necnon tercius partes terrarum de Sathlee
cum suis pertinenciis jacentes in baronia de Kynedward et infra vicecomitatum de Abirdene pro
fauore et singulari dilectione quam habui erga eum . . . Tenendas et habendas . . . de supremo
domino nostro Rege et successoribus suis in feodo et hereditate imperpetuum . . . Reddendo
inde . . . wardam et releuium ac seruicium consuetum . . . In cuius rei testimonium sigillum
meum proprium huic presenti carte mee est appensum vnacum subscriptione Magistri Johannis
Gordoun notarii cum manu mea ducente pennam apud Petlorge die mensis secundo Julii anno
Domini millesimo quingentesimo tricesimoprimo presentibus Duncano Gordoune in Knavin
Jacobo Gordoun in Davacht Roberto Forbes Domino Andrea Symson Magistro Johanne
Gordoun notario QUAMQUIDEM cartam . . . pro perpetuo confirmamus Saluis . . . juribus et
seruiciis . . . debitis et consuetis . . . In cuius rei testimonium huic presenti carte nostre confirmacionis magnum sigillum nostrum apponi precepimus . . . apud Edinburgh octauo die
mensis Octobris anno Domini millesimo quingentesimo tricesimo primo et regni nostri decimo
nono .

Carta Johannis Gordoun de Longar super terris de Tullochcarroune.—(A.D. 1536. *From the
Registrum Magni Sigilli*, lib. xxv., no. 322.)

14 Jacobus Dei gracia Rex Scotorum . . . Sciatis nos quandam cartam venditionis . . . factam
per Robertum Lamb de Tullocarroune dilecto nostro Johanni Gordoune de Longar . . . ad
plenum intellexisse sub hac forma OMNIBUS hanc cartam visuris vel audituris Robertus Lamb
de Tullocarroune salutem in Domino sempiternam Noueritis me . . . vendidisse . . . honorabili
viro Johanni Gordoune de Longar suis heredibus et assignatis . . . omnes et singulas terras
meas de Tullocarroune cum pendiculis earundem et suis pertinenciis jacentes infra vicecomitatum de Banf . . . Tenendas et habendas . . . de supremo domino nostro Rege et suis
successoribus in feodo et hereditate imperpetuum . . . Reddendo inde annuatim . . . supremo
Domino nostri Regi . . . jura et seruitia . . . debita et consueta necnon mihi et heredibus meis
et assignatis summam decem librarum tresdecem solidorum et quatuor denariorum vsualis
monete regni Scotie . . . In cuius rei testimonium sigillum meum huic presenti carte mee est
appensum vnacum subscriptione mea manuali apud Petlorg decimosexto die mensis Augusti
anno Domini millesimo quingentesimo trigesimo sexto Coram hiis testibus Alexandro Pater-
soune alias Talyeour Alexandro Gordoune in Litill Petlorg Thoma Paxtoune Domino Georgio
Michelsoun et Magistro Johanne Gordoun notario publico cum diuersis aliis QUAMQUIDEM
cartam . . . pro perpetuo confirmamus . . . In cuius rei testimonium huic presenti carte nostre
confirmacionis magnum sigillum nostrum apponi precepimus . . . Apud Striueling vicesimo
tertio die mensis Augusti anno Domini millesimo quingentesimo trigesimosexto et regni nostri
vicesimo tercio .

Carta feodifirme Johanni Gordoune de Longar concessa super terris de Petlurge.—(A.D. 1539.
From the Registrum Episcopatus Moraviensis, pp. 414, 415.)

15 Carta feodifirme ab Episcopo Moraviensi cum consensu capituli concessa Johanni Gordoune
de Longar et heredibus masculis de corpore legitimis quibus deficientibus Willelmo Gordoun et
Georgio Gordoun filiis naturalibus inter ipsum et Jonetam Maitland procreatis et eorum heredi-

bus masculis quibus omnibus deficientibus heredibus masculis dicti Johannis quibuscunque terrarum de Petlurge Ovir Auchquhorteis Nether Auchquhorteis cum crofta de Petruchnay in baronia de Keth et vicecomitatu de Banf Reddendo inde annuatim £22 6. 8. Apud ecclesiam cathedralem anno Domini 1539.

Carta confirmacionis Johannis Gordoune de Petlurg super terris de Crevethyn.—(A.D. 1541. *From the Registrum Magni Sigilli*, lib. xxvii., no. 227.)

16 Jacobus Dei gracia Rex Scotorum . . . Sciatis nos quandam cartam vendicionis . . . factam per dilectum et fidelem nostrum consiliarium Thomam Erskin de Brechin militem nostrum secretarium dilecto nostro Johanni Gordoun de Petlurg . . . ad plenum intellexisse sub hac forma Omnibus hanc cartam visuris vel audituris Thomas Erskin de Brechin mules ac supremi domini nostri Regis secretarius Salutem in Domino sempiternam Noueritis me dedisse . . . honorabili viro Johanni Gordoun de Petlurg heredibus suis et assignatis totas et integras terras meas de Crevethin cum singulis suis pertinentiis jacentes in parrochia de Dunblait et baronia de Strabogy infra vicecomitatum de Abirdene in verum et legitimum excambion omnium et singularum terrarum de Hiltoun cum portu et piscatione earundem ac singulis suis pertinentiis jacentium infra vicecomitatum de Kincardin Tenendas et habendas . . . de supremo domino nostro Rege et suis successoribus in feodo et hereditate imperpetuum . . . Reddendo inde . . . seruicia debita et consueta . . . In cuius rei testimonium sigillum meum huic presenti carte mee est appensum vnacum subscriptione mea manuali apud Edinburgh vicesimooctauo die mensis Maij anno Domini millesimo quingentesimo quadragesimoprimo Coram hiis testibus Jacobo Cleland de eodem Johanne Robertoun de Ernok Magistro Johanne Gordoun burgense de Abirdene Alexandro Gordoune Edwardo Buthquhannane Donaldo Fultoun Magistro Johanne Burnat et Alexandro Maknele notariis publicis cum diuersis aliis Quamquidem cartam . . . pro perpetuo confirmamus . . . In cuius rei testimonium huic presenti carte nostre confirmacionis magnum sigillum nostrum apponi precepimus . . . Apud Striueling penultimo die mensis Maii anno Domini millesimo quingentesimo quadragesimo primo et regni nostri vicesimo octauo .

Carta Johannis Gordoun filii et heredis apparentis Johannis Gordoun de Petlurg et Jonete Ogilvy sue sponse.—(A.D. 1543. *From the Registrum Magni Sigilli*, lib. xxix., no. 216.)

17 Maria Dei gratia Regina Scotorum . . . Sciatis nos . . . dedisse . . . dilectis nostris Johanni Gordoun filio et heredi apparenti Johannis Gordoun de Petlurg et Jonete Ogiluy sue sponse ac eorum alteri diutius viuenti in coniuncta infeodacione et heredibus suis . . . totas et integras terras subscriptas videlicet terras de Ovir Kynmundy Kynknoke et Milbrek cum tenentibus tenandriis et liberetenencium seruiciis earundem ac suis pertinentiis exceptis multuris dictarum terrarum jacentes in baronia de Kynedwart infra vicecomitatum de Abirdene Quequidem terre . . . fuerunt dicti Johannis Gordoune de Petlurg perprius hereditarie et quas idem . . . simpliciter resignauit . . . Tenendas et habendas . . . dicto Johanni Gordoune juniori et Jonete Ogiluy sue sponse ac eorum alteri diucius viuenti in coniuncta infeodacione et heredibus masculis inter ipsos legitime procreatis seu procreandis quibus deficientibus heredibus masculis dicti Johannis Gordoun de Pitlurg quibuscunque de nobis et successoribus nostris in feodo et hereditate imperpetuum . . . Reddendo inde annuatim . . . jura et seruicia . . . debita et consueta In cuius rei testimonium huic presenti carte nostre magnum sigillum nostrum apponi precepimus . . . apud Edinburgh septimo die mensis Decembris anno Domini millesimo quingentesimo quadragesimo tertio et regni nostri primo .

Carta confirmacionis Margarete Drummond relicte quondam Johannis Gordoun de Petlurg.—
(A.D. 1547. *From the Registrum Magni Sigilli*, lib. xxx., no. 308.)

18 Maria Dei gracia Regina Scotorum . . . Sciatis nos . . . quamdam cartam donationis factam
per Georgium Bard de Glencuthill Margarete Drummond relicte quondam Johannis Gordoun
de Petlurg . . . ad plenum intellexisse sub hac forma Omnibus hanc cartam visuris vel
audituris Georgius Barde de Glencuthill salutem in Domino sempiternam Noueritis me . . .
pro speciali fauore quem habeo et gero erga dilectam meam Margaretam Drummond relictam
quondam Johannis Gordoun de Petlurg et pro matrimonio inter me et eandem Margaretam Deo
annuente contrahendo dedisse . . . predicte Margarete in vitali reddittu pro toto tempore vite
sue in sua viduitate totas et integras terras meas de Glencuthill cum molendino earundem et
suis pertinenciis necnon totas et integras terras meas de Auchmedane cum suis pertinenciis
jacentes in baronia de Glendowaquhy et infra vicecomitatum de Abirdene Tenendas et habendas . . . a me et heredibus meis de suprema domina nostra Regina . . . Reddendo inde . . .
jura et seruicia . . . debita et consueta . . . In cuius rei testimonium sigillum meum proprium
huic presenti carte mee manu mea subscripte est appensum apud burgum de Perth vicesimo
quarto die mensis Januarii anno Domini millesimo quingentesimo quadragesimo sexto Coram
hiis testibus Vmfrido Rollok in Findony Georgio Rollock de Duncrub Dauide Maule Roberto
Watsoun Willelmo Baty Dominis Willelmo et Waltero Ramsayis capellanis et notariis publicis
cum diuersis aliis Quamquidem cartam . . . pro perpetuo confirmamus . . . In cuius rei
testimonium huic presenti carte nostre confirmacionis magnum sigillum nostrum apponi precepimus . . . apud Edinburgh vigesimooctauo Januarii anno Domini millesimo quingentesimo
quadragesimosexto et regni nostri quinto .

Preceptum carte confirmacionis Jacobi Gordoun fratris Johannis Gordoun de Petlurg super
terris de Auchleuchries.—(A.D. 1547. *From the Registrum Secreti Sigilli*, vol. xxi., fol. 10.)

19 Preceptum carte confirmacionis Jacobi Gordoun fratris germani Johannis Gordoun de Petlurg
super carta alienacionis per dictum Johannem facta sibi et heredibus suis masculis de corpore
suo legitime procreandis quibus deficientibus prefato Johanni et heredibus suis quibuscunque
reuersuris de totis et integris terris de Eistir Auchluchreis et Westir Auchluchreis cum suis
pertinenciis jacentibus in baronia de Ardendracht infra vicecomitatum de Abirdene Tenendis
de prefato Johanne et heredibus suis ac assignatis etc. Apud Striueling octauo Maij anno pre-
dicto [jᵐ vᵒ xlvijᵒ] . Per signetum .

Carta confirmacionis Jacobi Gordoune fratris germani Johannis Gordoune de Petlurg super
terris de Auchleuchries.—(A.D. 1547. *From the Registrum Magni Sigilli*, lib. xxx., no. 238.)

20 Maria Dei gratia Regina Scotorum . . . Sciatis nos . . . quandam cartam alienacionis et
vendicionis factam per Johannem Gordoun de Petlurg dilecto suo Jacobo Gordoun eius fratri
germano . . . ad plenum intellexisse sub hac forma Omnibus hanc cartam visuris vel audituris
Johannes Gordoun de Petlurg salutem in Domino sempiternam Noueritis me vtilitate mea in
hac parte vndique preuisa et diligenter considerata . . . vendidisse . . . dilecto fratri meo germano Jacobo Gordoune et heredibus suis masculis de corpore suo legitime procreandis quibus
deficientibus reuertendas michi et heredibus meis quibuscunque omnes et singulas terras meas
de Estir Auchluchreis et Westir Auchluchreis cum suis pertinenciis jacentes in baronia de Arden-

dracht et vicecomitatu de Abirdene pro quadam certa pecunie summa michi pre manibus dicti Jacobi bene gratanter et integre persoluta . . . Tenendas et habendas . . . de me heredibus meis et assignatis in feodo et hereditate imperpetuum . . . Reddendo inde annuatim . . . vnum denarium vsualis monete regni Scocie super solum dictarum terrarum nomine albe firme in festo Penthecostes si petatur tantum . . . In cuius rei testimonium huic presenti carte mee sigillum meum proprium est appensum vnacum subscriptione manuali apud Petlurg decimo quinto die mensis Marcii anno Domini millesimo quingentesimo quadragesimo sexto Coram hiis testibus honorabilibus et egregiis viris Magistro Johanne Gordoun vicario de Keith et Georgio Duncane notariis publicis cum diuersis aliis testibus QUAMQUIDEM cartam . . . pro perpetuo confirmamus Saluis nobis et nostris successoribus juribus et seruiciis de dictis terris . . . debitis et consuetis In cuius rei testimonium huic presenti carte nostre confirmacionis magnum sigillum nostrum apponi precepimus . . . Apud Striuiling octauo die mensis Maij anno regni nostri quinto .

Sasine of Ardendraught and superiority of Auchleuchries.—(A D. 1589.   *From the MS. Inventory of the Erroll Papers at Slaines.*)

21 Sasine of William Hay of Delgatty, grandchild and heir of William Hay of Delgatty, in the lands of Ardendraught and superiority of Auchleuchries, upon a precept by John, lord Glammis. 23 March, 1588.

The renunciatioun of the mid plewche of the landis of Eister Auchlewchries, in favouris of James Ogilwie of Blerok, presentit be the said James wpon the xiij day of July, 1603.—(*From the Secretary's Register of Seisins for Aberdeenshire*, vol. ii., fol. 272.)

22 By a deed, dated at Aberdein on the 13th of June, 1603, George Gordoun in Auchleuchreis acknowledges to have received from James Ogilwie of Blerak the sum of 1000 merkis Scottis, and therefore renounces all right and claim to the mid plewche of the toune and landis of Eister Auchlewchreis.

Ane instrument of saising givin to James Ogiluy, appeirand of Bleraik, and to Meriorie Gordoun his future spous, vpoun the landis of Auchluchres, with the milne and milne landis of the samen, presentit in his name be George Jope, noter, the tuentie day of September, 1604.— (*From the Secretary's Register of Seisins for Aberdeenshire*, vol. iii., foll. 365, 366.)

23 By a charter, dated at Aberdein on the 18th of August, 1604, (in presence of Abraham Forbes of Blaktoun, John Ogiluie, apparent of Glasauch, and Alexander Lautye, servitor to Master John Dempster, advocate, before the Lords of Council), James Ogiluie of Bleraik, grants to Mariorie Gordoun, daughter of George Gordoun of Coclarachie, and future spouse of James Ogiluy, son and heir apparent of the said James Ogiluy of Blerak, the town and lands of Eister Towne of Auchlewchres, with the milne and milne lands, in liferent for all the days of her life. Sasine was given on the 18th of August, 1604.

Instrument of seasing giwen to Mariorie Gordoun, guidwif of Blerack, of the waster pleuche of Auchluchreis, presentit be Walter Robertsoun, clark deput of Abirdene, vpoun the auchteint day of Februar, 1618.—(*From the Particular Register of Seisins for Aberdeenshire*, vol. i., foll. 116-118.)

24 By a charter, dated at Aberdeen on the 3rd of November, 1617, James Ogilvie of Blerack (with consent of Sir Alexander Hay of Delgatie, knight, overlord of the lands of Auchluchreis) granted to Mariorie Gordoun, his spouse, for all the days of her life, the waster pleuch of the toun and lands of Auchluchreis, under condition that the grant should fall whenever the granter redeemed the easter pleuch of Auchleuchreis, from the hands of George Hay, son of Alexander Hay of Brunthill, by payment of £1000 Scots. Sasine was given on the 12th of February, 1618, in presence of Gavin Cruikshank, notary public, and others.

Contract conteinnand reuersioun betuix George Ogilvie of Carnusies, and James Ogiluie, elder and younger of Blerok, on the ane and vther pairtis, off twa pleuchis of the landis of Waster Auchleuchreis, presentit be Peter Lawte in Auchleuchreis, vpone the twalt day of July, 1618.—(*From the Particular Register of Seisins for Aberdeenshire*, vol. i., foll. 230-233.)

25 By a deed, dated at Aberdeine on the 27th of May, 1618, James Ogiluy, younger, fiar of Blerok, (as well for himself as for Mariorie Gordoun, his wife), and James Ogiluy, elder of Blerok, his father, acknowledge to have received from George Ogiluy of Carnowseis the sum of 3300 merkis Scots, and for security of payment of the said sum bind themselves to infeft him in twa pleuchis or sextein oxingait of the toune and landis of Wester Auchleuchreis, to be holden of the granters in free blench ferme, and of their superiors in few ferme for payment of £5 Scots yearly.

Renunciatioune grantit be George Hay, brothir germane to the guidman of Brunthill, to James Ogiluy, now of Auchleuchreis, of the wastir pleuche of Eister Auchleuchreis, presentit be Mr. Williame Gordoune, sone to the guidman of Coklarachie, vpone the xxv day of May, 1619.—(*From the Particular Register of Seisins for Aberdeenshire*, vol. i., foll. 427, 428.)

26 By a deed, dated at Aberdeine on the 18th of May, 1619, George Hay, lawfull son to Alexander Hay of Brunthill, acknowledges to have received payment of £1000 Scots from James Ogiluie, now of Auchleuchreis, and therefore renounces all right and claim to the wastir pleuche of Eister Auchleuchreis.

Reuersioun grantit be Johne Gray at the Mylne of Leask to James Ogiluie of the landis of Wastir Auchleuchreis, presentit be Mr. Williame Gordone, sone to the guidman of Coklarachie, vpone the xxv day of May, 1619.—(*From the Particular Register of Seisins for Aberdeenshire*, vol. i., foll. 428-430.)

27 By a deed, dated at Auchleuchries, on the 13th of May, 1619, Johne Gray, at the Mill of Leask, binds himself to ane honorabill man, James Ogiluy of Auchleuchries, that notwithstanding the said James Ogiluy, with consent of Mariorie Gordoune, his spous, and bayth of them with consent of George Gordoune of Coklarachie, Alexander and Mr. Williame Gordones, his sonis, Mr. Robert Bisset off Lessindrum, and Andro Launtie of Innaltrie, hes sauld to him the twa pleuchis of Wastir Auchleuchries, yet quhow sone the said James Ogiluie payis to him the soume of 7200 merkis, he shall renounce all right and claim to the said twa pleuchis in favouris of the said James Ogiluie.

Instrument of sesing gewin to George Ogiluie, elder of Carnowses, of aucht oxingait of the toune and landis of Waster Auchleuchries, callit Muirtack, presentit be Williame Gordone, notar publict in Abirdeine, vpon the sexteine day of Junij *in anno* 1621.—(*From the Particular Register of Seisins for Aberdeenshire*, vol. iii., foll. 128, 129.)

28 By charter, dated at Abirden, on the 25th May, 1621 (in presence of John Ogiluie of Glassauch, Walter Ogiluy of Reidhytht, and William Ogiluy of Crowalis), James Ogiluie of Auchlewchries granted to George Ogiluye, elder of Carnowsies, the plough, or six oxgates of the town and lands of Wastir Auchlewchries, called the Muir Tak. Sasine was given on the 26th of May, 1621.

Reuersioune and grant of redemptioune of the toune and landis of Auchlewchries *alias* Murtak, maid be George Ogilvie, elder of Carnowseis, to James Ogiluy of Auchleuchries, presentit be Williame Gordone, noter publict in Aberdeine, vpon the third day of July, 1621.—(*From the Particular Register of Seisins for Aberdeenshire*, vol. iii., foll. 134, 135.)

29 By a deed, dated at Aberdeine, on the 25th May, 1621 (in presence of Walter Ogiluy of Reid-hywe, George Ogiluy, fear of Carnowseis, and Mr. Alexander Craig of Rosecraig), George Ogiluie, elder of Carnowsies, binds himself, on receiving payment of 1000 merks Scots, to renounce all right and claim to the pleuch or aucht oxingait of Wastir Auchleuchries, callit the Muir Tak, in favour of James Ogiluy of Auchlewchries.

Sasine of Ardendraught and superiority of Auchleuchries.—(A.D. 1622. *From the MS. Inventory of the Erroll Papers at Slaines.*)

30 Sasine of Alexander Hay of Delgatty, and Dame Isobell Lesley, his spouse, in the lands of Ardendraught, fishing on Cruden, and superiority of Auchleuchries, upon a charter and precept by John, earl of Kinghorn, superior thereof. 27 April, 1622. Charter whereon the sasine proceeded. 12 April, 1622.

Instrument of seasing giffin to Georg Hay, lawfull sone to Alexander Hay of Brunthill, wpon ane part of Auchleuchries, presentit be Johne Hay, burges of Abirdein, wpon the twantie fyft day of July, *anno Domini* 1623.—(*From the Particular Register of Seisins for Aberdeenshire*, vol. iv., foll. 187, 188.)

31 By charter, dated at Abirdene on the 6th of June, 1623, James Ogiluye of Auchleuchries, with consent of Mariorie Gordoun, his wife, grants to George Hay, lawful son of Alexander Hay of Brunthill, the middle plough of the toun and lands of Estir Auchleuchries. Sasine was given on the 3d of July, 1623.

Renunciatioun and grant of redemptioune be George Hay, sone lauchfull to vmquhill Alexander Hay of Brunthill, now stylit of Awquharnie, of the middle pleuche of land of Eister Auchleuchries, in fauoris of Johne Gordone, presentit be Mr. William Lumsden, advocat in Aberdene, vpone the tent day of Apryle, 1633. – (*From the Particular Register of Seisins for Aberdeen-shire*, vol. viii., foll. 184-186.)

32 By a contract, dated at Aberdene on the 6th of June, 1623, James Ogiluye of Auchleuchries bound himself to infeft George Hay, sone lauchfull to wmquhill Allexander Hay of Brunthill, now styllit of Awquharnie, in the middell pleuche of land of the said James Ogiluye, his toun and landis of Easter Auchleuchries, in the parochin of Cruden, and shire of Aberdene, in considera-tion of a sum of 2500 markis paid to him by the said George Hay : to be holden in frie blenche of the said James Ogilvie, and in few ferme of Sir Allexander Hay of Delgattie, knycht, his im-mediat superiore, for yeirlie payment of 26 schillingis : but redeemably by the said James Ogilvie upon payment of the said sum of 2500 markis.   By a deed, dated at Aberdene on the 2nd of Marche, 1633, the said George Hay acknowledges to have received payment of the said sum of 2500 markis from Johne Gordone, third lauchfull sone to wmquhile Patrick Gordone of Nathirmwir, assignay lawfullie constitut be the said James Ogiluye to the said contract, and renounces in his favour all right and claim to the said middel pleuche of land of Eister Auch-luchries.

Instrument of seasing giwen to Johne Gordon, and Marie Ogiluye, his future spous, of the toun and landis of Easter Auchlochries, with the milne theroff, the toun and landis of Waster Auchlochries, etc., presentit be Mr. William Lumsden, advocat in Aberdene, vpone the auchtene day of Apryle, 1633.—(*From the Particular Register of Seisins for Aberdeenshire*, vol. viii., foll. 187-189.)

33 By a charter, dated at Aberdene on the 2nd, and at Coclarachie on the 9th, of March, 1633, James Ogiluye of Auchlochries, proprietor of the lands afternamed, and Hew Gordone, lawful son to George Gordone of Coclarachie, with consent of Mariorie Gordone, spouse of the said James Ogiluye, granted to Marie Ogiluye, lawfull daughter of the said James Ogiluye, and future spouse of John Gordone, third son of the deceased Patrick Gordone of Nethirmwire, and to the said John Gordone in conjunct fee, and to the heirs lawfully begotten between them, whom failing to the heirs and assignees whomsoever of the said John Gordone, all and haill the two pleughs of Easter Auchlochries, occupied by George Hay, son of the deceased Alexander Hay of Brunthill, George Elleis, and Alexander Clark ; the pleugh of Easter Auchlochries, oc-cupied by the said James Ogiluye, John Moire, and Adam Leithe, with the milne of Auch-lochries, and the milne lands ; and the toun and lands of Wester Auchlochries, with the pendicle called the Muiretak, lying in the parish of Croden, and shire of Aberdene, under reservation to the said James Ogiluye and Mariorie Gordone, and the longer liver of them two, of the liferent and usufruct of the plough of Easter Auchleuchries, occupied by the said James Ogiluye, John Moire, and Adam Leithe.   Sasine was given on the 16th of March, 1633.

Instrument of seasing giwen to Hugo Gordone, lawfull sone to wmquhill George Gordone of Coclarachie, of the landis of Easter and Westir Auchleuchries, with the milne and pertinentis thairof, presentit be Mr. William Lumsden, notar tharto, vpon the penult day of October, 1633.—(*From the Particular Register of Seisins for Aberdeenshire*, vol. viii., foll. 328-330.)

34 By a charter, dated at Auld Deir, on the 19th of August, 1633, Sir Alexander Hay of Delgatie, knight, immediate superior of the lands afternamed, granted to Hew Gordone, lawful son to the deceased George Gordone of Coclarachie, the lands of Easter and Waster Auchleuchreis, with

the pendicle called Murris Tack, and the milne of Auchleuchries, with the milne lands, etc. Sasine was given on the 31st of August, 1633.

Instrument of seasing given to Johne Gordone, third lawfull sone to Patrick Gordone of Nethirmuir, and Marie Ogilvie, his spous, of tuo pleuches of land in Easter Auchleuchreis, etc., presentit be Mr. William Lumsden, noter thairto, wpone the penult day of October, 1633.—(*From the Particular Register of Seisins for Aberdeenshire*, vol. viii., foll. 327, 328.)

35 By a charter, dated at Old Deir, on the 19th of August, 1633, Sir Alexander Hay of Delgatie, knight, granted to John Gordone, third son of the deceased Patrick Gordone of Nethirmuir, and to Marie Ogilvie, his wife, in conjunct infeftment, and to the longer liver of them, and the heirs lawfully begotten between them, whom failing to the heirs and assignees of the said John Gordone whomsoever, the two ploughs of the toun and lands of Easter Auchleuchries, formerly occupied by George Hay, George Eleis, and Alexander Clark, the plough of the said toun and lands of Easter Auchleuchries, occupied by James Ogilvie, John Moir, and Adam Leithe, with the milne and milne lands, and the toun and lands of Waster Auchleuchreis, with the pendicle called Murres Tack. Sasine was given on the 31st of August, 1633.

Charter of Ardendraught and superiority of Auchleuchries.—(A.D. 1634. *From the MS. Inventory of the Erroll Papers at Slaines.*)

36 Charter by Sir Alexander Hay of Delgatty, to William Hay, his eldest lawful son, of the lands of Ardendraught, fishing on Cruden, and superiority of Auchleuchries. 9 November, 1634.

Instrument of saising gevin to Gawine Cruikshank in Ardiffrie, nottar publict, of the toune and landis of Eister Auchleuchries, presentit be the said Gawin, wpoun the tent day of Julij, 1637.—(*From the Particular Register of Seisins for Aberdeenshire*, vol. x., foll. 427-431.)

37 By a contract of alienatioun and dispositioun, dated at Aberdein on the 13th of June, and at Wester Auchleuchries on the sext day of July, 1637, Johne Gordoun of Auchleuchries, with consent of Marie Ogilvie, his spous, bound himself to infeft Gawin Cruikshank in Ardifferie in the toune and landis of Eister Auchleuchries, occupied by the said Johne Gordoun, and George Aelleis, his tenant, in security of payment of 200 merkis, 28 bollis meall, 12 capones, and 12 hennes yeirlie, redeemably by payment of £3000 Scots, after Whitsunday, 1640. Sasine was given upon the 6th of July, 1637.

Instrument of saisin giwin to Walter Bodie in Auchleuchries of the tounes, landis, maner plaice, milne, and milne landis of Auchleuchries, presentit be George Gordoun, burges of Aberdein, wpon the tent day of July, 1637.—(*From the Particular Register of Seisins for Aberdeenshire*, vol. x., foll. 432, 433.)

38 By a charter, dated at Aberdein on the 14th of June, 1637, Johne Gordoun of Auchleuchries, granted to Walter Bodie in Auchleuchries, the mains, milne, and milne lands of Auchleuchries, redeemably by payment of 2500 merks Scots. Sasine was given on the 6th of July, 1637.

Sasine of Ardendraught and superiority of Auchleuchries.—(A.D. 1638. *From the MS. Inventory of the Erroll Papers at Slaines.*)

39 Sasine of Gilbert, earl of Erroll, as heir of William, earl of Erroll, his father, in the lands of Ardendraught, fishing on Cruden, and superiority of Auchleuchries, upon a precept by John, earl of Kinghorn, superior thereof. 14 July, 1638.

Renunciatioune and grant of redemptioun, be Walter Bodie in Auchleuchries, of the Maynes of Auchleuchries, mylne, and mylne landis thairof, in fauoris of Johne Gordone of Auchleuchries, presentit be the said Johne himselff, vpoun the allevint day of Juni 1642.—(*From the Particular Register of Seisins for Aberdeenshire*, vol. xii., foll. 210, 211.)

40 By a deed, dated at Aberdeine on the 11th of June, 1642, Walter Bodie in Auchleuchries acknowledges to have received payment, from Johne Gordoun of Auchleuchries, of the sum of 2500 merkis, and therefore renounces all right and claim to the Maynes of Auchleuchries, milne and milne landis thairof.

Instrument of saising gevin to Mr. James Gordoun of Greinmyre and Annas Gordoun his spous, of the Maynes of Auchluchres with the mylne and mylne landis, presentit be the said Mr. James vpoune the nynteint day of September 1650.—(*From the Particular Register of Seisins for Aberdeenshire*, vol. xiv., foll. 437-439.)

41 By charter, dated on the tenth of September, 1650 (in presence of the granter's lawful sones, George and Patrick Gordounes) John Gordoune of Auchluchries granted to Mr. James Gordone of Greinmyre and Annas Gordone, his spouse, the Maynes of Auchluchries, with the milne, milne lands, multures, suckin, and knaivschipis, redeemably by payment of two thousand five hundred merks Scots. Sasine was given on the 16th September, 1650.

Innovatione of reversione, Johne Gordone of Auchluchries and Marie Ogilvie his spous, to Gawin Cruikschank in Ardiffrie, presented be the said Gawin vpon the sex day of Julij 1652.—(*From the Particular Register of Seisins for Aberdeenshire*, vol. xv., foll. 251, 252.)

42 By contract and appoyntment off the dait att Aberdeine and at Wester Auchluchries the thretteine and sex dayes of Junij and Julij j^m vj^o and threttie sevin yeres (registrat in the Buikis of Consall vpon the sexteine day of Apryll j^m vj^o and fiftie yeires), Johne Gordone of Auchleuchries and Marie Ogilvie his spous, for the sowme of thrie thousand pundis money, wodset to Gawin Cruikschank in Ardiffrie, the toune and landis of Eister Auchluchries (then possessed by the wodsetter Johne Gordone, and George Ailles his tenant). By deed dated at Aberdeine on the fourth day of Junij 1652 (in presence of Gilbert Skeine of Dyce Mr. William Lumsden of Pittiloche, and James Gordone, brothar to the wodsetter Johne Gordone of Auchluchries), the said Johne Gordone of Auchluchries and Marie Ogilvie his spous acknowledge to have received from the said Gawin Cruickshank a farther sum of ane thousand merkis, in respect whereof they declare that the said wodsett shall not be redeemable but be payment of the sowme of fyve thousand and fyve hundreth merkis

Instrument of seasing givin to James Gordoune brother german to John Gordoune off Auch-
leuchries, off the eistsyde of the Westertoun of Auchleuchries, presented be Mr. William
Lumsden off Pittullok, advocat in Aberdene, vpon the second day of Apryll 1655.—(*From the
Particular Register of Seisins for Aberdeenshire*, vol. xvii., foll. 421-423.)

43 By charter dated att Westertoune of Auchleuchries on the tuentie day of Julij 1654 (in presence
of William Lumsdene, sone to Mr. William Lumsden off Pittullock, and John and George Gordones sones to the granter), John Gordoune of Auchleuchries granted to his brother german,
James Gordoune, the eistsyde of the toune and landis of Westertoune of Auchleuchries. Sasine
was given on the twelfth of February, 1655.

Instrument of seasing given to Johne Gordone younger in Westertoune and Margaret Forbes
his spous, in lyfrent, of the pendicle of land of Wester Auchleuchries called the Muretack,
presented by Johne Gordone forsaid, vpon the fyiftenth day of March 1665.—(*From the
Particular Register of Seisins for Aberdeenshire and Kincardineshire*, vol. iii., foll 372, 373.)

44 By charter, dated at Auchleuchries on the fifth day of April, 1664, (in presence of James
Gordone of the Westertoune of Auchleuchries), Johne Gordone of Auchleuchries granted to his
son Johne Gordone, younger, in Westertoune of Auchleuchries, and to Margaret Forbes his wife,
the longest liver of them tua, in conjunct fie and lyfrent, and to the bairnes laufullie gotten,
or to be gotten, betuixt them tuo, that pendicle of land of Wester Auchleuchries called the
Muretack. Sasine was given on the last day of February, 1665.

Instrument of seasing given to Marie Ogilvie, spous to Johne Gordone of Auchleuchries, in
lyfrent, and James, Patrick, and Alexander Gordones, ther laufull sones, in fee, of the westsyde of the toune and landes of the Westertoune of Auchleuchries, presented be Johne
Gordone, younger, in Westertoune of Auchleuchries, vpon the fyftenth day of March, 1665.
—(*From the Particular Register of Seisins for Aberdeenshire and Kincardineshire*, vol. iii.,
foll. 373-375.)

45 By charter, dated at Auchleuchries on the twenty third day of March, 1665, (in presence of
his son, Johne Gordone in Westertoune), John Gordone of Auchleuchries granted to Marie
Ogilvie, his spouse, in conjunct fie and lyfrent dureing all the dayes of hir lyftyme after his
deceiss, and to Patrick, James, and Alexander Gordones, his sones, ther aires and assigneys
equallie amongst them after the deceiss of himself and the said Marie Ogilvie, in fie and
heritage, the westsyde of the said Johne Gordone of Auchleuchries his toune and landes of
Westertoune of Auchleuchries, presentlie occupied by the said Johne Gordone of Auchleuchries
himselff. Sasine was given by Johne Gordone, younger, in Wester Auchleuchries, as bailie
of the granter, to James Gordone, fourth laufull sone of the granter, for himself, and as
actornay for the said Marie Ogilvie, his mother, and Patrick and Alexander Gordones, his
brethren, on the third day of March, 1665.

Seasing, William Hay and Elizabeth Gordone, his spouse, of the lands of Auchleucharies, presented by Mr. Alexander Robertsone, advocat in Aberdein, on the first day of December,

16 5.—*(From the Particular Register of Seisins for Aberdeenshire and Kincardineshire, vol. iv., foll. 81, 82.*

46 By charter, dated at Buthlay, on the fifteenth day of June, 1665, Master James Gordoun, now of Buthlay, and John Gordone of Auchleucharies grant to William Hay of Ardenrit and Elizabeth Gordone his wife, the Maynes of Auchleucharies, the Milne of Auchleuchries, mill lands, multures, and sequels, now occupied by Henry Patersone, Alexander Martine, and Thomas Gray, redeemably by the said John Gordone of Auchleucharies and his heirs, by payment of the sum of five thousand merks Scots. Sasine was given by John Gordone, younger in Wastertoune, bailie of the granters, to the said William Hay, the granter, on the eleventh day of November, 1665, in presence of James Cuming, notary public, William Hay of Sandend, Alexander Perke, John Christie, and George Myllne in Aucleuchries.

Seasing, Collonell Patrick Gordone and Katharine Van-Bock-Hovin, his spous, of the lands of Auchlewchries, presented be Mr. Alexander Robertsone, advocat in Aberdein, on the twentyfyft day of Januar, 1671.—*(From the Particular Register of Seisins for Aberdeenshire and Kincardineshire,* vol. vii., foll. 232-234.)

47 By charter, dated at Wastertoune, the twentie day of November, jᵐ vjᵉ and seavintie yeares (in presence of James Gordoune in Artrachie, James Gordoune, the granter's youngest lawfull sone, John Hay in Auchlewchries and James Gordone, sone to the deceast Mr. Thomas Gordoune, the granter's brother), Johne Gordone of Auchlewchries, with consent of Marie Ogilvie, his wife, granted to his second lawfull sone, Collonell Patrick Gordone, and to Katharine van Bockhoven, his spouse, the longest liver of them, in lyfrent, and to the heirs gotten or to be gotten betwix them, in fee, the landis of Auchlewchries, Eister and Waster, with the pendickles theroff callit Marestack, Milne of Auchlewchries, milne landis, multures, and sequellis thereof, reserving to the granters their lyfrent of the wester pleugh of Auchlewchries then possest by them. Sasine was given on the twenty ninth day of December, 1670, in presence of James Gordone, son of umquhill Mr. Thomas Gordone in Turnalow, and Walter Cruickshank, gardener at Wastertoune.

Sasine, Collonell Patrick Gordone and Katharin Van-bock-hovin, of the lands of Eister Auchleuchries etc., presented by Mr. Alexander Robertsone, advocat in Aberdeine, on the tent day of Januar, 1672.—*(From the Particular Register of Seisins for Aberdeenshire and Kincardineshire,* vol. vii., foll. 442-444.)

48 By disposition, dated at Ellone on the fyfteint day of November, 1671, Gavin Cruickshank in Maines of Barra, and Gilse Smith, his wyfe, sell to Collonell Patrick Gordone, second lawful sone of John Gordone of Auchlewchries, and to Catharine Wan-bock-hoven, his wife, and the longer liver of them, the toune and lands of Eister Auchlewchries, redeemably be payment of fyve thousand fyve hundreth merkis. Saisin was given on the fourth day of January, 1672, to Johne Gordone, younger in Wastertoune, attorney for the grantees, in presence of James Gordone in Westertoune.

Sasine, John Gordone, younger in Wester Auchlewchries, and Margaret Forbes, his spous, of the lands of Auchleuchries, presentit be Mr. Alexander Robertsone, advocat in Aberdeine, the twentieth day of May, 1674.—(*From the Particular Register of Seisins for Aberdeenshire and Kincardineshire*, vol. viii., foll. 400, 401.)

49 By disposition, dated at Milne of Ardendret, the threttein day of May, 1674 (in presence of William Hay, son to the granter), William Hay of Sandend sells to John Gordone, younger, in Wester Auchlewchries, lawfull sone of Johne Gordone of Auchleuchries, and Margaret Forbes, his wife, the pendickle of land of Wester Auchlewchries called Muirtack, redeemably by payment of certain sums of money. Seisin was given on the thirteenth day of Apryll, 1674.

Charter of Ardendraught and the superiority of Auchleuchries.—(A.D. 1677.—*From the MS. Inventory of the Erroll Papers at Slaines.*)

50 Charter by George, earl of Panmure, to John, earl of Erroll, and his heirs, of the lands of Ardendraught, fishing on Cruden, and superiority of Auchleuchries, upon the resignation of Gilbert, earl of Erroll, to be holden in feu for payment of £82 Scots yearly. 24. September, 1677.

Renunciatioun, James Gordon, younger in Wastowne, to Major Generall Patrick Gordone, presented by Thomas Forbes, servitor to George Patoun of Grandham, on the twantie sevent day of June, 1682.—(*From the Particular Register of Seisins for Aberdeenshire and Kincardineshire*, vol. xi., foll. 253-255.)

51 By band of provisione, dated at Achlewchries, the twantie thrid day of March, 1665, John Gordon in Achlewchries, now deceast, bound himself to infeft Marie Ogilvie, then his spous, in lyfrent, and Patrick Gordon, James Gordon, and the now deceast Allexander Gordon, his second, fowrt, and youngest lawfull sones, equally among them thrie, in fee, in the westsyd of the said John Gordon, the father, his towne and lands of Westertowne of Achlewchries, then occupied by him, redeemably from his said sones, or any of them, by payment to ilk ane, or any of them, of fowrtie shilling Scots, and, after his deceas, by his aires, by payment to ilk ane of his said sones of ane thowsand punds Scots. Sasine was given upon the 23d March, 1665. By disposition, dated on the twantie day of November, 1670, the said John Gordon of Achluchries, and Marie Ogilvie, his spous, sold to their said secund lawfull sone, Collonell Patrick Gordon, and the now deceast Catharin Vanbuckowen, then his spowse, and the longest liver of them two, in lyfrent, the lands of Achlewchries, Easter and Wester, with the pendicles therof, called Murstack, the Milne of Achluchries, milne lands, multures, and sequelles, under burden of payment to the said James Gordone, fourth sone of the granter, of ane thowsand punds Scots (in caece he wer not wtherwayes provyded be his said father, the granter). By deed, dated at Ellon, the 30th of May, 1682 (in presence of John Gordon in Westertowne), the said James Gordone (now younger in Wastowne), fourt lawfull sone to the deceast John Gordon in Achlewchries, acknowledges that James Gordon of Westertowne, his unquhill [uncle] laite factor to the said Collonell Patrick Gordone, had, by order of the said Collonell (now designed Major Generall) Patrick Gordon, made payment to him of the said sowme of ane thowsand punds Scots, and therefore renounces, in favour of the said Major Generall Patrick Gordon, that thrid part and portioune of the said westsyde of the said towne and lands of Westertowne of Achlewchries, in which he was seised under the band of provisione aforesaid.

Sasine, John Gordone, sone of Generall Patrick Gordone, in the lands of Auchlewchries and others, presented by Williame Gordone, merchant in Aberdein, upon the eight day of September, 1692.—(*From the Particular Register of Seisins for Aberdeenshire and Kincardineshire,* vol. xiv., foll. 216-218.)

52 By disposition, dated at Moscovia the elevent day of Januarie, 1692 (in presence of Major Generall Paull Menzies, Collonell Alexander Livingstoun, and Major Harie Gordone, all in the service of ther Imperiall Majesties of all Russia), Generall Patrick Gordone of Auchleuchries, commander in chief of the select regiments of their Imperiall Majesties of all Russia, grants to John Gordone, his eldest lawful sone, the touns and lands of Auchleuchries, Easter and Wester, with the pendicles thereof called Muirtak, the Milne of Auchleuchries, milne lands, multuris, sequells, sucken, and knaveshipes of the samine, in the barronie of Ardenred, parochine of Crouden, shireffdome of Aberdeine, and kingdome of Scotland; reserving to the granter, and to Elizabeth Barnoe Roonaer, his wife, and to the longest liver of them two, an annuitie of thrie hundreth merks Scots, furth of the tuo pleughes of Easter Auchleuchries, during their lyftyme, to be paid at Whitsunday yearly to James Gordone, the granter's uncle, John Gordone of Nethermuir, and Patrick Gordone of Cults. Sasine was given on the twentieth day of August, 1692, by George Low, miller at the Milne of Leask, bailie of the granter, to William Milne, gardener, in the Westertowne of Auchleuchries, attorney of the grantee (designed honorabilis juvenis Johannis Gordone filii legittimi primogeniti honorabilis et prepotentis generosi viri Patricii Gordone de Auchleuchries summi strategi selectarum legionum Imperialium Majestatum totius Russie), in presence of James Middletoun, notary public, Robert Alexander in the Westertoun of Auchleuchries, William Lendrum there, Alexander Lendrum there, Robert Gairdin, his servant, and Johne Chalmer in Kilnary.

Sasine of Elizabeth Grant, ladie Auchleuchries, off her lyfrent right of the lands thereof and wthers, presented by William Gordone, merchant in Aberdein, upon the sext day of October, 1692.—(*From the Particular Register of Seisins for Aberdeenshire and Kincardineshire,* vol. xiv., foll. 233-236.)

53 By contract matrimoniall, dated the 27th of August, 1692 (witnessed by Patrick Leslie of Balquhan, Patrick Gordone of Barrack, John Gordone of Nethermuir, and William and James Grants, sones to William Grant of Creichie), between John Gordone of Auchleuchries, with consent of James Gordon of Westertoun, his granduncle, and Elizabeth Grant, eldest lawful daughter to William Grant of Creichie, with consent of the said William, her father, it was agreed that the said Elizabeth Grant, promised and affedat spouse to the said Johne Gordone of Auchleuchries, should be seised in lyfrent, after the decease of her said husband, of the manor place of Auchleuchries, yairds and orchards thereof, and of ane annuitie of thrie hundreth merks Scots, and thrie chalders of ferme meall yearly furth of the toune and lands of Wester Auchleuchries, the toun and lands called Muirtack, and the Milne of Auchleuchries. Sasine was given on the 15th of September, 1692, by William Mill, gardener in Westertoun of Auchleuchries, bailie of the said John Gordon of Auchleuchries, to Arthur Bruce, his servitor, attorney of the said Elizabeth Grant, in presence of John Middletoun, notary public, Alexander Ronald in Moortack, William Lendrum in Westertoun, William Milne, younger there, and George Arthur, servitour to the said John Gordon of Auchleuchries.

Seasine, Generall Patrick Gordone, and James Gordone, his second sone, of the lands of Westertoun of Auchleuchries, presented by Thomas Forbes, advocat in Aberdein, on the 28th of
February, 1696.—(*From the Particular Register of Seisins for Aberdeenshire and Kincardineshire*,
vol. xv., foll. 238-240.)

54 By a disposition, dated at Westertoune on the eighth day of September, 1682 (in presence of
John Gordone and James Gordone in Westertoune, brothers german to Generall Patrick
Gordone, John Gordone, sone to the said John Gordone, and James Cuming, notary public),
James Gordone of Westertoun sold to Generall Patrick Gordone, second lawful sone to the
deceast John Gordone of Auchleuchries, in lyferent, and to James Gordone, second lawful sone
of the said Generall Patrick Gordone, in fee, the eastsyde of the toun and lands of Westertoun of
Auchleuchries, reedemably by the heirs of the said deceast John Gordone of Auchleuchries, by
payment of thrie thousand and sex hundreth merks Scots, and reserving to the said James
Gordone his lyfrent of the said lands. Sasine was given upon the fifteenth of February, 1696,
by George Godsman in Westertoun of Auchleuchries, bailie of the disponer, to Alexander
Godsman, servitor to George Gordone in Westertoune, attorney for the disponees, in presence
of James Middletoun, notary public, John Gordone at Bridge of Gourdoun, Alexander Paull in
Auchmad, George Robertson, his servitor, and John Middletoun, younger, in Leask.

Sasina, Joannis Gordone de Auchleuchrie, annui redditus levandi e terris de Creichie, presentata
per Alexandrum Hay, scribam in Aberden, 24 Januarij 1706.—(*From the Particular Register of
Seisins for Aberdeenshire and Kincardineshire*, vol. xviii., foll. 195, 196.)

55 By heritable bond, dated at Rothiemay on the nynth day of November, 1696 (in presence of
John George, sone to William George, boatman of Rothiemay, and Adam Watt, servitor, and
James Grant, sone to the granter), William Grant of Creichie granted to John Gordon of Auchleuchrie, an annual rent of three hundreth merks Scots out of the lands and barony of Creichie,
mains, tower, fortalice, and manor place of the same, the toun and lands of Andrewsfoord, Burn-
gairnie, Bowrehillock, Easter Creichie, Machieshillock, Midsummer Cairnes, Cromlet, Lawhill,
Starbridg, Creichmeleids, and Milne of Creichie, in the barony of Creichie, parish of Fyvie, and
shire of Aberdeen, redeemably by payment of five thousand merk Scots. Sasine was given
on the 19th of December, 1705.

Sasina Jacobi Gordon de Ellon in terris de Muirtack cum pertinentiis, presentata 1 Septembris
1712.—(*From the Particular Register of Seisins for Aberdeenshire and Kincardineshire*, vol. xix.,
foll. 592-595.)

56 By charter, dated at Edinburgh on the 6th of June, 1712, Charles, earl of Erroll, Lord Hay and
Slaines, Great Constable of Scotland, grants to James Gordone of Ellon the toun and lands of
Muirtak (being a pendicle of the lands of Wester Auchleuchries), as they were possessed by the
deceased Sir John Forbes of Watertoun, and Thomas Forbes of Watertoun, his son; which
toun and lands of Muirtak formerly belonged to the deceased John Gordone of Auchleuchries,
holden by him of the aforesaid Charles, earl of Erroll, and were by the said deceased John
Gordone, with consent of Elizabeth Grant, his wife, on the 15th May, 1711, resigned into the
hands of the said Charles, earl of Erroll, as immediate superior of the same, in favour of the
said James Gordone of Ellone: To be holden of the said Earl of Erroll in feuferme, fee, and

heritage : Paying yearly the sum of twenty shillings Scots, as part of the sum of twelve pounds Scots of feu duty due to the said Earl yearly from the whole lands of Auchleuchries and Muirtak, lately belonging to the said John Gordon. Sasine was given on the 4th of August, 1712.

Sasine of Patrick Gordon, on Auchleuchries, presented by James Elphinstone of Wartle, on 7 September, 1722.—(*From the Particular Register of Seisins for Aberdeenshire and Kincardineshire,* vol. xxi., part ii., foll. 232, 233.)

57 Precept of clare constat (dated at Slains on 4 August, 1722,) by Mary, countess of Erroll, with consent of Mr. Alexander Hay of Delgaty, her husband, in favour of Patrick Gordon, now of Auchleuchries, son and heir of the deceased John Gordon of Auchleuchries, for sasine of the lands of Auchleuchries, Easter and Wester, with the grain mill of Auchleuchries, mill-lands, etc., in the barony of Ardendraught, regality of Slains, parish of Cruden, and sheriffdom of Aberdeen, holden of the Countess as immediate superior in feuferme, fee, and heritage, for payment of eleven pounds Scots yearly. Sasine was given on the twenty second of August, 1722.

Sasine, Elizabeth Gordon, on ane annualrent out of Westertoun of Auchleuchries, etc., presented on the 22nd May, 1723.—(*From the Particular Register of Seisins for Aberdeenshire and Kincardineshire,* vol. xxi., part ii., foll. 301, 302.)

58 By a bond, dated at Auchleuchries on the 16th January, 1723, Patrick Gordon of Auchleuchries acknowledged himself indebted to Elisabeth Gordon, his sister german, daughter of the deceased John Gordon of Auchleuchries, and Elizabeth Grant, his wife, in the sum of 2000 merks Scots, and, for security of payment, became bound to infeft her in the Westertoun of Auchleuchries, etc. Sasine was given on the 7th of April, 1723.

Sasine, Katharine Gordon, on ane annualrent out of Westertoun of Auchleuchries, etc., presented on the 22nd May, 1723.—(*From the Particular Register of Seisins for Aberdeenshire and Kincardineshire,* vol. xxi., part ii., foll. 302, 303.)

59 By a bond, dated at Auchleuchries on the 16th January, 1723, Patrick Gordon of Auchleuchries acknowledged himself indebted to Katharine Gordon, his sister german, daughter of the deceased John Gordon of Auchleuchries, and Elizabeth Grant, his wife, in the sum of 1600 merks Scots, and, for security of payment, became bound to infeft her in the Westertoun of Auchleuchries, etc. Sasine was given on the 17th of April, 1723.

Sasine, James, John, Alexander, and Charles Gordons, on an annuallrent out of Westertoun of Auchleuchries, presented on 22 May, 1723.—(*From the Particular Register of Seisins for Aberdeenshire and Kincardineshire,* vol. xxi., part ii., foll. 303, 304.)

60 By a bond, dated at Auchleuchries on the 16th January, 1723, Patrick Gordon of Auchleuchries acknowledged himself indebted to James, John, Alexander, and Charles Gordons, his brothers german, sons of the deceased John Gordon of Auchleuchries, and Elizabeth Grant, his wife, in the sum of 2000 merks Scots, and, for security [of payment, became bound to infeft them in the Westertoun of Auchleuchries, etc. Sasine was given on the 17th of April, 1723.

Sasine, Alexander Gordon, on ane annualrent out of Easter Auchleuchries, presented 20 February, 1724.—(*From the Particular Register of Seisins for Aberdeenshire and Kincardineshire,* vol. xxi., foll. 348, 349.)

61 By bond, dated at Aberdeen on the 6th February, 1724, Patrick Gordon of Auchleuchries bound himself to infeft Alexander Gordon in Sandend in an annualrent of 275 merks Scots (corresponding to the principal sum of 5500 merks Scots), out of Easter Auchleuchries. Sasine was given on the 18th February, 1724.

Sasine, Alexander Gordon, on Auchleuchries, etc., presented 9 March, 1726.—(*From the Particular Register of Seisins for Aberdeenshire and Kincardineshire,* vol. xxii., foll. 63-65.)

62 By disposition, dated at Aberdeen on the 5th February, 1726, Patrick Gordon of Auchleuchries conveyed to Alexander Gordon in Sandend the toun and lands of Auchleuchries, Easter and Wester, with the pendicles of Muirtack and the Miln of Auchleuchries (excepting that part of Muirtack sold by the deceased John Gordon of Auchleuchries, father of the said Patrick Gordon, to James Gordon of Ellon), under burden of the jointure of Elizabeth Grant, mother of the said Patrick Gordon. Sasine was given, in presence of John Gordon, brother german of the said Patrick Gordon, on the 9th of March, 1726.

Discharge and renunciation, Katherine Gordon and her husband, to Alexander Gordon, presented 19 July 1729.—(*From the Particular Register of Seisins for Aberdeenshire and Kincardineshire,* vol. xxii., foll. 381, 382.)

63 By deed, dated at Blackwater, on the 10th and 25th June, 1729, Katherine Gordon, daughter of the deceased John Gordon of Auchleuchries and Elizabeth Grant his wife, with consent of Kenneth Mackenzie, at Blackwater, her husband, acknowledge to have received from Alexander Gordon, now of Auchleuchries, the sum of 1600 merks Scots, for security of payment of which her brother german, Patrick Gordon of Auchleuchries, had infeft her in the Westertown of Auchleuchries on the 7th April, 1723.

Discharge and renunciation, Alexander Gordon, to Patrick and Alexander Gordon, presented on 17 January, 1730.—(*From the Particular Register of Seisins for Aberdeenshire and Kincardineshire,* vol. xxii., foll. 437, 438.)

64 By deed, dated at Aberdeen on the 19th December, 1729, Alexander Gordon of Barrack, factor for James and Alexander Gordons, lawful sons of the deceased John Gordon of Auchleuchries, acknowledges to have received the sum of 1000 merks Scots as their share of the sum of 2000 merks, for security of payment of which they (with their brothers, John and Charles Gordon) were infeft by their brother, Patrick Gordon of Auchleuchries, in the Westertown of Auchleuchries, on the 17th of April, 1723.

Sasine of Alexander Gordon on Auchleuchries, presented on the 5th August, 1730.—*(From the Particular Register of Seisins for Aberdeenshire and Kincardineshire, vol. xxii., foll. 478, 479.)*

65 By charter, dated at Slains on the first of May, 1730, Mary, countess of Erroll, lady Hay and Slains, Great Constable of Scotland, with consent of Alexander Hay of Delgaty, her husband, granted to Alexander Gordon of Auchleuchries, the lands of Easter and Wester Auchleuchries, with the Muirtack and Mill of Auchleuchries (resigned by Patrick Gordon of Auchleuchries in favour of the said Alexander Gordon of Auchleuchries), excepting that part of the Muirtack disposed by the deceased John Gordon of Auchleuchries to James Gordon of Ellon; and ratified all former writs, and specially a contract as to the teinds of the said lands, dated the 15th and 18th December, 1648, between Gilbert, earl of Erroll, and John Gordon of Auchleuchries. Sasine was given on the 10th of July, 1730.

Sasine, Alexander Gordon, on annualrent out of Auchleuchries, presented on 5 August, 1730.— *(From the Particular Register of Seisins for Aberdeenshire and Kincardineshire, vol. xxii., foll. 479, 480.)*

66 By disposition, dated at Aberdeen on the 28th day of May, 1724, John Gordon, brother german to Patrick Gordon, some time of Auchleuchries, with consent of the now deceased Elizabeth Grant, his mother, granted to Alexander Gordon, then of Sandend, now of Auchleuchries, an annual rent of twenty five merks Scots, (corresponding to the principal sum of five hundred merks), out of the lands of Westertoun of Auchleuchries, with the croft on the Mains of Auchleuchries. Sasine was given on the 18th July, 1730.

INDEX OF PERSONS AND PLACES.

INDEX OF PERSONS.

INDEX OF PLACES.

244 INDEX OF PLACES.

Yarmy, 64.
Yaroslaw, 150.
Yasulbitsa, the village, 64, 156.
Yausa, the river, 51.
Yedro, 63.
York, 138.
Ythan, the river, 145, 146.

ZAGRODNIKY, the Sloboda, 49, 51.
Zagoria, 112, 155.

Zamoga, the river, 157.
Zanow, the town of, 118.
Zamoisiz, 36.
Zavidova, the village of, 157.
Zeeland, 74.
Zell, the town of, 70.
Zerick-Zee, 74.
Ziemna Gora, 63, 156.
Znin, 40.